Cooking at Home on Rue Tatin

COOKING AT HOME ON

Rue Tatin

SUSAN HERRMANN LOOMIS

WM
WILLIAM MORROW
An Imprint of HarperCollins Publishers

HarperCollins books may be purchased for educational, business, or sales promotional use. For information please write: Special Markets Department, HarperCollins Publishers Inc., 10 East 53rd Street, New York, NY 10022.

FIRST EDITION

Designed by Lee Fukui

Photographs by Martin H. M. Schreiber

Printed on acid-free paper

Library of Congress Cataloging-in-Publication Data

Loomis, Susan Herrmann.
    Cooking at home on rue Tatin / Susan Herrmann Loomis.
        p.   cm.
    Includes index.
    ISBN 0-06-075817-1
    1. Cookery, French—Normandy style.   I. Title.
    TX719.2.N67L63   2005
    641.5944'2—dc22

                                    2004061092

05   06   07   08   09   WBC/RRD   10   9   8   7   6   5   4   3   2   1

To Fiona, Joe, and Michael for loving me
through the prisms of stove and computer.
Yes, now we can play!

I swear that I was afraid to hurt Grandmother's recipes in writing them down. They were spoken, with images of a life that one had to know to understand, they were almost fairy tales. . . . Each evening, when I got to my room, I wrote my memories of the traditions that I had been initiated into that day. I tried to link them with my own experience, with that of other women of my profession. Faces emerged from the fog of time, it was like a group of fairies with blue aprons. There was the Grandma, the Menette, the Sister, Margoton, Mariette, and the others poor and old, with subtle palates that could distinguish vintage flours, water, and honey. . . . They gathered provisions without looking for glory, never suspecting in their simplicity that they were artists, that they guarded the regional art which today allows us to speak of gastronomy.

Magaridou, a Book of Reminiscences of an Auvergnat Cook,
Suzanne Robaglia

CONTENTS

ACKNOWLEDGMENTS

For me, friendship is in the details, and like any book, this one is built on details too numerous to mention. I have many people to thank for them, some of whom you will meet in these pages. But oh so many are the structure behind the scenes.

Thank you, then, to Kerrie Luzum, helper, friend, and assistant extraordinaire, for years of laughter, energy, and food sense.

To Brinn Moore for her unparalleled *nems*.

To Patricia Wells, my finest food friend.

To Elisabeth Hyde, Marie Keech, Beverly Crofoot, Babette Dewaele, Antonella Ricci, Eloise Peret, Annie Grodent, Bernadette Brière, Karen Malody, Marie-Agnès Gaudrat, and Marion Pruitt for mirth and constancy.

To Christian and Nadine; Stefana and Ziad; Edith and Bernard; Bernadette and Philippe, and their children, Michel and Chantal; and Babette and Jean-Lou for cheerful participation in meals that did not always follow French order and decorum because of the vagaries of recipe testing.

To the butcher, the baker, and the candlestick maker—Mr. Dragonelli, Mr. and Madame Guincêtre, and Mr. Burreaux.

To Hervé Lestage for his friendship and wine sense, and to Brice Lestage for his timely arrival.

To Alain Juvenon for his wisdom and insight.

To Lisa Jackson, who came on the wings of an angel.

To Ina Garten for her warm, generous counsel.

To Martin Schreiber for his joy.

To Angela Miller, my dear and understanding agent.

To Harriet Bell, my bright and shining editor.

To everyone else at Morrow who has helped bring this book to life.

My thanks come from the bottom of my heart!

INTRODUCTION

I've just finished my regular bike ride through the fields around Louviers, which brings me home through the heart of town. I try to bicycle between noon and 1 P.M. because at that hour people are pulling up their chairs to the table and the streets are empty, making it safe and pleasant to ride.

As I cycled through town, I smelled the most enticing aromas. They weren't the predictable aromas of French cuisine, however. There was the distinctive, vinegary aroma of Asian food on one block, and immediately after it one of peppers, onions, and cinnamon from a tagine or a big pot of couscous. I smelled hints of turmeric, cumin, and garlic. And I inhaled the comforting aroma of *rôti de boeuf* and grilled lamb.

By the time I arrived at our door, I was starving, and conscious of how the aromas I'd just been enjoying reflect the fabric of today's French culture, and French cuisine. French cuisine is no longer quantifiable or predictable. Rather, it is ever evolving—infused with curry, fragrant with lemongrass, spicy with harissa, and lively with lime, coconut milk, fresh ginger—the flavors of France's former colonies. France set out to conquer the world and that world has come to inhabit its culture. It is the new order of things, nowhere more obvious than in the country's cuisine.

When I first came to France more than twenty years ago, I was intrigued by the couscous parlors and the African and Asian restaurants tucked into every town and city, but I was so enthralled with classic French cuisine that I shrugged it off then as the exoticism of a foreign land. What captivated me about France was the way food fits into French life. A meal isn't just a moment taken on the sidelines to wolf down food, but a cherished experience where you pull up a chair to the table set with linens, and the experience takes on a certain order. Picture Thanksgiving: it is the one day in American life that is set aside to enjoy favorite dishes linked to history and tradition, to be enjoyed with family and friends. In France, such a meal is, if not a daily occurrence, something that happens at least once a week.

The French sense of food resonated with me. So did the fact that when I went shopping for my daily fare, I usually put my money in the hands of the person who produced it. The exchange was precious. I felt the sense of ownership and pride on the part of the producer, who not only cared about the quality of the product, but had the instinctive knowledge to tell me how best to use it.

I saw people shop daily for meals, wait for seasonal ingredients with a thrill of anticipation, and use them to prepare beautiful, often traditional dishes. Everywhere I went, food was a major topic of conversation, a thread woven through every aspect of French life.

Food is still primordial in France, but gone is any sort of predictableness. The cooking of Southeast Asia and the Maghreb has melded with traditional French home cooking. Dishes like couscous, tagine, and *nems* are now near-standard French fare. Rum, the elixir of the isles, is a common flavoring in pastries and wildly popular as the basis of a punch or cocktail. Classic French dishes like *blanquette de veau, raie au beurre noir,* and *daube de boeuf* are still the delicious heart and soul of French cooking, of course, but its humor and daring come from faraway lands and cultures.

What this means to me, and to any cook in France, is a world of excitement. Here I am, surrounded by delicious, satisfying, traditional dishes assembled using classic techniques that remain rigorous and ordered, and that allow flavorful ingredients to speak for themselves. Added to these are the gutsy, sparkling, aromatic newcomers that have insinuated themselves into this classic tradition, embellishing it, giving it class and nuance. It makes for a fine and flavorful world.

Effortless Cooking and Fabulous Eating

Although I've lived in France for more than fifteen years, I still marvel at the way my French friends put a meal on the table. It always looks so effortless, even though I know better.

I have come to believe that it looks so easy because French people do not consider cooking to be work. They cook because they want to eat well, they want their families and their friends to eat well, and they simply love the process.

There is more to it, of course. Behind the "effortlessness" is a *connaissance instinctive,* or knowing, which translates as supreme confidence and an innate understanding about ingredients and cooking.

The quality of knowing is linked to instinct, and that instinct is linked to education. Most French, male or female, young or old, have grown up around someone who cooked all the time, in a society where good, often lavish, meals are daily fare. They heard their mothers, grandmothers, aunts, and sisters talking about recipes and techniques, and their grandfathers, fathers, uncles, and brothers exclaiming over flavor and finesse. In this social context, where culinary information is freely passed around, it is normal to grow up knowing a lot about food and cooking, because food and cooking are so integral to life. In the same way that an American understands the game of baseball, a French person knows that to make a good *pot-au-feu* you need to use three different cuts of meat. Knowledge of food and cooking is simply part of the ambient information that swirls around the French home.

Not only do most French people still grow up in this atmosphere of culinary ease, but they also spend time in the kitchen learning at their mother's, grandmother's, sometimes father's and grandfather's elbows. Then they take the recipes they've learned and they make them their own.

I am convinced that the reason French families are tightly knit, that generations do not merely tolerate but actually enjoy each other, that French children have an awareness of and gusto about food, and that the French tend not to be as overweight as their contemporaries in the United States, has to do with this ease about food. They have a sense of security from eating together so frequently and taking the time to eat well. This healthy attitude towards food also has to do with the fact that the French understand where food comes from. If they haven't grown up on a farm, they have gone to the farmers' market from a very early age and seen food in its most raw form—just-butchered chickens with their heads still on, slabs of raw pork including head and tail, whole rabbits, and mounds of just-picked vegetables and fruit.

I saw this with Joe, my son, when he was younger, and I see it now with Fiona, my six-year-old daughter. When I walk through the market with her, she is riveted by the sounds and colors. We stand in line for vegetables or fruit, and inevitably the farmer gives her a carrot, a handful of raspberries, or a crisp apple. The butcher's wife cuts a round of garlic sausage for her. At the fish stand, she is entranced by the riot of whole glistening fish and fillets. Occasionally the fishmonger allows her to touch scales, or an eye, or the tip of a fin—which sends her into paroxysms of delight. Rachid, who sells the ethereal nut-and-spice-rich Algerian pastries his wife, Salima, makes at home, lights up when he sees Fiona, and greets her with a kiss and a cookie, then a fresh date, then a handful of almond candies. Fiona returns from the market not only physically satiated, but sensorialy too.

Satiation is important to the French, but it isn't linked with excess, because a good meal is a regular occurrence. In France, it isn't necessary to eat richly but to eat well, which means taking time at table. When you do so on a regular basis, there is no need to overdo.

How I Gathered the Recipes in This Book

I am very fortunate in my passion for food, for it opens doors for me, takes me places I might not otherwise go, inspires confidences that are made concrete in the form of recipes. Each of the recipes in this book is linked to a friend or an acquaintance who shares my passion, and each has a story behind it. Together they are a reflection of contemporary French cooking, which is the cooking I do in my own home. Enjoy them as much as I do, and as much as I have enjoyed compiling them for you.

As you read through the book, I would like to ask you to consider participating in an exercise that will give you a sense of the French way of life. Prepare a meal using recipes you find here. Invite some close friends, set the table, and make sure all your family is present. Sit down. Make the meal last at least fifteen minutes longer than one of your typical meals. Notice what happens. I wish you a hearty bon appétit from rue Tatin.

THE BEAUTY OF FRENCH TECHNIQUE

La Beauté de la Technique

As I blanch, brown, and braise my way through the preparation of meals, I often think about the many different techniques I use that turn something simple into something simply extraordinary. This is the beauty of French cuisine, for using techniques that are adapted to specific ingredients gently coaxes forth all of their innate flavors.

Using such techniques isn't difficult, nor does it usually require any special equipment. It simply demands concentration on what is at hand and, yes, a bit of time. But when the subject is food, the fuel that keeps our personal machines humming, it doesn't seem like a lot to ask!

The recipes in this book are technique-oriented, but not laborious or tiresome, for the techniques are natural steps that take ingredients from their raw state to their ultimate, most flavorful cooked state. As you follow these recipes you will see how this occurs, and you will be learning techniques without even realizing you are doing so.

Cooking and Entertaining the French Way

Just as a painter prepares a palette, so a cook must prepare ingredients and all of the details around a fine meal. Here are a few of my suggestions for making sure that your meal comes off without a hitch, that you have fun all along the way, and that it appears you have done everything with no effort. If you pull this off, you will be entertaining *à la Française*.

Decide what dishes you will cook, then assemble the recipes and read through them. Compile a shopping list and shop.

Sit down and make a list of everything you need to do to prepare for the evening. I make my list on a small blackboard in the kitchen and I'm quick to cross off things as I do them—nothing is more satisfying! If there is anything I can safely do well in advance—even the night before—then I do it. Wash and trim the vegetables, wrap them in a damp towel, and place them in a plastic container in the refrigerator; they will be perfect the next day. If you need a meat or poultry stock, a crème anglaise or other ice cream base, or any basic preparation that will keep, make it ahead. If there is advance preparation—brining a chicken, for example, or letting a terrine mature in the refrigerator—you will be prepared.

Set the table the night before (upturn the glasses so they don't gather dust). There is no pressure then and you can dawdle over the details—the silverware, the napkin colors, the tablecloth, the glasses. Decide what centerpiece you will put on the table, but do not make it until the following day—it should be fresh and enticing.

Read over the recipes again early the next day to be sure you have all the necessary ingredients. Then assemble serving platters and bowls, plates, any other dishes you will need for the meal, and put them at hand. This avoids last-minute panic.

Decide what you will serve as an apéritif. My philosophy about entertaining revolves around establishing a feeling of comfort and togetherness. To begin this process, I like to offer one drink rather than a variety, because I feel that if everyone is drinking something different, each person is having a separate experience. So I chill the white wine, the Champagne, the Mellow Orange Wine (page 298), or the white Cinzano or put out the red wine or the red Cinzano. I arrange glasses and napkins on a tray, set it aside, and don't give it another thought.

Make dessert first. This practice has nothing to do with uncertainty of life but with getting the end of the meal finished first, which is like giving yourself the gift of time.

Once dessert is made, do the mise-en-place for everything else, which is the weighing, slicing, dicing, grating, and measuring of the ingredients for each dish. If you are following well-written recipes, they will lead you by the hand through this process, for an ingredients list is basically a mise-en-place road map. By doing careful mise-en-place you will get your mind into each recipe so that when you begin cooking, there are no surprises.

Decide what you will use to garnish the plates and platters. Pick it from the garden or the windowsill, rinse, wrap it in a damp towel so it stays fresh, and set it aside.

Clean up as you go along, or at least organize and keep work surfaces clear. It is much easier to prepare food when your work space is unencumbered. If your ingredients aren't organized and your work space isn't clear, problems may ensue.

Invite guests for 8 P.M. or later. This leaves time for hosts and guests to shake off the workday, feed the children so calm reigns, and mentally prepare for the enjoyable evening ahead.

While you don't need to have everything finished by the time your guests arrive, you should know exactly what remains to be done and when you will do it. If guests want to help, let them, with simple things like cutting the bread right before you sit down, filling water pitchers, uncorking and pouring the wine. But don't let your guests do the dishes, no matter how much they insist: they don't really want to. Put yourself in their place—you don't want to do the dishes when you are invited out, do you?

Serve the apéritif in the kitchen, if you have the space. This puts people at ease because everyone loves being in the kitchen, and it allows you to do last-minute preparation or cooking without missing out on anything.

If you follow this general plan, your meals will come off without a hitch. You will also find that you are enjoying these occasions as much as everyone else!

THE APÉRITIF HOUR

L'Heure de l'Apéritif

A good meal must be as harmonious as
a symphony and as well constructed
as a Norman cathedral.

Ma Gastronomie,
Fernand Point (1897–1955)

Lemon Thyme and Honey Almonds

Amandes au Thym Citronné et Miel

❧ These almonds are one of my favorite little dishes to accompany an apéritif. They are salty and lightly sweet, redolent of the lemon thyme picked fresh from the garden, and ever-so-slightly addictive. I serve them often, and everyone always asks for the recipe! They are perfect with the Mellow Orange Wine on page 298.

3 cups (about 1 pound; 500 g)

3 cups (about 1 pound; 500 g) unblanched whole almonds

2 teaspoons extra virgin olive oil

1 tablespoon mild honey, such as lavender

1 teaspoon fine sea salt

2 tablespoons fresh lemon thyme leaves

1. Preheat the oven to 350°F (180°C).

2. In a medium bowl, toss the almonds with the olive oil until they are thoroughly coated. Spread them out evenly on a baking sheet and bake in the center of the oven until they begin to smell toasty and turn golden, about 15 minutes. Remove the almonds from the oven and transfer them to a large bowl. Leave the oven on.

3. While the almonds are baking, heat the honey and salt in a small saucepan over low heat until the honey is liquid. Keep warm.

4. Mince all but 2 teaspoons of the thyme. Stir the minced thyme into the honey mixture, then pour it over the almonds. Toss so they are thoroughly coated with the mixture, then return them to the baking sheet, spreading them out in an even layer, and bake until they are golden and smell deeply toasted, about 8 minutes.

5. Remove the nuts from the oven, transfer them to a bowl, and immediately toss with the remaining thyme leaves. Let cool to room temperature, and serve.

ASTUCES: Once roasted, these nuts freeze beautifully. If you are making them to freeze, omit the lemon thyme, then add it once they are thawed. Leftover almonds can be frozen, but you will need to add additional fresh lemon thyme before serving them again. ❧ These almonds are slightly sticky, which makes napkins a must.

Curried Pecans

Noix de Pecan au Curry

❧ I have never experienced an apéritif hour in France without toasted nuts, and the usual offerings are pistachios and peanuts. Pecans are considered chic and exotic because of their rarity in France, and this preparation makes them doubly so.

The curry powder gives them a spicy bite, which is perfect along with a lightly sweet wine like the Mellow Orange Wine (page 298) or an eye-opening pastis.

4 cups (about 13 ounces; 400 g)

2 tablespoons (30 g) unsalted butter

1½ teaspoons curry powder, such as Madras

1 teaspoon fine sea salt

4 cups (about 13 ounces; 400 g) pecan halves

1. Preheat the oven to 325°F (165°C).

2. In a small pan, melt the butter with the curry powder and salt over low heat. Stir until the salt is almost completely dissolved.

3. Place the pecans in a medium bowl and pour the melted butter over them. Toss well, until the nuts are thoroughly coated with the butter. Spread the nuts out on a baking sheet and bake in the center of the oven until they are golden and smell toasty, about 18 minutes. Remove them from the oven and let cool completely before serving. (These will keep well for a week in an airtight container, and they freeze very well too.)

ASTUCE: A low oven temperature is necessary for toasting pecans, which burn very easily. Your nose is always your best guide when toasting nuts, because an intense toasty aroma will tell you when they are ready.

Nut Care

The French are big consumers of nuts, which are folded into cakes and cookies, incorporated into savory dishes, and toasted, salted, sweetened, and blended with herbs to serve as apéritif. Nuts are appreciated for the way their flavors combine with and enhance other ingredients.

I use nuts whenever and wherever I can, simply because I love their flavors and textures. Since nuts are fragile and the fat they contain can easily turn rancid, I buy them fresh from a producer whenever I can, shortly after they are harvested. Or I purchase them from a reputable source where the turnover is high. I store nuts, carefully wrapped and airtight, in the freezer. Then I remove a specific amount and thaw the nuts before cooking.

All nuts are delicious when raw, but most are even better when lightly toasted, for then their deep, true flavors emerge. Following are specific techniques for toasting the most common nuts. Nuts can burn in an instant, so watch them carefully.

Hazelnuts

Preheat the oven to 375°F (190°C). Spread the nuts in a single layer in a baking pan and bake in the center of the oven until they smell toasty and the meat of the nuts is golden, 10 to 15 minutes. Immediately transfer the nuts to a cotton tea towel and wrap it up around them. Let the nuts steam in the towel for about 15 minutes, then vigorously rub them to remove the skins. Not all of the skin will come off the nuts, but rub off as much as you can.

Almonds

To skin unbleached almonds, bring a pan of water to a boil. Add the almonds, return the water to the boil, and boil for less than 1 minute. Drain the almonds and remove the skin by pinching each almond at the thicker end: it will shoot right out of the skin, so be sure you aim at a bowl or other receptacle.

To toast almonds, skin on or off, spread them on a baking sheet and bake in the center of a 375°F (190°F) oven until they smell toasty and the meat of the nuts is golden, 10 to 15 minutes.

Walnuts

Walnuts toast quickly due to their high fat content. Preheat the oven to 350°F (180°C), spread the walnuts out on a baking sheet, and toast them in the center of the oven for 10 to 12 minutes.

Pine Nuts

There are two major commercial varieties of pine nuts available, those from a Mediterranean pine, which are delicately flavored, elongated, and slightly torpedo shaped, and Chinese pine nuts, which are strong in flavor, triangular, and flat. Pine nuts toast faster than any other nut, so it is best to toast them atop the stove. Place them in a dry skillet over low heat and sauté them until they turn golden. (In saying sauté here, I mean it in the true sense of the word, which is to make an ingredient jump, or *sauter*, in a pan by shaking it so the nuts continuously move in the pan.) Continue stirring or they may burn.

Pistachios

The best ones come from Iran and Turkey. Their shells are darker than pistachios from other parts of the world, the nuts are slender, and they have a deeper, more buttery, toasty flavor. Their meats have a reddish-brown outer skin, a vivid green outer layer, and a creamy yellow interior.

Generally, pistachio nuts are sold already toasted and salted. If you find raw pistachios, follow the directions for walnuts, as they toast quickly.

Pecans

Preheat the oven to 350°F (180°C). Spread the pecans on a baking sheet and toast them in the center of the oven until they smell toasty and the meat of the nuts is a deep rust color, about 12 to 14 minutes.

Punch from Martinique

Punch de la Martinique

❧ **Punch (pronounced "ponsh") is common as a summer apéritif in the French home, offered by those nostalgic for their sunny vacations to France's tropical extensions, such as Ile de la Réunion, Nouvelle Caledonie, Guadeloupe, and Martinique. I never cared for punch until I tasted this one, which Jean-Claude Chaudron, who is originally from Martinique, brought to a dinner party given by friends. I didn't think I liked rum, but I realized when I tasted this that I'd never had good rum, for this is lovely, exotic, and refreshing. If your guests drink more than a glass or two of this punch, you may want to offer them a bed for the night.**

The yield depends on how much you serve in each glass, but this makes enough for many punches

2 cups (440 g) packed light brown sugar

2 cups (500 ml) mineral or filtered water

1 vanilla bean, slit down its length (so the seeds can escape), and cut into ½-inch (1.3-cm) lengths

2 limes, preferably organic, well washed

1 bottle *"rhum agricole,"* preferably St. James or Three Rivers

Ice cubes

1. Place the sugar, water, and vanilla bean in a small saucepan and bring to a simmer over medium heat. Cook, stirring frequently, just until the sugar dissolves. Remove from the heat and let the syrup cool to room temperature, then refrigerate it, covered, until cold.

2. Cut 1 of the limes into eighths. Cut the other lime into thin rounds, then cut the rounds in half.

3. To serve the punch, place 1 tablespoon of the chilled syrup in each glass, preferably with a piece of vanilla bean. Squeeze a lime wedge into the glass, then discard the lime, and add rum to taste (usually about 2 tablespoons). Add 2 lime half-rounds and an ice cube, stir, and serve.

ASTUCES: Excellent rum is necessary for any punch. Look for a bottle that has *"rhum agricole"* on the label, for this ensures that the rum has been made according to specific methods that guarantee its quality. ❧ Be sure that all the ingredients for the punch are well chilled. ❧ The recipe for sugar syrup may make more than you may need. If you have leftover syrup, squeeze some lemons and add their juice to the syrup for lemonade. ❧ I call for mineral water here because tap water often has an accentuated chlorine taste, which dulls the flavor of the punch.

Melon and Lime Parfait
Parfait de Melon et Citron Vert

❧ The credit for this delightfully refreshing and extravagantly simple little *amuse-bouche*, or palate teaser, goes to chef Patrice Barbot at restaurant l'Astrance, in Paris.

Like much of Chef Barbot's food, it is closely linked to milk. Milk? (It's the secret to the airy froth that makes this dish look as if it is dressed for a party.)

The success of the dish rests on the quality of its ingredients, so find the most flavorful melon you can, the best yogurt, and a good Banyuls or other white wine vinegar.

6 servings

1 small Cavaillon or Charentais melon or cantaloupe (about 1.25 pounds; 525 g), rind and seeds removed, cut into chunks

½ cup (125 ml) plain full-fat yogurt

The zest of ½ lime, minced

½ cup (125 ml) 2% milk

½ teaspoon Banyuls or other flavorful white wine vinegar

1. Puree the melon in a food processor. Transfer to a nonreactive airtight container and refrigerate for at least 1 hour and up to 3 hours.

2. In a small bowl, whisk together the yogurt and lime zest. Divide the mixture evenly among six glasses that hold at least ¾ cup (185 ml) each, such as wineglasses. Place the glasses in the refrigerator, covered loosely with a towel, to chill for at least 30 minutes.

3. Just before serving, remove the glasses and melon from the refrigerator and divide the melon puree among the glasses, pouring it carefully atop the yogurt mixture.

4. In a milk frother (or in the chilled bowl of a food processor), combine the milk and vinegar and froth or process until solidly foamy on top. Place a generous tablespoon of the foam in each glass, and serve immediately.

ASTUCES: The array of "frothers" on the market continues to increase: try a Frothmatic or a Bonjour Primo Latte for this. Two-percent milk froths much better than whole milk. ❧ Banyuls vinegar, with its light hint of honey flavor, is made with the fortified wine from the Collioure area in the Languedoc called Banyuls and a vinegar starter culture. The mixture is aged for a year in oak barrels while it achieves the 6 percent acidity necessary to be wine vinegar.

A Homemaker's Chicken Liver Terrine

Terrine de Foie de Volaille Ménagère

❧ I call this homemaker's chicken liver terrine because it is unlike any terrine from a charcuterie. Chunky and lively, it has the freshness of flavor that comes from being made in a small quantity, at home, with love.

I first tasted this with the Maudry family, owners of Domaine Maltaverne, which puts its label on one of the most interesting Pouilly Fumé wines in the Loire Valley appellation. Martine Maudry had made it several days before and left it to ripen in the refrigerator before serving it on a hot summer evening. Occasionally when I love a dish, I wonder if it is simply the magic of the moment, the people with whom I enjoyed it, the sense of place and purpose. The terrine withstood the test of being made at home, however, and we continue to enjoy it.

Serve the terrine either along with an apéritif with cornichons, small French pickles (page 296), or Onion Marmalade (page 275), or as a first course with green salad.

6 to 8 servings

1 pound (500 g) chicken livers, trimmed of any veins and gristle and coarsely chopped

8 ounces (250 g) boneless pork shoulder, cut into ½-inch (1.3 cm) pieces

8 ounces (250 g) ground pork

3 tablespoons Armagnac, Cognac, or Calvados

2 tablespoons tawny port or dry sherry

2 garlic cloves, green germ removed if necessary, minced

1 teaspoon fresh thyme leaves

Generous pinch of freshly grated nutmeg

1 teaspoon sugar

1. In a medium, nonreactive bowl, mix together the livers, pork shoulder, and ground pork with your hands. Add the Armagnac, port, garlic, thyme leaves, nutmeg, sugar, salt, and pepper and mix until thoroughly blended. Cover and refrigerate for 24 hours.

2. Preheat the oven to 350°F (180°C).

3. Lay 2 bay leaves and half the thyme sprigs on the bottom of a 4-cup (1-liter) terrine mold. Place the pork mixture atop the herbs, pressing it down lightly. Top the pork with the remaining bay leaves and thyme sprigs. Place the cover or a piece of parchment paper and a piece of aluminum foil on the mold, and place the mold in a pan large enough to hold it with room to spare. Pour in enough boiling water to come halfway up the sides of the terrine mold.

4. Bake until the terrine registers about 170°F (75°C) on an instant-read meat thermometer inserted into the

1 tablespoon (10 g) fine sea salt

12 grinds of black pepper (about ½ teaspoon freshly ground)

4 fresh bay leaves from the *Laurus nobilis*, or dried imported bay leaves

About 20 sprigs fresh thyme

center, about 1½ hours. Remove the terrine from the oven, remove from the water bath, and let cool slightly.

5. When the terrine is cooled, but not yet at room temperature, after about 30 minutes, cover the top of the terrine with parchment paper, if you have not already done so, and place a piece of cardboard cut to fit the terrine atop it. Place several—up to three—1-pound (500-g) weights on the cardboard. When the terrine has reached room temperature, refrigerate it, with the weights on it, for at least 24 hours, up to 3 days.

6. Serve the terrine chilled, from the terrine mold, with plenty of cornichons alongside.

ASTUCES: I bake the terrine and refrigerate it for at least three days before I serve it so it has a chance to mellow. Regardless of how long it sits or how heavy the weights set upon it, the terrine crumbles when you cut it. That is the price to pay for its toothsome texture.
✿ *Terrine* and *pâté* are interchangeable terms used for mixtures of meat, poultry, fish, or vegetables that are usually eaten chilled. Formally, however, a pâté is enclosed in pastry and served either hot or cold, and a terrine is like this dish, cooked in an earthenware mold also called a terrine, and eaten chilled.

Not Just Any Chicken Liver Pâté
Pâté de Foies de Volailles Pas Comme les Autres

❧ **Unbelievably delicious, smooth, and flavorful, you might think this pâté was foie gras if you didn't know better. I discovered it through a friend, Pierre-Yves Pieto, whose grandfather was a charcutier. Drink a Monbazillac with this, or Champagne—either is worthy.**

A generous 3 cups (750 ml), about 20 servings

1 pound (500 g) chicken livers, trimmed of any veins and gristle

⅓ cup (80 ml) tawny port

1 pound (500 g) unsalted butter, cut into chunks, softened

2 teaspoons fleur de sel

Several grinds of white pepper

Fresh chervil or flat-leaf parsley sprigs

1 baguette, sliced and toasted just before serving

ASTUCE: Warm freshly toasted bread is a must with this as it makes the pâté soft, giving it a seductive edge.

1. Place the chicken livers and port in a nonreactive bowl and stir well. Cover and refrigerate for at least 24 hours, and up to 48 hours.

2. Transfer the chicken livers and port to a small saucepan and bring to a gentle boil over medium-high heat. Reduce the heat so the livers are simmering gently, cover, and cook until the livers are cooked through and no longer red in the center, 12 to 15 minutes. Remove the pan from the heat and drain the livers, reserving the cooking liquid.

3. Place the chicken livers and 3 tablespoons cooking liquid in a food processor and puree. If the puree is still very stiff, add a little more cooking liquid—the puree should be the thickness of very heavy cream. Set the remaining liquid aside. Cool the puree, then press it through a sieve to remove any tough bits.

4. Return the puree to the cleaned bowl of the processor, add the butter and salt, and puree until the mixture is very smooth. If necessary, add 1 additional tablespoon of the cooking liquid to lighten the pâté. Season with the pepper, and additional salt if necessary. Transfer the pâté to a serving bowl, cover, and refrigerate for at least several hours, or overnight. (The pâté will keep for several days, tightly covered.)

5. To serve the pâté, garnish it with the herbs and serve chilled, with the warm toasts.

Hummus

Hommos

Hummus has become part of the French culinary landscape, contributed by the substantial Middle Eastern population living in France. Good hummus should taste of the chickpeas, with the right balance of garlic to lemon juice and a hint of cumin. This recipe is from a friend, Ziad Hatahet, a Syrian who makes it often as a dip for vegetables, crackers, or slices of bread.

A nicely chilled rosé from the Languedoc goes well with hummus.

About 7 cups (1.75 l)

2½ cups (1 pound; 480 g) dried chickpeas, or three 1-pound cans of chickpeas

1 teaspoon baking soda

1 tablespoon cumin seeds

¼ cup (60 ml) tahini (sesame paste)

4 large garlic cloves, green germ removed if necessary

¼ cup (60 ml) freshly squeezed lemon juice

3 to 6 tablespoons (60 to 90 ml) extra virgin olive oil

2 teaspoons fine sea salt

Freshly ground black pepper

½ cup (5 g) minced flat-leaf parsley leaves

¼ cup pomegranate seeds, optional

1. Place the chickpeas in a nonreactive bowl or pot, cover with water by 2 inches (5 cm), and stir in the baking soda. Let sit for at least 8 hours, and up to 12 hours.

2. Drain the chickpeas, rinse them, and place them in a large pot. Cover them with water by about 3 inches (7.5 cm), add the cumin, and bring to a boil over medium-high heat. Reduce the heat to medium so the water is softly boiling and cook, partially covered, until the chickpeas are tender through but still hold their shape, about 1½ hours. Drain the chickpeas, reserving the cooking liquid.

3. Place the chickpeas in a food processor and process to a chunky puree. Add the tahini, garlic, lemon juice, and about 3 tablespoons olive oil and puree until almost smooth. Add 6 tablespoons (90 ml) reserved cooking liquid and puree the mixture until light and smooth. Add the salt and pepper to taste, then add up to 3 tablespoons more olive oil, if desired. Adjust the seasoning, then transfer to a serving dish.

4. Sprinkle the parsley leaves and pomegranate seeds over the hummus if using. Serve immediately.

ASTUCES: If possible, use organic, recently dried chickpeas. Dried chickpeas more than a year old tend to be less tender and flavorful (but adding baking soda to the water tenderizes chickpeas of any age). Hummus keeps, refrigerated in an airtight container, for about 1 week.

Crisp Anchovy Toasts

Toasts Croquants aux Anchois

✤ It was a dark, cold winter night as we picked our way through the tightly planted pine trees outside Christian and Nadine Devisme's home out in the country, heading for the golden light of their veranda. Through the trees we glimpsed the old wooden bar inside, where four glasses and a bottle of Champagne sat, the round table set for four, and a flickering flame in the ornate woodstove in the corner. As soon as we wrestled off our coats, scarves, hats, and gloves, Christian handed each of us a glass of Champagne and a warm anchovy toast, oozing with butter and the flavor of delicious *anchois de Collioure,* the best in France. The four of us pulled up our chairs to the woodstove and nibbled these toasts well into the evening; Christian kept us well supplied.

4 to 6 servings

12 to 18 thin slices baguette

1 small garlic clove, green germ removed if necessary

1½ tablespoons (22 g) unsalted butter, softened

6 best-quality anchovy fillets, from Collioure or Sicily, cut into 1½-inch (3.75-cm) pieces

Flat-leaf parsley leaves

1. Preheat the oven to 400°F (200°C).

2. Place the bread slices on a baking sheet and toast in the oven until they are golden, turning them once if necessary, about 6 minutes total. Remove from the oven and rub the hot toasts lightly with the garlic. Spread the toasts with the butter, and lay a piece or two of anchovy fillet on top. Arrange the toasts on a platter, and garnish the platter with the parsley leaves. Serve immediately, while the toasts are still very warm.

ASTUCES: While soaking is not necessary if you are using excellent-quality anchovies packed in oil, you do need to soak salted anchovies. Set them in a shallow dish and cover them with white wine. Soak for 15 minutes, then drain and pat them dry. ✤ These toasts must be served warm.

Garlic Tips

Keep garlic at room temperature away from bright daylight. Depending on the variety and where you store it, garlic will last from the moment it is harvested in July, to as late as May of the following year.

What is the green germ inside the garlic clove? It's a budding garlic plant, and it can lend a bitterness to the flavor of the garlic. I recommend removing it, a simple matter. Slice the garlic clove lengthwise in half and pry it out, then use your garlic.

To mince or not to mince is not really the question. The more accurate question is with what does one mince? There are garlic presses, which I shy away from because they mash the garlic into a purée with a muffled flavor and no texture. When I call for minced garlic, I mean garlic that has been chopped into tiny bits with a very sharp knife.

During winter, simply plant a few garlic cloves in a window box or a flowerpot with potting soil (shallots work well, too), and husband them until their green shoots are well above the soil. Snip these to add to salads, sprinkle atop soups, or garnish vegetables.

Dried Fig and Hazelnut Bread
Cake aux Figues et aux Noisettes

❧ Sweet, savory *cakes* (pronounced *kek*) like this are typically served as an apéritif. I was inspired to combine these particular flavors by a cake I tasted at the *salon de thé* in the garden of the Musée de la Vie Romantique in Paris's 9th arrondissement. Serve this with a chilled glass of Savennières or a flute of Champagne.

10 to 12 servings

1½ cups (210 g) unbleached all-purpose flour

1 tablespoon baking powder

1 mounded teaspoon fine sea salt

6 large eggs

8 tablespoons (1 stick; 120 g) unsalted butter, melted and cooled

8 dried figs (7 ounces; 210 g), coarsely chopped

6 ounces (180 g) Gruyère or Emmenthal, finely grated (2 cups)

½ teaspoon fennel seeds, crushed

½ cup (2 ounces; 60 g) hazelnuts, toasted and skinned (see page 12)

Generous ¼ teaspoon freshly ground black pepper

1. Preheat the oven to 425°F (220°C). Butter an 8½ × 4½ × 2½-inch (21 × 11 × 6-cm) loaf pan. Line it with parchment paper, butter the parchment paper, and dust it lightly with flour.

2. Sift the dry ingredients onto a piece of parchment paper.

3. In a large bowl or the bowl of an electric mixer, whisk the eggs until they are combined, then slowly whisk in the dry ingredients. Using a wooden spoon, fold in the melted butter until it is thoroughly blended, then stir in the figs, cheese, fennel seeds, hazelnuts, and pepper, making sure they are well distributed throughout the batter.

4. Pour the batter into the prepared pan and rap it sharply on a work surface to release any air bubbles. Bake until the top of the bread is golden and a thin-bladed sharp knife stuck in the center comes out clean, 40 to 45 minutes.

5. Remove the bread from the oven and turn it out onto a wire cooling rack. After about 5 minutes, peel off the parchment paper, let it cool, and serve.

ASTUCE: To serve, cut in thin slices, then cut the slices into quarters on the diagonal.

Red Pepper Bread

Cake aux Poivrons Rouges

❧ This savory cake is a playful version of a recipe I got from a good friend, Héloise Tuyéras, a vibrant woman in her seventies from the Bordelais. Each time I serve it, it is greeted like an old friend. "Oh, I remember my mother or my grandmother making cakes like this," someone will say.

Get very creative with this by adding a tiny dice of ham or cooked bacon, or a Swiss-type cheese, or any number of spices.

Serve this with a Sauvignon Blanc from Château Turcaud.

About 10 servings

1½ cups (210 g) all-purpose flour

1½ teaspoons fine sea salt

2 teaspoons baking powder

½ teaspoon hot paprika

1 cup (10 g) gently packed flat-leaf parsley leaves

6 large eggs

¼ cup (60 ml) extra virgin olive oil

2 large red bell peppers (about 1 pound; 500 g total) roasted (see page 24), peeled, seeded, finely chopped, and patted dry

⅔ cup (2 ounces; 60 g) finely grated Parmigiano-Reggiano

1. Preheat the oven to 400°F (200°C). Oil an 8½ × 4½ × 2½-inch (21 × 11 × 6-cm) loaf pan. Line it with parchment paper, lightly oil the paper, and dust it with flour.

2. Sift the dry ingredients, including the paprika, onto a piece of parchment paper.

3. Mince the parsley leaves.

4. In a large bowl, whisk the eggs until combined. Add the oil and whisk until combined, then whisk in the flour mixture just until combined. Fold in the roasted peppers, Parmigiano-Reggiano, and parsley. Turn the batter into the prepared pan, and rap it once on a work surface to release any air bubbles.

5. Bake in the center of the oven until the top of the bread is golden and your finger leaves a slight indentation when pressed, about 50 minutes. Remove the bread from the oven and turn it out onto a wire rack. After about 10 minutes, peel off the parchment paper and let the bread continue to cool to room temperature.

ASTUCE: This bread keeps well, if thoroughly wrapped, for 2 days; it freezes well for up to a month. To serve, cut into thin slices, then cut the slices into quarters on the diagonal.

Roasting a Pepper

Les Façons de Rotir un Poivron

Roasting a red bell pepper brings out its sweet softness. If you roast it over a flame, it takes on a delectable smoky flavor. Once the skin, seeds, and pith—or membranes—have been removed from the pepper, do not rinse it, for you will rinse away flavor. Instead, using a sharp knife or plastic scraper, scrape away any residual skin or seeds.

Method 1

1. Place the pepper directly over the gas flame of a stove and roast it, turning it frequently, until the skin is completely black all over. Transfer it to a paper bag or wrap it in a cotton tea towel or a piece of aluminum foil, and let it sit until it has come to room temperature, so the steam from the pepper can loosen the skin from the flesh.

2. Rub off all of the black skin (it will come away easily), then cut away the stem end and pull out the "heart" of the pepper, which will bring most of the seeds and pith with it. Cut the pepper lengthwise into quarters. Trim away any pith that remains, and scrape away any remaining seeds and pieces of black skin.

Method 2

Preheat the broiler. Place the pepper on a piece of aluminum foil 3 inches (7.5 cm) from the heat element and roast, turning frequently, until the skin has blackened evenly all over. Remove the pepper from the oven, wrap it up in the foil, and let sit until it has cooled to room temperature. Proceed as directed above.

Method 3

1. Prepare a small fire on a grill.

2. When the coals are red and covered with ash, place the pepper 3 inches (7.5 cm) above the coals and grill, turning it frequently, until the skin is evenly blackened all over. Proceed as directed above.

Eggplant Caviar and Red Pepper Toasts
Toasts au Caviar d'Aubergine et Poivron Rouge

❧ **This lovely apéritif was served to me by Renaud Ducher, a young landscape architect in Lyon who lives to cook. The minute he gets on his bicycle heading for home in the evening, he is already composing supper's menu in his head, and his dishes are always unusual and full of imagination.**

I serve these toasts with a chilled dry Muscat or a fruity Chinon from Les Grezeaux.

20 toasts

20 slices Walnut Bread (page 214), about 3 by 2 inches (7.5 by 5 cm), lightly toasted

5 teaspoons top-quality walnut oil or extra virgin olive oil

Eggplant Caviar (page 276)

1 red bell pepper, roasted (see page 24), peeled, seeded, and cut into tiny dice

Fresh cilantro or basil leaves

Place the toasts on a serving platter. Drizzle each one with ¼ teaspoon of the oil. Top each toast with 1 tablespoon eggplant caviar, spreading it to the edges. Sprinkle an equal amount of the roasted pepper atop the eggplant, garnish with the herbs, and serve.

> **ASTUCE:** Each element of this recipe can be prepared in advance: the peppers as early as the night before, the eggplant caviar 2 to 3 days in advance, and the toast up to an hour ahead, as it needs to be fresh but not hot.

Savory Feta Rolls

Rouleaux de Jambon Sec à la Feta

⚜ I borrowed the idea for these brilliant little appetizers from a charcutier in Provence. One day I was walking past our neighborhood charcutier when I saw the very same rolls in his front window. I realized then that they weren't a personal brainchild, but a recipe made available to charcutiers France-wide, in some sort of professional capacity.

It doesn't really matter whose creation they once were, for these no longer resemble what I saw in the charcuterie window. With my experimenting, they have become herb-rich and bite-sized, the perfect, flavorful accompaniment to an apéritif. They go beautifully with a glass of lightly chilled rosé and a napkin.

About 40 rolls

4 ounces (120 g) thinly sliced prosciutto, cut into 1-inch (2.5-cm)-wide strips

4 ounces (120 g) feta, cut into 1 × ¼ × ¼-inch (2.5 × 0.6 × 0.6-cm) pieces

About 20 fresh sage leaves, cut lengthwise in half

⅓ cup (80 ml) extra virgin olive oil

Freshly ground black pepper

1. Lay out several strips of the prosciutto, and place a piece of feta at one end of each. Lay half a sage leaf across each piece of feta so the tip of the leaf sticks out beyond the edge of the prosciutto, then roll up the prosciutto around the feta and sage. Stand the rolls in a shallow bowl, so that the cheese shows, crowding them together to keep them from unrolling. Continue until all of the feta and sage are rolled inside the prosciutto.

2. Pour the olive oil over the rolls and marinate at room temperature for 1 hour.

3. Just before serving sprinkle the rolls with black pepper. Serve with toothpicks to skewer the rolls.

ASTUCE: Use any air-cured ham such as prosciutto di Parma or prosciutto di San Daniele, though be sure it is very thinly sliced. As for feta, I prefer a rich-tasting, creamy version from Turkey. However, Greek feta, which is saltier and more crumbly, makes a worthy substitute.

Goat Cheeses in Olive Oil

Fromages de Chèvres Marinés dans l'Huile d'Olive

❦ Good marinated goat cheese is the result of fine extra virgin olive oil, fresh and pungent herbs, flavorful goat cheese, and the time it takes for them to meld. I keep marinated goat cheese in my pantry because it can turn an ordinary meal into something special. The cheese can be sliced or cut into pieces for an apéritif, crumbled on a salad for a first course, wrapped inside a piece of pastry and baked, or sliced atop a pizza.

This recipe reflects my preferred herbs, but vary the flavor by using your favorites. Let the cheeses marinate in a cool, dark place for at least a week, and up to a month. Beyond a month they lose their freshness, though they will keep almost indefinitely in the oil.

4 marinated cheeses

Four small (about 3 ounces; 90 g) round slightly firm goat cheese

2 fresh bay leaves from the *Laurus nobilis*, or dried imported bay leaves

2 branches fresh rosemary

3 sprigs fresh sage

10 branches fresh lemon thyme

1½ generous cups (375 ml) extra virgin olive oil, or as needed

Place the goat cheeses in a jar that is large enough to hold them with room to spare, interspersing the herbs among them. Pour the oil over the cheeses, making sure it completely covers them. Cover the jar and let it sit in a cool, dark place for at least 1 week, and up to 1 month-before serving.

> **ASTUCES:** Look for firm, round goat cheeses. In France I use Crottin de Chavignol from the Loire Valley, because they have enough flavor to stand up to the marinade. ❦ If you plan to serve all the cheeses at once, remove them from the oil, strain it, and taste it. If it has a good, fresh flavor, you may want to use it to marinate another batch of cheese, along with additional fresh herbs. Or try it in a salad dressing, as a dip for fresh bread, or a seasoning for steamed vegetables. ❦ You may refrigerate the cheeses in oil, but it isn't necessary and it will hold back the maturation of their flavor. Once the cheeses have achieved the flavor you desire, you may refrigerate them.

Salmon Rillettes
Rillettes de Saumon

❧ Generally rillettes, a pâté-like delicacy made either on the farm or purchased at the charcuterie, are made of a blend of fatty and lean pork, often enriched with either goose or duck. The meats are cooked together slowly with herbs and spices, then left to cool. These rillettes have gone uptown, for they are made with fresh and smoked salmon. The idea is similar to traditional rillettes; the result totally different, bright, and sparkling.

They are the inspiration of our gardener, Franck Pecqueux, one of those unusual French men who loves to cook, takes an interest in interior design, and loves gardening and taking care of his new young son. Ideal before a fine meal with still-warm thinly sliced toasts and a slightly sweet Lombard white from the Côtes du Rhône.

2⅓ cups (580 ml); 10 to 12 servings

8 ounces (250 g) thick salmon fillet, preferably from a wild salmon, skin and bones removed

Fine sea salt

5 tablespoons (75 g) unsalted butter, softened

1 tablespoon (30 ml) extra virgin olive oil

4½ teaspoons (45 ml) freshly squeezed lemon juice

1 small bunch fresh chives

4 ounces (125 g) smoked salmon, cut into thin slices, then cut into strips that are ½ inch × ¼ inch (1.3 × 0.6 cm)

Toasted baguette, or crackers

1. Rinse the salmon fillet under cold water, pat it dry, and refrigerate until ready to use.

2. Bring about 3 cups (750 ml) water to a boil in the bottom of a steamer. Lightly salt the fresh salmon on all sides, then place it in the top of the steamer, cover, and steam until it is opaque through, about 13 minutes. If it is nearly but not quite opaque through when you check it, simply leave it in the steamer with the top off to cook in the residual steam for an extra minute or two. Once it is cooked, remove the salmon from the steamer and let it cool to room temperature.

3. In a medium bowl, whisk together the butter and olive oil until smooth and thoroughly combined, then whisk in the lemon juice until combined. Mince the chives (you should have 2 tablespoons), then whisk them into the butter mixture. Fold in the smoked salmon with a wooden spoon or spatula, and reserve at room temperature.

4. As soon as the cooked salmon fillet is thoroughly cool, crumble it over the smoked salmon mixture, and fold it in carefully. Season to taste with salt. Refrigerate the rillettes, covered, for at least 2 hours, or overnight.

5. At least 20 minutes before serving, remove the rillettes from the refrigerator and let sit until softened and serve on rounds of toasted baguette or crackers.

Mackerel Rillettes
Rillettes de Maquereaux

❧ Mackerel, one of my favorite fish, is available much of the year in Normandy, fresh off the boat, its dazzling steely blue skin stretched thin and taut over its firm flesh. Some say it is too strong; I say it is full of flavor, moist, easy to prepare, and easy to cook. Unlike so many of its cousins, it is forgiving too, for its high fat content means that a moment of overcooking will not destroy its texture.

Mackerel turned into rillettes makes an accompaniment for an apéritif that will surprise you with its delicacy and its popularity. Make this at least eight and up to twenty-four hours before you plan to serve it so the flavors can mellow, then serve with a chilled Pouilly-Fumé.

About 10 servings

Three 1-pound (500-g) mackerel; or about 2 pounds (1 kg) fish fillets or steaks

For the court bouillon

3 cups (750 ml) dry white wine

¼ cup (60 ml) white wine vinegar

2 cups (500 ml) water

1 medium carrot, peeled, trimmed, cut into thin rounds

1 fat leek, well rinsed, and trimmed, cut into thin rounds

1 large bunch fresh lemon thyme or regular thyme (about 40 sprigs)

3 bay leaves

Large pinch of fine sea salt

Several grinds of white pepper

1. Clean the mackerel and remove their heads. Rinse the belly cavity very thoroughly, and refrigerate until ready to cook.

2. To make the court bouillon, place all the ingredients in a large heavy-bottomed skillet or Dutch oven with sides at least 4 inches (10 cm) high. Bring to a boil over medium-high heat, then cover, reduce the heat so the liquid is simmering, and cook for 20 minutes.

3. Add the mackerel and increase the heat under the court bouillon so it is simmering merrily. Simmer the mackerel for about 3 minutes, then turn them and cook until they are opaque through, about 2 additional minutes. Transfer the mackerel to a plate to cool.

4. When the mackerel is cool enough to handle, remove the skin, remove the fillets from the bones, and then remove any small bones or pinbones from the fillets. Be very thorough: mackerel bones are fine and can be almost invisible.

To finish the rillettes

1/2 cup (125 ml) crème fraîche or heavy cream, preferably not ultra-pasteurized

2 tablespoons Dijon mustard

3 tablespoons grainy mustard

Fine sea salt and freshly ground white pepper

To serve the rillettes

Fresh herbs, such as cilantro or flat-leaf parsley, basil, or sage leaves

1 baguette, cut into thin rounds and toasted

5. In a medium bowl, whisk together the crème fraîche and mustards. Season to taste with salt and white pepper, then fold in the mackerel, mixing until thoroughly combined. Taste for seasoning—the rillettes should be slightly salty as they will be served cold and the seasoning will be less noticeable. Place the rillettes in a bowl, cover, and refrigerate for at least 8 hours, and up to 24 hours.

6. To serve the rillettes, transfer to a serving dish and garnish with the herbs. Serve with the toasted baguette slices.

ASTUCES: You can substitute fresh tuna, bonito, or any other full-flavored fish for the mackerel. If so, you may want to add additional cream for moisture—your palate will be your judge. ✤ Cooking fish in a court bouillon is the most gentle way to prepare it. In the case of mackerel, which is very full flavored, it enhances both flavor and texture.

Potatoes Roasted in Ashes, with Foie Gras
Pommes de Terre dans les Cendres, au Foie Gras

⚜ This is an idea that comes from years of cooking alongside Danie Dubois at her farm kitchen in the Dordogne. She produces the most marvelous goose foie gras, and I formed my palate on it years ago, when I went there each weekend to help her cook at the family's bed and breakfast. Danie uses foie gras in many ways, and slipping a slice into a hot potato fresh from the coals is my way of honoring her creativity and largesse.

There are many ways to roast a potato. I bury mine directly into the wood ashes, then quickly and carefully brush them off when they are baked, before adding the foie gras. No fireplace? Bake them in a very hot oven.

I serve these around the island in the kitchen, with Champagne and many napkins.

About 8 servings

24 small (about 2 ounces; 60 g each) Yukon Gold or Kennebec potatoes, scrubbed

6 to 8 ounces (180 to 250 g) fresh foie gras, cut in 24 thin slices and chilled

Fleur de sel

Freshly ground pepper blend (white, black, and green)

1. Build a large fire in the fireplace, or prepare a fire in a grill using wood, not charcoal briquettes. Do not start the fire with fire starter, or there will be a residue of petroleum flavor in the ashes.

2. When the fire has created a deep layer of ashes, carefully move the logs and bury the potatoes in the ashes. If they aren't completely buried, it doesn't matter—but you'll need to rotate them once so they roast evenly. Roast them until they are tender through, about 20 minutes.

3. About 10 minutes before you remove the potatoes from the fire, remove the foie gras from the refrigerator so it loses its chill but doesn't soften too much.

4. Remove the potatoes and brush the ashes from them. Slit each one down the center with a sharp knife, and push the ends toward the center to open up the potato. Insert a slice of foie gras into the potato, and season it with the salt and pepper or leave that for your guests to do. Eat immediately!

ASTUCES: Foie gras is easier to cut when chilled. Keep the sliced foie gras chilled to ensure that it will melt slowly when it hits the hot flesh of the potato. Using a blend of peppers gives a lively dimension to the foie gras and potato combination.
❧ Yukon Gold or Kennebec potatoes are both good for this, as they are wonderful baked, yet they hold their shape.

Tapenade Dressed Fit to Kill

Tapenade sur sa Trente-et-un

❧ This is an alternative way to serve tapenade, the Provençal olive puree that is usually served by itself. I got the idea many years ago at a small restaurant in Paris, where a dish similar to this was served just after we'd ordered our meal, to keep us busy while we waited. I loved the idea, and have played with it to get the flavors and proportions just right.

The rich tang of the yogurt cheese softens and highlights the salty depth of the tapenade, making a dish that is dressed up in its *trente-et-un,* or very best. This works at a formal dinner party as well as at a simple meal among friends, for it is beautiful and unusual.

I serve this with a lightly chilled Sauvignon Blanc, a perfect foil for the salty, rich blend of anchovy and olives and the creamy yogurt.

About 12 servings

3 cups (750 ml) plain full-fat yogurt

Tapenade (page 292)

Thyme or other edible flower blossoms

1. Line a sieve with two layers of cheesecloth and place it over a bowl. Turn the yogurt into the sieve and let drain for 24 hours.

2. Transfer the yogurt into a shallow serving bowl, and mound the tapenade atop it. Garnish with the flower blossoms and serve.

ASTUCE: Whole-milk yogurt makes the best yogurt cheese. Once you've tried yogurt cheese, you'll think of many uses for it. I like to fold fresh herbs and minced garlic into it for an appetizer, or serve it as dessert, topped with fresh berries, sugar, and a touch of crème fraîche, or with Dried and Fresh Apricot Compote (page 234).

Wild Mushrooms on Toast

Croûte Forestière

✤ I first tasted this at the Bois Gourmand, an alpine restaurant, outside Champagnole in the Jura region of eastern France, on a cool, sunny spring day. It was easy to imagine then, as we sat outside gazing over meadows and cattle far below, how this would satisfy the woodworkers, coal makers, shepherds, alpine walkers, and skiers of the Jura.

Though this is traditionally a rustic dish made with seasonal, regional ingredients at hand, I find it extraordinarily special because fresh morels are such a delicacy.

Try it with a lovely wine from the Jura.

4 servings

8 to 10 ounces morel mushrooms or other fresh mushrooms such as chanterelles or oyster mushrooms brushed clean, trimmed, and thickly sliced, or 1 ounce (about ½ cup; 30 g) dried morels

1 cup (250 ml) boiling water if using dried morels

1 pound (500 g) button mushrooms, trimmed, wiped clean, and thinly sliced

1 cup (250 ml) buttery white wine, such as an Arbois or light Chardonnay

2 tablespoons (30 g) unsalted butter

1 tablespoon all-purpose flour

½ cup (125 ml) crème fraîche or heavy cream, preferably not ultra-pasteurized

1. If using dried morels, place them in a medium bowl and pour the boiling water over them. Let sit for 1 hour, then lift the mushrooms from the soaking water and set aside. Strain the water through several thicknesses of cheesecloth and reserve.

2. Place the morels and button mushrooms in a large heavy-bottomed sauté pan, pour the wine over them, and bring to a boil over medium-high heat. Cook the mushrooms at a vigorous boil, stirring from time to time, until all but about 1 tablespoon of the wine has evaporated but the mushrooms are still moist, 8 to 10 minutes. Lower the heat to medium, add the butter, and stir until it has melted, then sprinkle the flour over the mushrooms and stir constantly for about 2 minutes so the flour is completely mixed into the mushrooms and cooked enough to lose its raw taste.

3. Add the reserved mushroom soaking liquid or, if using fresh morels, ¾ cup (185 ml) water to the mushrooms and cook, stirring, until the sauce has begun to thicken, about 4 minutes. Stir in the crème fraîche and cook until the sauce has thickened slightly again and the

Fine sea salt and freshly ground black pepper

8 large (about 6 × 4 × ¼ inch; 15 × 10 × 0.6 cm) slices crusty bread

Fresh chervil sprigs

mushrooms are tender but not limp, 4 to 5 minutes. Season to taste at this point.

4. While the mushrooms are cooking, toast the bread lightly on both sides, and place 2 pieces on each of four plates. Spoon the mushrooms and sauce over the bread. Garnish the plates with the chervil, and serve immediately.

ASTUCE: Do not rinse fresh wild mushrooms, as they are likely already quite damp, and putting them under water will harm their texture and flavor. Instead, to clean fresh mushrooms, tap them sharply but gently over a bowl, to dislodge any unwelcome material they may contain. Brush them clean with a pastry brush, working very carefully, as the mushrooms tend to be fragile.

A BOWL OF SOUP

Un Bol de Soupe

Cuisine is both an art and a science: it is an art when it strives to bring about the realization of the true and the beautiful, called *le bon* [the good] in the order of culinary ideas. As a science, it respects chemistry, physics, and natural history. Its axioms are called aphorisms, its theorems recipes, and its philosophy gastronomy.

La Table au Pays de Brillat-Savarin,
Lucien Tendret (1825–1896)

Creamy Fava Bean Soup

Soupe de Fèves à la Crème

❦ An ode to spring, this delicious soup was inspired by a cool, sunny lunch at Le Grand Véfour in the Palais Royale in Paris. There, chef Guy Martin dedicates himself to preparing dishes with flavors that are pure distillations of their simple ingredients, such as this one.

I wait with impatience for fava season, which begins in France in early June. I buy the small, tender favas from the first harvest, which offer elegant, sweet, and pure flavor and texture. Once favas get too large, they become starchy and are not as good in this soup.

Serve this with a chilled Pinot Grigio.

6 servings

2 pounds (1 kg) fava beans in their pods, shelled

1 tablespoon (15 g) unsalted butter

1 small white onion, diced

4 cups (1 l) Herb Broth (page 261)

½ cup (125 ml) crème fraîche

Fine sea salt

12 good-sized basil leaves

1. To peel the fava beans, bring a medium pot of water to a boil over high heat. Add the fava beans, return the water to a boil, and boil for about 1 minute, then drain the beans. When they are cool enough to handle, slit the skin of each and gently squeeze out the bright green bean within. Reserve 12 of the smallest fava beans.

2. Melt the butter in a medium, heavy-bottomed saucepan over medium heat. Add the onion, stir, cover, and cook until it is translucent and tender, about 11 minutes; check to be sure the onion isn't browning or sticking to the bottom of the pan.

3. Add the fava beans and broth and bring to a boil, increasing the heat if necessary to do so, then reducing it so the broth is simmering merrily. Cover, and cook until the fava beans are completely tender, about 15 minutes depending on their size; check the fava beans to determine their tenderness.

4. When the fava beans are tender, puree the mixture with an immersion blender or transfer it to a food processor to puree, then return it to the saucepan. Whisk in

the crème fraîche and cook just until the soup is hot through; do not let it boil. Season to taste with salt, and remove from the heat.

5. Meanwhile, just before serving, place 2 fava beans, separated into halves, in each of six soup bowls. Cut the basil into a chiffonnade, very fine strips.

6. Divide the soup among the bowls and top each with a few strips of basil. Serve immediately.

Gazpacho with Mustard Ice Cream

Gaspacho et sa Glace à la Moutarde

❧ Mustard ice cream? Sounds awful? Wrong, in this gazpacho, it is the crowning element, a huge and yummy surprise.

This dish is the brainchild of three-star chef Alain Passard at the Parisian restaurant Arpège, who shocked the French culinary world several years ago when he decided to serve an all-vegetarian menu. Who, he reasoned to the press at large, would want to eat meat in this day and age?

It was, as the French say, *osé*, or daring, but it has worked out, for clients continue to fill his cool, calm, restaurant in the 7th arrondissement.

This is a mid-to-late summer soup, made when tomatoes are ripe and filled with the sun's warmth, cucumbers are crisp and flavorful, and bell peppers sing with sweetness. It is perfectly seasoned by the tang of the distinctively flavored ice cream.

Serve a lightly chilled Gamay with the gazpacho.

6 servings

For the ice cream

1 cup (250 ml) whole milk

½ cup (125 ml) heavy cream, preferably not ultra-pasteurized

3 large egg yolks

2½ tablespoons Dijon mustard

For the gazpacho

6 medium ripe tomatoes, peeled, seeded, and diced

¼ red bell pepper, diced

8 ounces (250 g) cucumber, peeled and diced

1 small onion, quartered

1. To make the ice cream, first place a fine-mesh strainer over a medium bowl. Whisk together the milk, cream, and egg yolks in a medium saucepan and cook over medium heat, stirring constantly but slowly in a figure-eight pattern with a heatproof spatula or wooden spoon, until the mixture thickens enough to coat the back of the spoon and your finger leaves a definable trace when wiped across it. This should take about 5 minutes. Pour the custard through the strainer into the bowl. Let cool to room temperature, whisk in the mustard, then refrigerate. (You can make the ice cream up to this point the night before you plan to serve it.)

2. To make gazpacho, place all the vegetables and the garlic in a food processor or blender and process to a coarse puree. Transfer the mixture to a fine-mesh sieve placed over a bowl to drain, and refrigerate for at least 2 hours, and up to 4 hours.

1 small fennel bulb, trimmed and coarsely chopped

1 small clove new garlic

1 tablespoon freshly squeezed lemon juice

½ cup (125 ml) extra virgin olive oil

Pinch fine sea salt

3. Remove the soup from the refrigerator. Discard the juices, and transfer the solids to a medium bowl. Stir in the lemon juice and olive oil, then season to taste with the salt. Return to the refrigerator.

4. Remove the custard from the refrigerator. Freeze the mixture in an ice cream maker according to the manufacturer's instructions. If the ice cream is too soft to hold a shape, freeze it until it is firm.

5. To serve the soup, divide it among six chilled shallow bowls. Using two soupspoons, scoop out the ice cream, shaping it into elongated ovals and place one oval in the center of each bowl of soup. Serve immediately.

ASTUCES: If you don't use all of the ice cream for the soup, I suggest using the mixture unfrozen to make a sauce for chicken or fish. Just make sure that you cook it gently so the egg yolks don't curdle. The ice cream recipe makes about 1¾ cups (435 ml). ✿ New garlic has been harvested when it is fully formed but not yet dry. Its outer skins are moist and thick, the inner cloves tender and almost juicy, and filled with pungent garlic flavor. Look for new garlic mid-to-late May through June.

Fresh Spring Pea Soup

Soupe aux Petits Pois de Printemps

❧ The very first harvest of fresh peas is the best, hands down. I buy two kilos and then we all shuck them. I boil the peas in lightly salted water and top them with a big nut of fresh butter. I can't bear to do anything with the first peas in spring, other than enjoy them in all their purity. Fortunately, my family feels as I do; we serve ourselves big bowls of peas and call it supper.

Peas from subsequent harvests are made into this luscious soup—which is deep green with a pure pea flavor.

Serve a light, delicate Sauvignon Blanc with this light, delicate soup.

6 servings

4 pounds (2 kg) fresh peas in the pod, shucked (to give about 4¾ cups)

½ teaspoon fine sea salt

Freshly ground white pepper

1½ tablespoons (22 g) unsalted butter

12 small fresh mint leaves

1. Place the peas in a medium saucepan and cover with water by 1 inch (2.5 cm). Add the salt, bring to a boil, cover, and cook until the peas are completely tender, about 20 minutes.

2. Puree the peas with an immersion blender or in a food processor, then press them through a fine-mesh sieve to remove their skins. Return the soup to the saucepan if necessary and gently reheat. If it is too thick for your liking, thin it slightly with water, but do not add too much, or you will dilute the flavor of the peas. Season to taste with salt and pepper.

3. Ladle the soup into six warmed shallow soup bowls. Garnish each bowl with a bit of butter, and place 2 mint leaves next to the butter. Serve immediately.

ASTUCE: Late spring peas are perfect for this soup, for they have ample flavor and sweetness, and their slightly tough skins are removed before serving. Mint is the ideal herb to accompany pea soup, though chive blossoms are delightful too. Don't be tempted to add cream to this soup, as it would muffle the fresh pea flavor.

The Cucumber Soup of Summer
La Soupe au Concombre d'Été

⚜ I look forward to making this soup each summer with fresh cucumbers, grown by our friend Baptiste Bourdon, a farmer who sells at our local market. There is something about his firm yet juicy cucumbers that is so alluring and refreshing.

This frothy soup was inspired by Isabelle Devisme, a friend who readily admits she doesn't like to cook. Whenever a French person says that, my ears prick up, for I find these are the people who come up with the most imaginatively simple recipes. Why? Because they love to eat, they just don't want to spend time in the kitchen so they develop recipes that fit their needs.

This soup couldn't be simpler. It is a perfect summer tonic, particularly on a scorching day.

Serve with a chilled Sauvignon Blanc.

6 servings

2 long firm European or Asian cucumbers (about 2¼ pounds; 1 kg 120 g total), peeled, halved lengthwise, seeds removed, and coarsely chopped

4 small fresh onions, or 6 scallions, white part only

1 cup (250 ml) heavy cream or half-and-half, preferably not ultra-pasteurized

Fine sea salt and freshly ground black pepper

¼ cup firmly packed flat-leaf parsley leaves

6 fresh mint leaves

1. Place the cucumber in a food processor fit with a steel blade, and process.

2. Add the onion and process until the mixture is a frothy puree. Add the cream and process to blend. Transfer to a bowl and season to taste with salt and pepper.

3. Mince the parsley and mint together and stir them into the soup. Cover the soup and refrigerate for at least 2 hours before serving, and up to overnight (8 hours).

ASTUCE: I refrigerate the cucumbers because they froth better when they are chilled and hold their froth longer. This soup has amazing durability; it is just as refreshing and delicious the day after it is made. To remove the cucumber seeds, scrape them out gently with a soupspoon.

Chorba

⚜ The ninth month of the Muslim year, called Ramadan, is given over to fasting. Our friends, Salah and Dalila Boufercha fast all day and then like their fellow believers worldwide, feast once the sun goes down. The first time we joined them for a Ramadan meal it was completely dark by 6 P.M., very early for dinner by French standards, unless you have been fasting all day. The apéritif was a cup of sweet café au lait with a plateful of date cakes called *makroute*.

"We drink café au lait to coat and protect the stomach," Dalila explained. "That way it doesn't suffer after being empty all day."

We then had bowls of chorba, this cilantro-, mint-, and cinnamon-scented vegetable and lamb soup. "Ramadan wouldn't be Ramadan without chorba," said Dalila. "I have such fond memories of sitting around the table when I was a girl in Algeria, and eating the chorba my grandmother and mother had made. We eat it every single night of Ramadan, but I make it at other times of the year too."

The traditional accompaniment for this is water, since alcohol is forbidden according to Islam. Otherwise, it goes well with a lovely rosé from the Touraine.

8 to 10 servings

⅓ cup (80 ml) extra virgin olive oil

14 ounces (400 g) lamb shoulder or neck, trimmed of excess fat and cut into bite-sized pieces

4 medium onions, finely diced

2 large celery branches with leaves or 4 regular celery branches, trimmed and sliced paper-thin

1 good-sized bunch fresh cilantro

1 teaspoon ground cinnamon

1 tablespoon coarse sea salt

1. In a heavy-bottomed saucepan or Dutch oven, heat the oil over medium heat. When it is hot but not smoking, brown the meat on all sides. Add the onions and celery and stir, then reduce the heat slightly and cook, covered, until the onions are translucent and softened, stirring occasionally to be sure they don't stick, about 8 minutes.

2. Mince half the cilantro leaves and stems and add it to the pan, then sprinkle the cinnamon over the ingredients, season with the salt and pepper, and stir. Add the tomatoes, increase the heat slightly, and bring to a boil. Cook, covered, for about 5 minutes, then stir in the tomato paste and 2 cups (500 ml) of the hot water. Cook, covered, for about 10 minutes so the flavors blend, then add the remaining 2 quarts (2 l) hot water. Bring to a simmer, then add the bulgur, stir, and then

1 teaspoon freshly ground black pepper

One 14-ounce (425-ml) can peeled tomatoes, with their juice (or 3 to 4 fresh tomatoes, cored and diced)

5 tablespoons (2 ounces; 60 g) tomato paste

2½ quarts (2.5 l) hot water

½ cup (75 g) bulgur wheat

1 large bunch fresh mint, tied together with kitchen string

add the mint. Bring to a boil, reduce the heat to low so the soup is simmering, cover, and cook until the bulgur is tender through and all the flavors have blended nicely, about 30 minutes.

3. Just before serving, mince the remaining cilantro leaves. Remove and discard the mint, stir the cilantro into the soup, and adjust the seasoning. Serve immediately.

ASTUCES: There are as many versions of chorba as there are cooks who make it. Dalila has several others as well, but this is the one she makes most often. Lamb neck is a little-appreciated part of the animal, which is a shame because it gives wonderful flavor and texture. ✤ This soup cooks for a relatively short time, so its flavor remains fresh and sparkling.

Soup for Couscous
Soupe de Couscous

❧ **An aromatic broth that goes with Couscous (page 278); this soup speaks of exotic, faraway lands and boisterous groups, of family and friends around a laden table.**

Dalila Boufercha, who taught me to make Chorba (page 44), loves entertaining, and when she does, her meals go on forever. A couscous evening begins with a lively tomato salad and Flat Semolina Bread (see page 196). She makes dozens and dozens of *gâteaux makroute,* substantial little semolina cakes stuffed with pureed dates, for dessert, along with ice cream for the children. Couscous is a happening, an event, a wonderful dish to share with friends. I make it when I have the whole day ahead of me, for while it is a very simple meal, it demands time and patience.

The traditional drink with couscous is water or fermented milk. A Beaujolais or a red Sancerre are my choices.

8 to 10 servings

1⅓ cups (250 g) dried chickpeas

½ teaspoon baking soda

3 tablespoons (45 ml) extra virgin olive oil

2½ pounds (1 kg; 250 g) lean lamb or cow's shoulder or neck, cut into about ¾-inch (2-cm) pieces

5 medium onions (1 pound 6 ounces; 180 g), diced

2 generous pinches saffron

1 tablespoon coarse sea salt

2¼ quarts (9 cups; 2¼ l) hot water

2 tablespoons (30 g) tomato paste

1. Place the chickpeas in a saucepan, cover with water, by 2 inches (5 cm), add the baking soda, and stir. Bring the water to a boil, remove the pan from the heat, cover, and let sit for 1 hour.

2. Drain the chickpeas and cover them with fresh water. Bring to a boil over medium-high heat, reduce the heat so the water is boiling gently, and cook until the chickpeas are nearly tender, about 1 hour. Remove from the heat and reserve, undrained.

3. Heat the oil in a large heavy saucepan or Dutch oven over medium heat. When the oil is hot but not smoking, add the meat and brown it well on all sides, about 9 minutes. Add the onions, stir so they are coated with oil, and cook until they are deep golden, about 10 minutes. Crumble the saffron over the mixture, season with the salt, stir, and add 1 cup (250 ml) of the hot water. Stir and cook for 4 to 5 minutes to blend the ingredients and allow the saffron to soften.

2 pounds (1 kg) carrots, cut on a slight diagonal into 1-inch (2.5-cm) lengths

1½ pounds (750 g) turnips, peeled and cut into quarters if small or into 1-inch (2.5-cm) pieces if large.

1½ pounds (750 g) zucchini, trimmed and cut on a slight diagonal into 1½-inch (3.75-cm) lengths

1½ pounds (750 g) potatoes, peeled and cut into 1½-inch (3.75-cm) pieces

4. Add the tomato paste and stir. Then add the remaining 2 quarts (2 l) hot water and bring to a boil. Cover, reduce the heat so the liquid is simmering merrily, and cook until the meat begins to turn tender, about 30 minutes.

5. Add the carrots and chickpeas, cover, and bring to a boil. Reduce the heat so the liquid is boiling gently and cook until the carrots resist only slightly when tested with a sharp knife, about 15 minutes. Add all the remaining vegetables and only cook until they are tender, about 30 minutes. Check the seasoning and remove from the heat.

6. The soup is ready to serve, but it will benefit from sitting for an hour or two and then being reheated.

ASTUCES: The best meat for couscous soup is lamb neck, which is toothsomely gelatinous. You can use a mix of meats, but no pork, since it is forbidden in Islam. ✤ Baking soda added to dried legumes as they pre-cook tenderizes them. ✤ You will notice that the carrots and zucchini are cooked until quite soft, which is how they are meant to be. If you want your vegetables a bit more al dente, add them later in the cooking time.

SEA SALT

Most salt can rightly (and legally, I believe) be called sea salt since, whether it sits well below the earth's surface or out in a salt marsh in Brittany, it is the product of the sea. That said, the sea salt that I am referring to is gray in color and moist, and the best comes from waters off the coast of southern Brittany near the town of Guérande. It is the best sea salt I have ever tasted: its intense but full and well-rounded saltiness make it a food rather than a simple seasoning.

The four thousand acres of salt marsh near Guérande look like silver panes of glass separated by dark brown dikes. Sea water is run through canals into a series of cantilevered coastal marshes. The water evaporates as it goes, leaving sea salt behind. In summer, the height of the salt harvest, the *paludiers*, or salt rakers, tanned, lean, barefoot, and windswept, literally rake by hand mound after mound of salt up onto dikes. There the salt rests in gray pyramids until the salt rakers return at the end of the day to load it into wheelbarrows and transport it to the storage shed.

Why is sel de Guérande gray? The color comes from the hard-packed clay and the algae in the marshes, both of which contribute minerals to the salt. *Gros sel,* or coarse gray salt, contains almost 7 percent humidity, 55 percent chloride, 35 percent sodium, and trace amounts of potassium, calcium, and magnesium. Each kilo (2.2 pounds) of sea salt contains 2.5 milligrams of copper, 5 milligrams of zinc, almost 7 milligrams of manganese, 85 milligrams of iron, and traces of iodine. While this cocktail of minerals doesn't supply much of a person's daily requirement, it is what helps give this salt its uniquely satisfying flavor.

Both coarse and fine gray sea salt are wonderful for cooking. I use the coarse salt in dishes where exact amounts aren't important—soups and stews, for example, as well as in pasta water, water for blanching vegetables, and bread doughs. I also strew coarse salt over roasted poultry once it is removed from the oven, on grilled meats, and on some fish. Coarse gray salt is ideal for use as a salt crust, though outside France the cost tends to be prohibitive. As a less expensive alternative, I suggest kosher salt.

When I need a more precise amount of salt, I use fine gray sea salt, which I can easily buy, but which you might have to make yourself by first drying out coarse gray salt, then grinding it in a mortar and pestle or a coffee grinder. If you use a coffee grinder, be sure to wipe it out carefully afterwards so that no trace of salt or moisture remains to corrode the workings.

Fleur de Sel

Fleur de sel is also sea salt, but is not derived from evaporated sea water. Instead, it forms on top of the water in the salt marshes, in a sparkling layer of crystals that is carefully, delicately scraped away.

In Guérande, the salt rakers say that fleur de sel forms only when the east wind blows. They smell the wind before it arrives, as the air fills with a delicate scent of violets, then they watch carefully. When they see a glint on the water, they take to the marshes, carefully walking along the dikes that separate them, scraping off platelets of salt with a tool that resembles a wide rake but without tines. They mound the salt on the dikes to drain, then transport it to hangars where it will further drain before they package and sell it.

Fleur de sel is capricious, and the day I watched it being harvested the east wind wasn't just blowing, it was howling with a threat of rain. A *paludier* next to me explained: "You'll notice the rakers are mostly women," he said. "They are best at harvesting fleur de sel because their hands feel it better on the handle of the rake, and it is very fine work. They have to work quickly too, because weather conditions may change in an instant." Should a squall pass overhead, all the salt would melt away.

It was twilight and the sun was a red ball on the horizon, casting its pink glow on the clouds, the water, the marshes, and the piles of salt, which looked from a distance like cotton candy. I learned later that the intense pink hue in fleur de sel is primarily due to a plankton called *Dunaliella salina*. What I witnessed was the color of plankton amplified by the sunset. The female rakers worked steadily and without conversation until all the crystals were captured. I turned to leave, chilled to the bone. I would never again take fleur de sel for granted, I thought as I drove away, looking in my rearview mirror at the teams of *paludiers* now arriving with wheelbarrows to collect their salt.

Fleur de sel is highly esteemed for its pure and intense saltiness, and its marvelous, multifaceted crunch. It is not a salt to cook with but a salt to use for seasoning, added to a dish just before serving.

Provençal Vegetable Soup

Soupe au Pistou

⚜ On any given summer or fall day in any given home in Provence or on the Côte d'Azur, *soupe au pistou* is likely to be on the menu. And as with any local recipe, each cook has her own version. All of them include a palette of seasonal vegetables, cooked in water and seasoned at the very end with a puree of basil, garlic, olive oil, and, sometimes, cheese. The puree, called pistou, gives the thick soup its name.

Monique Tourette, an old friend who lives in the charming hilltop village of Venasque in Provence, has been my pistou guru. She makes it the way many of her neighbors make it, except that she uses a much bigger pasta than the angel hair pasta that is usually called for, which I love for its textural contrast, and she adds hot paprika to the soup to give it a lively zing!

Some cooks add the grated cheese to the pistou, then stir the pistou right into the soup. I like participatory dishes, so I serve the pistou and the cheese separately from the soup.

About 6 servings (with plenty of pistou)

1½ cups (8 ounces; 250 g) fresh white shell beans (from 1 pound; 500 g beans in the pot; or use 4 ounces; 120 g dried cannellini or other dried white beans—see Astuces)

1½ cups (8 ounces; 250 g) fresh red shell beans (from 1 pound; 500 g beans in the pod; or use 4 ounces; 120 g dried kidney or other red beans—see Astuces)

8 ounces (250 g) green beans, trimmed and cut into ½-inch (1.3 cm) lengths

2 medium waxy potatoes, cut into ½-inch (1.3 cm) cubes

1. Place all the vegetables in a large stockpot and cover with at least 2 inches (5 cm) of water. Bring to a boil over medium-high heat, then reduce the heat so the liquid is simmering and cook, partially covered, until the shell beans are tender, about 20 minutes.

2. Add the paprika, salt, pasta, and the cooked dried beans if using, and stir, return the liquid to a gentle boil, then increase the heat to medium-high and cook until the pasta is al dente, 8 to 10 minutes. Remove from the heat and adjust the seasoning.

3. While the soup is cooking, make the pistou: Place the garlic cloves and salt in a mortar or a food processor and grind or process until the garlic is mashed almost to a paste. Add the basil leaves and continue to pound or process until they make a sort of paste with the garlic — the paste will not be smooth or uniform, but the leaves should be completely crushed. Stir in the olive oil, or

1 medium zucchini, trimmed and cut into ½-inch (1.3 cm) cubes

2 medium carrots, peeled and cut into ½-inch (1.3 cm) cubes

1 medium leek, trimmed, well rinsed, and cut into ½-inch (1.3 cm) pieces

1 generous pinch of hot paprika

1 teaspoon coarse sea salt

¾ cup (260 g) penne

For the pistou

Makes about 1⅓ cups (265 ml)

3 large garlic cloves, green germ removed if necessary

Pinch of fine sea salt

4 cups (about 40 g) gently packed fresh basil leaves

⅔ cup (160 ml) extra virgin olive oil

½ cup (about 1 ounce; 22 g) finely grated Parmigiano-Reggiano

add it slowly with the processor running, until it is well mixed with the basil and garlic. The pistou will be quite liquid. Transfer it to a small serving bowl.

4. To serve, ladle soup into six warmed serving bowls and pass the pistou and cheese alongside.

ASTUCES: If you use dried beans, place them in a large pot and cover them with water by 2 inches (5 cm). Bring to a boil, then drain and return to the pot. Cover the beans with fresh water, add ½ teaspoon baking soda, bring to a boil over high heat, reduce the heat to medium, and cook, partially covered, until the beans are al dente, about 50 minutes. Drain and add to the soup along with the pasta. ❖ The pasta takes longer to cook in the soup than it would in salted water. ❖ Consider making a double recipe of the pistou. Everyone always wants more, and if there is leftover pistou, it freezes beautifully.

Chicken Soup with Tamarind

Soupe de Poulet au Tamarin

⚜ Leang Chhing owns an Asian grocery store in Val de Reuil, a new town near us that was built in the 1970s. Mr. Chhing draws forth amazing ingredients from behind his small vegetable counter, including galangal; *menthe aquatique* (*Mentha aquatica*), or water mint; and tamarind paste, all of which are blended into this light, refreshing soup. He gave me the recipe one day when I was asking him how to use much of the produce, telling me it assuaged his nostalgia for Cambodia, which he fled twenty years ago.

My son, Joe, was with me when Mr. Chhing carefully noted down the recipe in his precise handwriting, gathering the ingredients as he wrote, measuring the length of galangal I needed before weighing it, inspecting the tamarind paste to decide how much I should use, sorting through his bunches of water mint. Joe caught my eye at one point. "He's so proud of this recipe," he mouthed.

Joe was right. Mr. Chhing, who is normally taciturn, literally beamed as he showed us from his shop. The next time I went there, I told him how much we all had loved the soup, including Joe (who was eleven at the time). Mr. Chhing looked at me. "But did your husband really like it? Did he like it?" When I said he did, Mr. Chhing replied, "Well, then that's all right."

Serve this with a dry white wine or a blond Asian beer.

4 to 6 servings

6 cups (1.5 l) water

1 teaspoon coarse sea salt

1 small piece galangal (3 inches; 7.5 cm long), cut into coins, or 1 cinnamon stick

1 pound (500 g) skinless chicken breast (from a free-range chicken), cut into 1 × ½-inch (2.5 × 1.3-cm) strips

1. Put the water, salt, and galangal in a large saucepan and bring to a boil. Add the chicken, pineapple, onion, fish sauce, sugar, and tamarind paste, stir, reduce the heat so the water is simmering, and simmer until the chicken and onion are tender, about 20 minutes.

2. Meanwhile, place the garlic and oil in a small heavy-bottomed saucepan and cook over medium heat, stirring, until the garlic is golden, about 8 minutes. Remove from the heat and reserve.

3. Slice the water mint crosswise into thin slices and add it, along with the tomatoes and garlic, to the soup. Stir and cook just until the tomatoes are hot through and

6 ounces (180 g) fresh pineapple, peeled and cored if necessary, cut into ½-inch (1.3-cm) rings, then cut into wedges about ½ inch (1.3 cm) on the wide end

1 small onion, cut into 6 wedges

2 teaspoons *nuoc mam* (Asian fish sauce), or to taste

1 teaspoon sugar

2½ ounces (75 g) tamarind paste

2 garlic cloves, green germ removed if necessary, minced

2 teaspoons mild cooking oil, such as safflower

10 slim branches water mint, cut into 3-inch (7.5-cm) lengths, or 12 fresh peppermint leaves

4 small tomatoes, cored and cut into quarters

slightly softened but still have some texture, 3 to 5 minutes.

4. Ladle the soup into warmed soup bowls and serve immediately.

ASTUCES: If the tamarind paste is very solid, you may have to gently pound some boiling water into it before adding it to the soup to loosen it up so that it blends in well. ✤ Note that the water mint—a semisucculent variety of mint—is sliced just before adding it to the soup and not one second sooner, so that none of its essential oils and flavor are lost. A "coin" is roughly the size of a quarter.

Leek Potage
Potage aux Poireaux

✤ *Potage* is to French home cooking what orange juice is to the American breakfast. I would wager that potage is on most French tables every winter evening, as a prelude to something more substantial. All of my friends feel potage is the key to health during the winter, when illnesses lurk in every draft and drop in temperature.

Potage is easy, makes use of seasonal vegetables, and my family loves it. There are certain constants to potage—leeks, for their flavor; carrots, garlic, and onions for sweetness; potato as a thickener. I always include these, then add other ingredients like Belgian endive, an apple, shallots, or squash. Don't add broccoli, cauliflower, or Brussel sprouts, because their flavors are too distinctive.

Norman cooks add a small dollop of cream right before serving potage, and I do as well on occasion. Sometimes I mince a blend of fresh herbs to stir in right before I serve it.

Serve a chilled hard apple cider along with this potage.

6 to 8 servings

2 good-sized leeks (about
1 pound; 500 g), well rinsed and
cut into ½-inch (1.3 cm) slices

1 large carrot, peeled and cut
into ½-inch (1.3 cm) slices

1 small onion, diced

3 garlic cloves, green germ
removed if necessary, diced

1 large potato, peeled and diced

1 Belgian endive, rinsed and cut
into ½-inch (1.3-cm) pieces

20 sprigs fresh thyme tied in a
bundle

2 fresh bay leaves from the
Laurus nobilis, or dried imported
bay leaves

Coarse sea salt

1. Place all the vegetables and herbs in a Dutch oven and cover with water by 2 inches (5 cm). Season with salt and bring to a boil over medium-high heat, then reduce the heat so the liquid is simmering and cook, partially covered, until the vegetables are tender about 45 minutes. Remove from the heat.

2. Remove the herbs from the pot, and using an immersion wand blender or a food processor, puree the soup. Season to taste with course salt and pepper. Transfer to a warmed soup tureen, whisk in the crème fraîche, if using, then adjust the seasoning if needed.

ASTUCES: Potage is never left over, as it doesn't maintain its freshness for more than a day. ✤ Just one potato gives the potage its smooth texture, and the cream, which is added right before serving so it maintains its delicate flavor, rounds out the flavor.

Freshly ground black pepper

2 to 3 tablespoons (30 to 45 ml) crème fraîche, optional

3. Ladle the soup into six to eight warmed soup bowls, and serve immediately.

How to Eat Like the French

I am often asked how the French eat so well, yet look so thin and healthy. Here are some tips I've learned.

1. Buy ingredients as close to the source as you can. Go to a farm, a farmers' market, a shop featuring farm ingredients. Buy organic ingredients whenever you can. They may cost more, but realize that their cost is the real cost of producing food, for most organic farmers don't get government subsidies.

2. Serve a green salad with lunch and dinner.

3. Serve bread without butter at mealtimes.

4. Drink plenty of water throughout the day.

5. Avoid snacking between meals.

6. Always have seasonal fruit available. I often cut up fruit—apples, pears, melons, peaches—when my children are agitating for a meal and I haven't quite finished preparation.

7. Serve vegetable soup often; it is a delicious and satisfying way to enjoy vegetables.

8. Have a glass of wine with your meal. Wine, particularly red wine, is believed to have health benefits when taken in moderation.

9. Avoid processed foods and soft drinks.

10. Don't be afraid of your food. If you are comfortable with your food, you will enjoy it more and eat less.

11. Take time at the table so you can enjoy the meal you've prepared.

HOT AND COLD
FIRST COURSES
Entrées Chaudes et Froides

Everything ends this way in France—
everything. Weddings, christenings, duels,
funerals, swindles, diplomatic affairs—
everything is a pretext for a good dinner.

Cécile,
Jean Anouilh (1910–1987)

Asparagus Omelet
Omelette aux Asperges

⚜ With its tender, narrow stalks of green asparagus, bacon, fresh spring onions, and touch of cheese, this is a typical omelet from Provence. Omelets are lunch or dinner food in France and they are always *baveuse*, or moist and succulent in the center. Follow the directions to the letter, and yours will be that way as well. If you prefer your omelet cooked through, simply lower the heat a touch and increase the cooking time.

The omelet may be served as a main course, accompanied by a salad of tender lettuce leaves. Serve with a lightly chilled Coteaux de Tricastin.

4 servings

6 large eggs

1 ounce (30 g) Parmigiano-Reggiano, finely grated (about ⅓ cup)

Fine sea salt and freshly ground black pepper

8 ounces (250 g) asparagus, trimmed

3 ounces (90 g) slab bacon, rind removed, cut into 1 × ¼ × ¼-inch (2.5 × 0.6 × 0.6-cm) pieces

2 spring onions, trimmed and thinly sliced, or the white part of 4 scallions, thinly sliced

1. Whisk the eggs together in a medium bowl just until they are blended but not foamy. Whisk in the grated cheese and season with salt and pepper to taste. Set aside.

2. Bring about 3 cups (750 ml) water to a boil in the bottom of a steamer over high heat. Place the asparagus in the top of the steamer, cover, and steam until the asparagus is tender through, about 7 minutes. Remove from the heat and let cool slightly. Cut off the tips, slice the stems into thin rounds, and reserve.

3. In a large heavy-bottomed omelet pan, preferably nonstick, sauté the bacon over medium-high heat until it is lightly golden and cooked through, 2 to 3 minutes. Drain off all but 1 tablespoon of the fat from the pan, and add the onions. Sauté the onions until tender and translucent, 4 to 5 minutes. Add the asparagus tips and stems, stir, and cook until they are hot through and sizzling. Spread the ingredients evenly over the bottom of the pan, season them lightly with salt and pepper, and then pour the eggs over them, rotating the pan so the eggs cover the bottom. As the eggs set, use a spatula to pull the eggs from the edges toward the center of the

ASTUCES: The asparagus should
be cooked until it is tender through
so its full flavor melds with the
omelet. Don't give in to the tendency
to cook the asparagus just tender-
crisp, for the effect isn't the same.
✣ Gruyère is typically used in an
omelet like this, but I much prefer
Parmigiano-Reggiano for its sharper
flavor and drier, less elastic texture.
Also, Gruyère tends to make the
omelet stick to the pan, so if you
substitute it, don't mix it with the
eggs, but sprinkle it over the filling.

pan, tipping the skillet as you do so, so the uncooked egg flows toward the edge; make sure
as you do this that the asparagus and onions
remain evenly distributed throughout the
eggs. If the eggs are browning too much on the
bottom, reduce the heat to medium.

4. When the eggs are cooked to your liking, tip
the pan over a warmed platter and start to
slide the omelet onto it until half is on the platter, then fold the remaining half of the omelet
over the part on the platter. Serve immediately.

Simple Family Omelet
L'Omelette Familiale

❧ Like any working mom, I'm sometimes so busy that dinnertime sneaks up on me. When it does, I do what French moms do; I make an omelet for supper.

This omelet is one of our favorites because it's hearty and we love the combination of flavors. If I have leftover potatoes, I use them; otherwise it's a quick fifteen minutes from raw to cooked potatoes. With a big green salad or a pile of green beans, dinner is on the table in less than a half hour.

This omelet isn't folded over but is served "in the round," like a pizza. It looks gorgeous on the plate, topped with a quick garnish of flat-leaf parsley or other garden herb.

Open a light Sauvignon Blanc from the Touraine, such as one from Domaine du Vieil Orme, to enjoy here.

4 servings

6 large eggs

Fine sea salt and freshly ground black pepper

1½ tablespoons (22 g) unsalted butter

4 ounces (120 g) slab bacon, rind removed, cut into 1 × ½ × ½-inch (2.5 × 1.3 × 1.3-cm) pieces

8 ounces (250 g) waxy potatoes, cooked, peeled, and sliced

1 small bunch fresh chives

3 ounces (90 g) fresh goat cheese

1. In a medium bowl, whisk the eggs until just blended. Whisk in salt and pepper to taste.

2. Place the butter, bacon, and potatoes in a 12-inch (30-cm) nonstick omelet pan and heat over medium-high heat until the bacon and potatoes are sizzling and the butter is foaming. Continue to cook until the bacon and potatoes are beginning to turn golden at the edges, 3 to 4 minutes. If the bacon gives up a great deal of fat, drain off all but 2 tablespoons. Add the eggs to the pan and stir once. As the eggs begin to set, working all around the pan at least twice, bring the cooked edges of the eggs toward the center so the uncooked egg runs to the edges, meanwhile gently spreading out the bacon and potatoes.

3. Mince the chives.

4. Crumble the goat cheese over the omelet.

5. Sprinkle all but 1 tablespoon of the chives over the omelet.

6. When the omelet is mostly set but still somewhat runny, or when it is cooked to your liking, invert a large plate on top of the pan and turn the pan over so the omelet falls onto the plate. Garnish with the remaining chives and serve immediately.

An Artichoke, a Poached Egg, and a Dash of Cream

Artichaut et son Oeuf Poché avec un Soupçon de Crème

❧ Artichokes from Brittany, which is where the bulk of France's artichokes are cultivated, are huge and tender, with an incomparable nutty flavor that comes from the soil, the gentle sea air, and the specific variety.

I adore a simple steamed artichoke with garlic cloves tucked down in among its leaves. Gilles Maudry, who makes a palate-tingling Pouilly-Fumé in the Loire Valley, shared this simple yet sumptuous, rustic yet refined recipe. What's great about this dish is that you can make just one for yourself or make fifty for a crowd.

Artichokes are usually anathema to wine, but this dish goes very well with a Pouilly-Fumé, from Gilles' domain, Domaine Maltaverne.

4 servings

4 garlic cloves, green germ removed if necessary, each cut lengthwise into 6 pieces

4 large artichokes, stems trimmed flush with bottoms and ends of leaves snipped

2 generous tablespoons white wine vinegar

4 large eggs

1 small bunch fresh chives

Fine sea salt and freshly ground black pepper

¼ cup (60 ml) plus 2 teaspoons crème fraîche or heavy cream, preferably not ultra-pasterized

Chive blossoms, nigella flowers and leaves, or other edible flowers for garnish

1. Insert 6 slices of garlic down in among the leaves of each artichoke, interspersing them evenly around the artichoke. Place the artichokes in a heavy-bottomed nonreactive stockpot, pour about ½ inch (1.3 cm) water around the artichokes, and place the pot over medium-high heat. Cover and bring to a boil, then reduce the heat so the water remains at a steady simmer and cook the artichokes until the hearts are tender but not at all soft or mushy, about 45 minutes, checking occasionally to be sure there is enough water in the bottom of the pot, and that the artichokes aren't sticking. To test for doneness, remove an artichoke and pierce the heart with a sharp knife: if the knife goes through easily, the artichokes are cooked. Remove from the heat.

2. Meanwhile, fill a medium, wide saucepan with at least 4 inches (10 cm) water and bring to a boil over high heat. Add the vinegar and return the water to a boil. Break an egg into a small bowl, then slide the egg into the boiling water right where it makes a whorl.

Continue with the remaining three eggs, keeping the water at a gentle boil, and poach the eggs until the whites are set and the yolks are pale yellow on top but still soft, 3 to 4 minutes.

3. While the eggs are poaching, fill a large bowl half full with warm water. When the eggs are cooked, with a slotted spoon or ladle, transfer them one at a time into the bowl of warm water. They will stay warm in the water without continuing to cook.

4. When the artichokes are cooked, transfer them to a plate. Holding an artichoke with a tea towel so you don't burn your hands, use tongs to pull out the center leaves and the choke; you may need to use a stainless steel spoon to scrape away some of the choke. Repeat with the remaining artichokes, keeping them in a warm spot.

5. Mince the chives.

6. Season each artichoke cavity with salt and pepper and a sprinkling of chives, then spoon or pour 1 tablespoon cream into each one. One at a time, remove the eggs from the water, pat dry, and set inside the artichokes. Spoon or pour ½ teaspoon of the remaining cream atop each egg and season with salt and pepper. Divide the remaining chives among the artichokes, sprinkling them over the eggs.

7. Set an artichoke in the center of each warmed plate, garnish with the herbs and flower blossoms, if desired, and serve. To eat, remove the leaves one at a time from the artichoke, dip them into the egg yolk, and scrape the flesh from the leaves with your teeth; when you finish the leaves, trim the heart and eat it as well!

Leek Salad

Poireaux en Salade

❧ Since I am always looking for novel ways to use leeks, this salad intrigued me when chef Guy Martin, at Le Grand Véfour in Paris, described it. He enjoys playing in the kitchen on weekends when the restaurant is closed, and one of his more whimsical ideas is to make "color-themed" meals. This is the first course of a "green" meal, which might be followed by the Steamed Chicken with Cilantro Oil (page 118).

This has become a regular at our house, though (shhh!) I sometimes serve red, brown, or white food after it!

4 servings

6 leeks, white part only (generous 2 pounds, 6 ounces; 1 kg 180 g of white parts) halved lengthwise and well rinsed

1½ tablespoons freshly squeezed lemon juice

2½ teaspoons hazelnut oil or walnut oil

1 tablespoon mild vegetable oil, such as grapeseed

2 cups (20 g) firmly packed fresh herb leaves, such as basil, tarragon, lemon thyme, sweet cicely, and garlic and/or regular chives

½ teaspoon coarse sea salt, or to taste

1. Bring about 3 cups (750 ml) water to a boil in the bottom of a steamer. Put the leeks in the top of the steamer, cover, and steam until they are tender, 8 to 10 minutes. The sharp blade of a knife should go through them easily when they are cooked. Transfer them to a colander and let them drain for at least an hour and up to two hours, then transfer them to a shallow bowl.

2. In a medium bowl, whisk together the lemon juice and the oils. Taste to check the balance of flavors—the nut oil should be obvious but not overpowering. Mince the herbs, and whisk them into the mixture. Whisk in the salt.

3. Pour the dressing over the leeks and gently toss them in it. Transfer to a serving dish and serve with more coarse salt on the side.

ASTUCES: Note that the oils and lemon juice may be mixed together in advance, but the herbs should not be added until the last minute, or the lemon juice will bleach out their color and flavor. ❧ If you find thin, young, tender leeks, use them here. Just double the quantity, and leave some of the pale green part attached to the white. Use the green part of the leeks in the Leek and Bacon Quiche (page 72).

Michel's Melon Salad

Salade de Michel au Melon

❧ I first tasted this melon salad during the hottest French summer in recent history, that of 2003, when our friend Michel Deplanche and his wife, Annique, served it under the oak tree in their garden. I had never eaten anything so refreshing, and made it every chance I got during that hot summer. It is so cool, so lovely, so delicious at the beginning of a meal that it works not only as a palate opener, but as a refresher between courses.

6 servings

Generous 3 pounds (1.5 kg) ripe Cavaillon or Charentais melons or cantaloupes (about 3 small ones), cut in half and seeds removed

4 pounds (2 kg) ripe watermelon, honeydew, or Crenshaw melons, cut in half and seeds removed

¼ cup (60 ml) freshly squeezed orange juice

1 teaspoon freshly squeezed lemon juice

¼ cup fresh mint leaves

Freshly ground black pepper, preferably Tellicherry

1. Using a melon baller, scoop out the flesh of all the melon into a large bowl. (Alternatively, cut the melon into bite-sized squares.) Pour the orange juice and lemon juice over the melon and toss well. Cover and refrigerate until well chilled, at least 1 hour, and up to 3 hours.

2. To serve, add the mint leaves to the melon, toss, and divide the salad among six chilled shallow bowls. Sprinkle with a light shower of black pepper and serve immediately.

ASTUCES: Mixing several varieties of melons makes for great eye appeal here, though more important than variety is the ripeness of the fruit. Melons are notoriously difficult to choose. As Claude Mermet, a French writer in the 1600s, said, "A melon is like a friend—you have to try fifty before finding a single good one." The perfect melon is heavy for its size, an indication of juiciness, and emits a sweet aroma from its blossom end. If it has a bit of the stem end still on it, on a perfectly ripe melon this will easily break away. ❧ The Cavaillon melon, from Provence, is the same variety as the Charentais, from the Charente, near Bordeaux.

Oven-Roasted Potato Slices
with Herbes de Provence

Tranches de Pommes de Terre aux Herbes de Provence

❧ This idea for potatoes came from Bernadette Tourrette, who owns a bed and breakfast in the tiny hilltop town of Venasque, in Provence. When she brought my breakfast to the table in her charming garden overlooking acres of her olive trees, we began talking food. I left with a handful of her delicious recipes.

These are a sort of cross between fried and baked potatoes, and they are also the perfect accompaniment to grilled and roasted meats and fish.

4 servings

2 pounds (1 kg) waxy potatoes, peeled and cut into ½-inch (1.3-cm)-thick slices

3 tablespoons (45 g) unsalted butter

Fleur de sel or fine sea salt

¾ teaspoon Herbes de Provence (page 269)

For the salad

1 tablespoon red wine vinegar

Fine sea salt

1 garlic clove, green germ removed if necessary, minced

¼ cup (60 ml) extra virgin olive oil

Freshly ground black pepper

10 cups curly endive, cut into large bite-sized pieces

1. Preheat the oven to 425°F (220°C).

2. Scrape each slice of potato across its surface with the tines of a fork, then divide the butter among the potatoes, setting a nugget atop each one. Sprinkle the potatoes with fleur de sel to taste and the herbes de Provence and place on a baking sheet or in a roasting pan.

3. Bake in the center of the oven until the potatoes are cooked through and turning golden brown at the edges, about 25 minutes.

4. While the potatoes are baking, make the salad. In a large bowl, whisk together the vinegar, salt to taste, and garlic, then slowly whisk in the oil. Season with pepper. Add the curly endive and toss until it is coated. Adjust for seasoning. Divide the salad among four plates.

5. When the potatoes are cooked, remove them from the oven and divide them among the plates, laying them to the side of the salad. Shower with freshly ground pepper and serve immediately.

ASTUCE: The best potato for this dish is the Yukon Gold or Kennebec, which are both starchy and waxy.

Goat Cheese Squares

Carrés au Fromage de Chèvre

⚜ I once thought that if I didn't cook every single thing from scratch, my life wasn't complete. Two children and two businesses later, I've changed my mind! Now, when I see a recipe that calls for puff pastry, I head to the baker and order a pound, or to the grocery store to buy a package, and feel no shame.

Brilliantly simple, this recipe comes to the table with an aura of elegance. Serve it as a first course atop a green salad or as a generous accompaniment to an apéritif.

Serve a chilled Sancerre, from Domaine de Reverdy if you find it, or Pouilly-Fumé from Domaine de Maltaverne.

8 servings

About 12 ounces puff pastry (360 g)

8 ounces (250 g) fresh goat cheese, cut into 8 equal rounds

1 large, ripe tomato, cored and cut into 8 slices

8 large or 16 small anchovy fillets (cut them in half lengthwise if using large fillets from Collioure or Sicily; or see Astuces)

2 teaspoons Herbes de Provence (page 269)

2 teaspoons extra virgin olive oil

Fresh flat-leaf parsley or basil leaves

1. Preheat the oven to 425°F (220°C).

2. Roll out the puff pastry until it is ⅛ inch (0.3 cm) thick. Cut it into eight 4-inch (10-cm) squares. Place the squares of puff pastry on a baking sheet. Top each square with a slice of goat cheese, then a slice of tomato. Lay 2 anchovy fillets atop each tomato slice, crossing them so they make an X, then sprinkle the squares with the herbes de Provence.

3. Bake in the center of the oven until the pastry is puffed and baked through, the cheese is softened, and the tomatoes are nearly cooked through, 15 to 20 minutes. Remove from the oven and let sit for about 10 minutes to cool slightly.

4. Transfer the squares to a warmed serving platter or eight warmed plates. Drizzle each pastry with an equal amount of olive oil, garnish with herbs, and serve.

ASTUCES: If you can't find Crottin de Chavignol, use a goat cheese that is quite soft yet set and aged at least one week, so it will hold together. ♣ Buy puff pastry that contains pure butter, not margarine. ♣ Anchovies packed in oil do not need soaking. If your anchovies are packed in salt, rinse them and soak them in white wine to cover for 15 minutes. Rinse again and pat dry before using.

Tomato Salad with Mozzarella and Pistachios

Tomates Coeur de Boeuf à la Mozzarella et aux Pistaches

⚜ Trust a Frenchman to take the inspired Italian combination of tomatoes and mozzarella and make it divine. Claude Colliot, chef and owner of the restaurant Claude Colliot/Bambouche in Paris, stacks slices of tomato with slices of buffalo milk mozzarella, then drizzles it with that elegant deep-green elixir, pistachio oil.

The *Coeur de Boeuf* (beef heart) tomato Claude uses has extremely tender and flavorful flesh, a quality that drives farmers crazy because it makes the tomatoes extremely fragile. They must be picked very ripe to have flavor, but when they are that ripe, they are almost impossible to transport because they blemish if you even look at them for a moment too long. Because of this, very few actually get to market.

4 to 6 servings

2 very large (about 9 ounces; 270 g each) ripe tomatoes, cored, and cut into thick slices

8 ounces (250 g) fresh mozzarella, cut into 8 equal slices

¼ cup (25 g) salted pistachios, dark skins rubbed off and coarsely chopped

3 tablespoons (45 ml) pistachio oil or extra virgin olive oil

Fleur de sel

Sprig of fresh basil

1. Arrange the tomato and mozzarella slices alternately on a serving platter. (If there aren't enough slices of mozzarella to alternate with all the slices of tomato, work it out so the salad looks balanced and lovely.)

2. In a small bowl, stir the pistachio nuts into the oil, then drizzle the mixture evenly over the tomatoes and cheese. Season with fleur de sel, and garnish with the basil sprig. Serve at room temperature.

ASTUCES: There are several types of tomatoes, called Oxhearts in English, that resemble the *Coeur de Boeuf*, including the Bull's Heart, Hungarian Heart, Anna Russian, and German Red Strawberry. All are excellent prepared this way because they have the characteristic tender skin, sweet flesh balanced by a slight acidity, and few seeds. If you cannot find any of these tomatoes, use the most flavorful perfectly ripe and juicy tomatoes you can find. ❀ Goat cheese makes a fine substitute for the mozzarella.

An Alsatian Country Smorgasbord
Bibeleskaes

❧ Just the name of this first course dish starts my mouth watering. It is composed of simple farm ingredients, what Alsatians have always had on hand, from tiny fingerling potatoes to fresh, tangy cheese. The potatoes are cooked in their skins, what the French call their *robe des champ*, or "field dresses." Everyone peels their own — no French person would consider eating a potato skin! — at the table, then smothers them in the cheese and condiments. *Bibeleskaes* can be either a first course or a one-dish meal in the Alsatian home; however it is served it turns a simple supper into something special.

Drink a chilled Pinot Gris with *bibeleskaes*.

6 servings

1⅓ cups (330 ml) Fromage Blanc (page 264; or see Astuces)

2 pounds (1 kg) small waxy potatoes or fingerling potatoes, scrubbed

1 cup (10 g) flat-leaf parsley leaves

1 bunch fresh chives

1 garlic clove, green germ removed if necessary, minced

½ small onion, minced

3 ounces (90 g) thinly sliced air-cured ham such as Black Forest ham cut into thin strips

Fleur de sel and freshly ground black pepper

1. Place the fromage blanc in a bowl and refrigerate.

2. Bring a large pot of salted water to a boil over high heat. Add the potatoes and return to a boil, then reduce the heat so the water is boiling gently and cook until the potatoes are tender through, 15 to 20 minutes. Drain the potatoes and keep warm in the hot pan.

3. While the potatoes are cooking, mince the parsley and chives separately, and place in two small dishes. Place the remaining ingredients in individual bowls.

4. Serve the hot potatoes and chilled fromage blanc with all the accompaniments.

> **ASTUCES:** Fromage blanc is a fresh cheese similar to cottage cheese, though without the curds. Make it according to the recipe on page 264, or blend together ½ cup (125 ml) each cottage cheese and sour cream, then add ⅓ cup (80 ml) crème fraîche. ❧ Serve *bibeleskaes* as a prelude to a main course, as is done in Alsatian restaurants, or as a one-dish supper.

Award-Winning Country Pâté
Pâté de Campagne Récompensé

What would the French culinary tradition be without pork pâté? A shadow of itself for certain, for pâté is often an integral part of the casual French meal.

I make pâté because I enjoy playing with flavors and textures, and I love dishes, like this, that emerge and ripen over time! There is something so satisfying about taking the pâté from its mold, smelling its good, fresh aroma, and serving it with pride. I have to say that our French friends are unbelieving when I serve homemade pâté—it is something they would not think of making, because good pâté is so readily available at the butcher, the charcuterie, or the market. But it never seems as fresh and intensely flavored as this, which is why it is such a treat.

I call this "award winning" because the recipe is based on one from a local charcutier that won "best of the year" in 2001.

Pâté is served as a first course or tucked into a baguette for a substantial sandwich. Try a lightly chilled Gamay, or a good micro-brewery beer with this.

About 10 servings

2¼ pounds (1 kg 125 g) coarsely ground pork (ask the butcher for a mix of half lean and half fatty)

2 tablespoons extra virgin olive oil

2 shallots, minced

1 small onion, minced

40 sprigs fresh thyme

9 bay leaves from the *Laurus nobilis*, or dried imported bay leaves

10 black peppercorns

¼ teaspoon ground allspice

5 allspice berries

1. Place the pork, olive oil, shallots, onion, all but 6 sprigs of the thyme, 3 of the bay leaves, the spices, and the salt in a large bowl and toss until thoroughly combined. Cover and refrigerate for 24 hours.

2. Preheat the oven to 350°F (180°C).

3. Remove the bay leaves and thyme sprigs from the pork mixture.

4. Place the liver in the food processor and puree it. Add it to the pork, and stir gently until all of the ingredients are thoroughly combined. Cook a teaspoonful of the mixture in a small pan over medium heat, then let it cool and taste it for seasoning—keeping in mind that when the pâté is chilled, the seasonings will be slightly muted. Adjust the seasonings with salt if necessary and test again. Mix in the hazelnuts until they are well distributed.

2½ teaspoons fine sea salt, or to taste

14 ounces (420 g) fresh pork liver

½ cup (75 g) hazelnuts, toasted and skinned (see page 12)

Cornichons, homemade (page 296) or store-bought

> **ASTUCES:** Pâté gets better as it sits, and I advise waiting for at least 72 hours before serving it. It keeps quite well in the refrigerator for a week, and it freezes just fine. ❦ Pâté is always served with cornichons and mustard, and often with a green salad on the side.

5. Arrange 3 of the remaining bay leaves and 3 generous sprigs of thyme in the bottom of a 2-quart (2-l) porcelain terrine mold or other nonreactive container. Top with half the pork mixture, smoothing and pressing it into the terrine. Remove the leaves from the remaining thyme sprigs and sprinkle them atop the pork. Cover with the remaining pork mixture, smoothing it out and pressing it down into the terrine, then top that with the remaining 3 bay leaves. Cut a piece of parchment paper to fit over the meat, lay it over the top, and cover with the lid of the mold or a piece of aluminum foil.

6. Place the terrine mold in a baking pan large enough to hold it with room to spare, and pour in boiling water to come halfway up the sides of the mold. Bake in the center of the oven until the terrine is cooked through, 2 to 2½ hours; it should register 170°F (77°C) on an instant-read thermometer inserted into the center. Remove the pan from the oven and remove the mold from the water. Let it cool slightly.

7. Cut a piece of cardboard to fit on top of the pâté, and set it atop the parchment paper. Place at least three 1-pound (500-g) weights on it to weight down the pâté, and let cool to room temperature. Refrigerate the weighted pâté for at least 24 hours, and preferably up to 3 days.

8. To serve the pâté, remove the weights, the cardboard, and the parchment paper, and turn it out onto a cutting board and cut into slices, or serve it right from the mold. Serve chilled, with cornichons and mustard alongside.

Leek and Bacon Quiche

Quiche aux Poireaux et au Lard Fumé

❧ Danie Dubois, who lives on a farm in the Dordogne region of France, showed me how to make this quiche when I used to help her cook for visitors at her guest house. She dressed the white parts of the leeks with vinaigrette and then, like any good farm wife who doesn't waste a thing, used the green parts in this quiche.

In France, quiche is served as a first course. I sometimes like to serve this one as a side dish, since it is so vegetable-rich, alongside Roasted Leg of Lamb with Herbs and Mustard (page 170).

6 to 8 servings

Pâte Brisée (page 256)

4 ounces (120 g) slab bacon, rind removed and cut into ½ × ¼-inch (1.3 × 0.6-cm) pieces

1 pound 10 ounces (800 g) leeks, green parts only (about 14 ounces; 400 g; reserve the whites for another use), well rinsed and diced

1 tablespoon extra virgin olive oil, optional

Fine sea salt and freshly ground black pepper

⅔ cup (170 ml) whole milk

6 large eggs

⅓ cup (80 ml) heavy cream, preferably not ultra-pasteurized

1. On a floured surface, roll out the pastry to a 12-inch (30-cm) round. Line a 10-inch (25-cm) pie plate with the pastry, crimp the edges, and trim the excess dough. Prick the bottom of the pastry shell with a fork or the tip of a sharp knife and refrigerate for 1 hour, or freeze for 30 minutes.

2. Preheat the oven to 425°F (220°C).

3. Line the pastry with aluminum foil, and fill it with pastry weights. Bake in the lower third of the oven until the edges of the pastry turn light golden, about 12 minutes. Remove from the oven and remove the foil and the weights. Return to the oven and bake until the pastry is pale golden all over, an additional 8 to 10 minutes. Remove from the oven and set aside on a rack.

4. Place the bacon in a large heavy-bottomed skillet over medium heat and cook, stirring occasionally, until the bacon has given off some of its fat, 3 to 4 minutes. Drain the excess fat. Add the leeks, stir, cover, and cook, stirring occasionally so the leeks don't stick to the bottom of the pan, until the leeks are tender, about 20 minutes. If the bacon you are using isn't fatty, you may need to add up to 1 tablespoon olive oil to help

keep the leeks from sticking. Remove from the heat and season to taste with salt and pepper.

5. In a medium bowl, whisk the milk into the eggs, then whisk in the cream and continue whisking until the mixture is homogeneous. Season lightly with salt and pepper.

6. Place the prebaked pastry shell on a baking sheet. Spread the leek and bacon mixture evenly over the bottom of the pastry. Add the custard mixture and, using a chopstick or a fork, move the bacon and leeks so the custard runs down into and around them.

7. Bake the quiche in the center of the oven until the custard is golden and puffed, and a sharp knife blade stuck into the center of the quiche comes out clean, 22 to 25 minutes. Remove from the oven and immediately take the quiche to the table so your guests can see it before it falls. Then wait about 10 minutes before serving, as it is blistering hot when it emerges from the oven.

Quiche Lorraine

❧ At our Saturday market, I buy individual quiches from Madeleine, who, with her husband, Hubert, sells them from a truck equipped with an oven so they are baked on the spot and emerge bubbling hot. Fiona and Joe have both grown up nibbling on them as we continue through the market.

Quiche is part of the French culinary anthem, a homey dish that is made year-round and typically served as a first course. This quiche is extraordinary, made as it is with Madeleine's custard recipe, which she divulged one day. I've used it for a classic quiche Lorraine, originally from the Lorraine region in eastern France, which remains my favorite, but you can put just about anything in a quiche. Madeleine likes smoked salmon and onions, or tomatoes, garlic, and zucchini, or just plain Gruyère. Armed with this custard recipe, your imagination need know no limit.

Serve with a lightly chilled Pinot Gris.

6 to 8 servings

Pâte Brisée (page 256)

4 ounces (120 g) slab bacon, rind removed and cut into 1 × ¼ × ¼-inch (2.5 × 0.6 × 0.6-cm) pieces

6 large eggs

1 cup (250 ml) whole milk

⅔ cup (160 ml) heavy cream, preferably not ultra-pasteurized, or crème fraîche

Fine sea salt and freshly ground black pepper

8 ounces (250 g) Gruyère, Emmenthal, or other Swiss-type cheese, grated (2½ cups)

¼ teaspoon freshly grated nutmeg, optional

1. On a lightly floured surface, roll out the pastry to 12-inch (30-cm) rounds. Line a 10-inch (25-cm) pie plate with the pastry and trim the excess dough. Crimp the edges and prick the bottom of the pastry all over with a fork or the tip of a sharp knife. Place the pastry in the refrigerator for 1 hour, or in the freezer for 30 minutes.

2. Preheat the oven to 425°F (220°C).

3. Sauté the bacon in a small heavy-bottomed pan over medium heat until it is cooked through, about 5 minutes. Remove from the heat and transfer the bacon to a plate lined with a brown paper bag or paper towels to absorb the excess fat.

4. Line the pastry with aluminum foil, and fill it with pastry weights. Bake in the lower third of the oven until the pastry is golden at the edges, about 12 minutes. Remove from the oven and remove the aluminum foil and weights. Return the pastry to the oven and bake until

the pastry is pale golden all over, an additional 8 to 10 minutes. Remove from the oven and set aside on a rack.

5. In a medium bowl, whisk together the eggs, milk, and cream, until thoroughly blended. Season with salt and pepper. Sprinkle the bacon and cheese evenly over the bottom of the pastry shell. Pour the custard mixture into the pastry shell and sprinkle the top with nutmeg if you've used a Swiss-type cheese.

6. Bake the quiche in the center of the oven until the filling is golden, puffed, and completely baked through, about 35 minutes. To test for doneness, shake the quiche gently—if it is set, without a pool of runny filling in the center, it is done. Or stick a sharp knife blade into the center of the filling; if it comes out clean, the quiche is done.

7. Remove the quiche from the oven and take it immediately to the table, as it deflates rapidly. Wait for about 10 minutes before serving it, to give it a chance to cool slightly.

Franco-Vietnamese Spring Rolls

Nems Franco-Asiatiques

❧ *Nems,* or Vietnamese spring rolls, have become part of the French culinary tradition. The connection is obvious, with the French colonization of Vietnam and ensuing Vietnamese immigration to France, which occurred over a long period of time.

Our friend Jean-Lou Dewaele, whose wife, Babette, owns La Maison des Simples, an herbalist shop in Louviers, began trying to re-create the *nems* we all buy at the Louviers market, and he prepared them for us one night. Jean-Lou shared his recipe, which I've tweaked further.

Serve a chilled Riesling from Dopff et Irion.

16 nems; *4 to 5 servings*

For the dipping sauce

2 small garlic cloves, green germ removed, minced

½ teaspoon sugar

½ cup (125 ml) *nuoc mam* (Asian fish sauce)

¼ cup (60 ml) freshly squeezed lemon juice

2 dried bird's-eye peppers, crushed, or to taste

For the filling

2 tablespoons hijiki

¼ package (2 ounces; 60 g) bean threads, preferably Lung Kow brand

8 dried shiitake mushrooms

1 tablespoon mild vegetable oil, such as safflower

6 spring onions (about 7 ounces; 210 g) or large scallions, trimmed and cut into very small dice

1. To make the dipping sauce, whisk together all the ingredients in a small bowl. Reserve.

2. To make the filling, place the hijiki, bean threads, and shiitake mushrooms in three separate small bowls. Cover them with warm water so they are floating freely, and set aside to soften. The hijiki will take about 10 minutes, the bean threads at least 15 minutes, and the shiitake from 15 to 30 minutes, depending on their dryness; test them frequently for tenderness after 15 minutes. Drain all three, squeezing each gently to remove the excess water, and reserve.

3. Place the 1 tablespoon oil in a large nonstick skillet over medium heat. Add the onions, garlic, carrots, turnips, hijiki, and 2 tablespoons water, stir, cover, and cook until the carrots and turnips are beginning to turn tender, 6 to 8 minutes, stirring occasionally to be sure the vegetables aren't sticking to the pan and adding a little additional water if necessary. Don't add too much water: you don't want the vegetables to be soggy. Add the cabbage, stir, cover, and cook until the cabbage is tender, about 12 minutes. Stir in the fish sauce and taste for seasoning. Transfer the vegetables to a medium bowl.

2 garlic cloves, green germ removed if necessary, minced

2 medium carrots, peeled and finely grated

2 small turnips, peeled and cut into very small dice

3 small Napa or Savoy cabbage leaves, minced (3 cups; 30 g)

2 tablespoons *nuoc mam* (Asian fish sauce)

½-inch (1.3-cm) piece fresh ginger, peeled and finely minced

1 dried bird's-eye pepper, crushed

Sixteen 9-inch (22.5-cm) round rice wrappers

¾ cup (8 g) lightly packed fresh cilantro leaves

4 cups (1 l) mild vegetable oil, such as grapeseed or safflower, for deep-frying

1 small bouquet fresh mint leaves

16 large, crisp lettuce leaves, such as Romaine

ASTUCE: The vegetables in the *nem* filling are variously grated, diced, and minced. This is by design, as the different textures play an important part in the finished texture and flavor of the *nems*.

4. Dice the shiitake mushrooms and add them to the vegetables, along with the bean threads, ginger, and bird's-eye pepper. Stir and taste for seasoning.

5. Place 1 rice wrapper in a pan of very warm water and let it sit until it is pliable, about 2 minutes. Transfer it to a tea towel laid out on a work surface and pat it dry. Place about ¼ cup (60 g) of the filling on the bottom third of the wrapper and lay several cilantro leaves atop the filling. Working quickly and carefully, roll up the bottom edge to enclose the filling, pressing on it gently, fold the sides of the rice wrapper over to completely enclose the filling, and then continue rolling from the bottom to make a nice, firm rectangular roll. Place the roll seam side down on a plate or work surface, and continue with the remaining rice wrappers and filling.

6. Heat the oil for deep-frying in a medium heavy-bottomed saucepan over medium heat. When the oil is hot but not smoking (a cube of bread added to the oil will cause it to bubble and rise up), place only as many spring rolls as will fit easily into the pan without overcrowding, and cook, turning them regularly so they brown evenly, for 4 to 6 minutes. Transfer the rolls to a plate or dish lined with plain brown paper to drain, and cook the remaining rolls in batches.

7. Transfer the *nems* to a serving platter and arrange the mint leaves and lettuce leaves around them. Serve with the dipping sauce on the side. To eat the *nems*, place one in a lettuce leaf, top it with fresh mint, roll the lettuce leaf around it, and dip it into the sauce before taking a bite.

Mussels in Cider Vinegar

Moules à la Normande

❦ Mussels are cultivated off the coast of Normandy as well as dragged from coastal waters. They are so tiny, sweet, and tender I prepare them often, steaming them in local hard apple cider and apple cider vinegar.

Make sure you have plenty of fresh bread on hand for dunking, and chilled hard cider to drink.

6 to 8 servings

6 pounds (3 kg) mussels

1 cup (about 10 g) firmly packed flat-leaf parsley leaves

2 small shallots, sliced lengthwise in half, then cut into paper-thin slices

4 bay leaves from the *Laurus nobilis*, or dried imported bay leaves

2 tablespoons apple cider vinegar

¼ cup (60 ml) hard apple cider or fresh apple juice

Freshly ground black pepper

1. Just before cooking the mussels, debeard them. Rinse them well in cool water and place them in a large pot. Coarsely chop the parsley and add it, along with the shallots, bay leaves, cider vinegar, and apple cider. Shake the pot so that all the ingredients are blended. Bring the liquid to a boil and reduce the heat to medium-high, cover the pot, and cook the mussels until they just open, shaking the pot from time to time so they cook evenly. Once the mussels are open, cook for an additional minute or so, checking the mussels frequently and removing those that are wide open so they don't overcook. If there are any mussels that refuse to open after 2 to 3 minutes, discard them, as they are either dead or empty.

2. Transfer the cooked mussels to a large serving bowl, or simply return all of them to the pot to serve. Shower them with pepper and serve.

ASTUCES: To clean a mussel, scrub it to remove any barnacles or other foreign material, then gently but firmly pull out its beard, the tangle of byssal threads that hangs from its shell. Do this right before you plan to cook the mussels, because without their beards, they will die and could spoil. ❧ When cooking mussels, shake the pan vigorously from side to side so they don't fall out of the shells but they will be evenly cooked. ❧ Black pepper and mussels have a real affinity. Be generous as you grind it over them. To turn this into a truly Norman treat, add a little cream right at the end and shimmy the pan around so it mixes into the cooking juices.

Khlat (Beet Mix-up)

Khlat

✤ I wouldn't have guessed when we moved to a small town in France that we would become very close friends with a Syrian anesthesiologist passionate for current events and cuisine, Ziad, and his partner, Stefana, a Romanian political refugee/dermatologist.

Both are gourmands, devoted to the cuisines of their home countries. When Ziad found out I loved to cook he couldn't wait to make us a Syrian dinner, which began with this vividly colored and tangy, nutty flavored beet salad.

This makes a lovely first course with a wine from the Hérault in the Languedoc, such as Domaine Poujol. Serve with Flat Semolina Bread (page 196), or pita bread.

About 10 to 12 servings

3 medium beets

Fine sea salt and freshly ground white pepper

2 tablespoons tahini (sesame paste)

2 tablespoons freshly squeezed lemon juice

2 tablespoons extra virgin olive oil

1 garlic clove, green germ removed if necessary, minced

2 cups (500 g) thick, full-fat Middle Eastern yogurt or other excellent-quality yogurt

Flat-leaf parsley sprigs

1. Preheat the oven to 425°F (220°C).

2. Place the beets in a baking dish and season with salt and white pepper. Pour about ½ inch (1.3 cm) water into the dish around the beets, cover, and bake until the beets are soft through, 1 to 1½ hours. Test for doneness by inserting a sharp knife into the center of the beet; you should feel no resistance. Let the beets cool, then peel and cut them into large pieces.

3. Place the beets, tahini, lemon juice, oil, and garlic in a food processor and process until the beets are roughly chopped. Add the yogurt and process until the mixture is homogeneous but not too smooth; the beets should remain in tiny rough chunks. Season to taste, transfer to a bowl, and let sit for at least 2 hours before serving.

4. To serve, transfer the *khlat* to a serving dish and garnish with parsley sprigs.

ASTUCES: Leave the skin on the beets while they cook so they retain all of their flavor and color; otherwise, both tend to drain away. ✤ The best tahini is made from organic sesame seeds that have been toasted before being ground.

Mussels in Saffron Cream

Mouclade

Although Bordeaux is the capital of the most famous wine region in France, Le Bordelais, few realize it is also the home of France's finest cultivated mussels. This is the typical Bordelais way to serve them, drowned in a rich and gorgeous cream sauce tinted with saffron. Use the smallest mussels you can find.

This is a very elegant recipe that is generally served as a first course, though I find it a lovely main course as well, with a richly flavored white Bordeaux.

4 to 6 servings

Generous pinch of saffron threads

3 tablespoons freshly squeezed lemon juice

4 pounds (2 kg) mussels

1½ cups (375 ml) dry white wine, such as a white Bordeaux

¾ cup (350 ml) crème fraîche or heavy, non-ultra-pasteurized cream

3 large egg yolks

2 tablespoons (30 g) unsalted butter

3 shallots, finely minced

2 tablespoons (30 ml) Cognac or Calvados, optional

12 fresh chives

1. In a small bowl, combine the saffron and lemon juice; set aside.

2. Just before cooking the mussels, scrub them and remove their beards.

3. Combine the mussels and wine in a large pot and bring to a boil over medium-high heat. Cover and cook, shaking the pot, just until the mussels open. Remove from the heat.

4. Remove the mussels from the pot and remove and discard the top shell from each one. Place the mussels in their bottom shells on a large platter, in layers if necessary. Or arrange them in four to six shallow soup bowls. Cover the mussels with parchment paper and keep warm in a low oven. Strain the mussel cooking liquid through a sieve lined with several thicknesses of cheesecloth, and reserve.

5. In a small bowl, whisk together the crème fraîche and egg yolks; set aside. Melt the butter in a medium saucepan over medium-high heat. Add the shallots and sauté just until they soften and begin to turn translucent, about 5 minutes. If using the Cognac, add it to the shallots and flambé it (see "Flambéing," page 132). Add the saffron and lemon juice and the mussel cooking

liquid and bring to a boil. Let the liquid boil just enough to reduce it slightly, about 5 minutes, then reduce the heat to low so it is simmering. Whisk in the crème fraîche and egg yolk mixture and cook, stirring slowly and constantly to prevent the sauce from curdling, until the sauce is thickened, which will take just a few minutes. Immediately remove from the heat. (Note: if the sauce has begun to curdle, quickly strain it through a fine-mesh sieve.)

6. Pour the sauce over the mussels, lay the chives over the top at a diagonal, and serve immediately.

Spring Fava Beans and Turnips

Fèves et Navets de Printemps

❧ This dish makes me think of a pointillist painting, with its dots of vivid color from the begonia blossoms and the fava beans interspersed with the white turnips and dark green oregano leaves. It's an inspiration from Pascal Barbot, chef at Astrance in Paris. As the French would say, it's a *clin d'oeil*, a wink at spring!

The season for this dish is short, just those few weeks in spring when both favas and turnips are small and tender.

I serve this with a lightly chilled Pouilly-Fumé.

4 servings

1½ pounds (750 g) baby turnips, peeled and cut into quarters

1½ pounds (750 g) fava beans in the pod, shelled and peeled (about 1 cup)

1½ tablespoons (22 g) unsalted butter

Fine sea salt and freshly ground white pepper

A handful of fresh rosy pink or red begonia flowers

1 tablespoon fresh marjoram, oregano, or tarragon leaves

Fleur de sel

1. Bring a large pot of salted water to a boil over high heat. Add the turnips, return the water to a boil, and cook until the turnips are tender through, 18 minutes. Meanwhile, prepare a bowl of ice water. When the turnips are tender, drain and transfer to the bowl of ice water. When the turnips are completely cool, transfer them to a rack covered with a cotton towel to drain. Set the ice bath aside.

2. Bring a smaller pot of salted water to a boil over high heat, add the peeled fava beans, and cook them just until they are tender through, about 5 minutes. Drain and transfer them to the ice water. When they are chilled, fish them out gently and transfer them to the cooling rack.

3. Melt the butter in a medium skillet over medium heat. Add the turnips and sauté them for 1 minute, then add the fava beans and sauté until the two vegetables are hot through and glistening but not golden or dry, about 4 minutes, seasoning them with salt and white pepper as you sauté.

4. Transfer an equal amount of the vegetables to each of four warmed plates, arranging them so that they look pretty on the plates, with the fava beans strewn over the turnips. Sprinkle each plate with the begonia petals and marjoram leaves, add a tiny sprinkling of fleur de sel, and serve.

Dandelion Salad

Salade de Pissenlit

❧ Every Saturday morning when **Jean-Claude Martin** is at his family's vegetable stand, I can see the glimmer in his eyes from across the market. I like everyone in his family, but there is something special about this slight, energetic, ruddy-faced man with the brilliant blue eyes. He is always cheerful, always ready to kiss or shake hands with his customers, always humble about his work, and always ready to put *bon poids*, a little extra, into his customers' market basket. He is also always ready with a recipe, or at least an idea. When I ask him for precision, he turns to his equally charming wife, Monique. *"Monique, tu peux dire à Suzanne comment tu fais?"* he asks, deferring to her for the cooking techniques of his favorite dishes.

Ever since Monique gave me this idea for dandelion greens, I've served this salad in the winter, when the greens are at their best. Simple to make, it is such a nice change from other more typical ways of preparing dandelion greens, which usually call for them to be wilted or sautéed.

Most French cooks use cultivated dandelion greens, which differ from their wild cousins in both flavor and texture. I prefer wild dandelion greens, which are smaller, more refined, more delicately flavored, and scarcer. I get one crop from our garden each year and then I turn to the Martins for the cultivated variety.

4 to 6 servings

2 tablespoons red wine vinegar

Large pinch fine sea salt

1 small shallot, minced

1 tablespoon Dijon mustard

⅓ cup (80 ml) extra virgin olive oil

Freshly ground black pepper

6 ounces (180 g) slab bacon, skin removed, cut into 1 × 1¼ × ¼-inch (2.5 × 3 × 0.6-cm) pieces

1. In a large bowl, whisk together the vinegar, salt, and shallot, then whisk in the mustard. Slowly pour in the oil, whisking constantly, until the vinaigrette is quite thick. Season to taste with salt and pepper, and reserve.

2. Place the bacon in a large heavy-bottomed skillet over medium heat and cook, stirring, until it is golden brown and cooked through, 5 to 6 minutes. Remove from the heat and keep warm.

3. Meanwhile, using sharp scissors or a knife, cut the dandelion greens into ½-inch (1.3-cm) lengths.

1 pound (500 g) dandelion greens, well rinsed and patted dry

4. Place the bacon and dandelion greens in a large bowl. Pour the vinaigrette over all, and toss until the greens and bacon are thoroughly coated with vinaigrette. Adjust the seasoning with salt and pepper, and serve immediately.

ASTUCES: Mustard is the best aid to emulsifying a vinaigrette, so I use it when I need a salad dressing with both bite and clinging power. ❧ If you have a large garden or field that is full of dandelions—yes, the plants we often think of as weeds—don't hesitate to go out and harvest them. Be sure, however, that there are no animals who make that garden or field their home, particularly of the cloven hoof variety, for they can spread disease, or any pesticide use nearby.

Green Bean, Smoked Sausage, and Hard-Cooked Egg Salad

Salade de Haricots Verts, Saucisses Fumées, et Oeufs Durs

❧ The green beans I buy at our farmers' market beginning in mid-July are about the most satisfying vegetable I know. I buy a kilo or two and serve them throughout the week, simply steamed and dressed with extra virgin olive oil, tossed with toasted almonds, almond oil, and garlic, or in a simple vinaigrette.

The green beans I buy from local farmers are the same as we have in the United States. The slender *haricots verts* so prized on an elegant table are a specialty version of the same variety. I get them at my next-door neighbor's, Chez Clet the *épicier*, or grocer, where they sit carefully arranged in small wooden boxes, most of them shipped in from Kenya. They have their decorative uses, though little flavor compared with their larger cousins fresh from the farm.

This dish was inspired by my neighbor Brigitte Petit, who owns Laure Boutique, a little store whose wares spill out over the sidewalk on one of Louviers' main streets. She makes big batches in summer so that she and her husband, Alain, can eat it as leftovers during their busy work week. This salad is delicious warm or at room temperature.

Serve with a chilled hard apple cider.

8 appetizer servings or 6 main-course servings

14 ounces (400 g) cervelas (garlicky cured pork sausage) or other uncooked, lightly smoked sausage such as kielbasa

1½ pounds (750 g) green beans, trimmed, strings removed if necessary

1. Place the sausages in a medium saucepan and cover with water by 1 inch (2.5 cm). Bring to a boil, then reduce the heat so the water is simmering and simmer until the sausages are cooked, about 20 minutes (10 minutes if using kielbasa). Remove from the heat and leave the sausages in the poaching water to stay warm.

2. Bring about 3 cups (750 ml) water to a boil in the bottom of a steamer. Place the beans in the top of the steamer, cover, and steam until they are tender through, about 15 minutes.

3. While the beans are steaming, make the vinaigrette: Whisk together the vinegar, shallot, and salt and pepper

For the vinaigrette

1 tablespoon red wine vinegar

1 large shallot, cut lengthwise in half and then into paper-thin slices

Fine sea salt and freshly ground black pepper

¼ cup (60 ml) extra virgin olive oil

4 large hard-cooked eggs, cut into quarters

to taste in a large serving bowl. Add the oil in a thin stream, whisking constantly until the vinaigrette emulsifies and thickens.

4. Tip the steamed beans into the vinaigrette and toss until they are thoroughly coated. Season well with salt and pepper. Slice the sausages on the diagonal into ¼-inch (0.6-cm) slices and add to the beans, tossing thoroughly. Arrange the egg quarters on top of the salad. Serve the salad warm or at room temperature.

ASTUCES: The beans are steamed for a full 15 minutes, until they are tender through. This is the way the French, and I, prefer them, and there is reason for it: when they are thoroughly cooked, their flavor is full and round and not the least bit grassy, as it can be when they are crisp-cooked. ✤ If you use kielbasa, you can cut the poaching time here in half, to 10 minutes. If you don't want to use traditional kielbasa, try organic turkey kielbasa, which is surprisingly full-flavored and delicious! ✤ Cervelas is a fat, short pork sausage usually made with a blend of lean and fatty pork, and typically seasoned with garlic and black pepper. Often lightly smoked, it is usually served raw.

Gruyère and Smoked Sausage Salad

Salade de Gruyère au Cervelas

⚜ **A little bit of delectable excess on a plate, this salad was traditionally an efficient way to satisfy the hearty appetites of field and forest workers in Alsace, where it is a cornerstone of the regional cuisine. Today it is still a well-loved family dish that has migrated into the** *winstub,* **or Alsatian bistro. In Alsace it is served as a first course before a savory meat pie or a choucroute.**

Serve this with a cracklingly spry Gewürztraminer.

6 servings

For the vinaigrette

⅓ cup (80 ml) sherry vinegar

2 teaspoons Dijon mustard

2 shallots, minced

½ cup plus 1 tablespoon (135 ml) mild extra-virgin olive oil

1 cup (10 g) loosely packed flat-leaf parsley leaves

Fine sea salt and freshly ground black pepper

3 medium (about 7.5 ounces; 230 g each) cervelas (garlicky cured pork sausage) or lightly smoked sausages such as kielbasa

8 ounces (250 g) Gruyère, coarsely grated

For the greens

6 cups (4 ounces; 125 g) salad greens, such as a blend of Batavia and butter lettuce, rinsed and spun dry

1. To make the vinaigrette, whisk together the vinegar, mustard, and shallots in a small bowl. Slowly add the oil in a fine stream, whisking constantly until the vinaigrette is emulsified and thickened.

2. Mince the parsley and whisk it into the vinaigrette. Season to taste with salt and pepper. Set aside.

3. Place the sausages in a medium saucepan and cover with water by 1 inch (2.5 cm). Bring to a boil then reduce the heat so the water is simmering. Simmer until the sausages are cooked, about 20 minutes (10 minutes if using kielbasa).

4. Put the Gruyère in a medium bowl, pour half the vinaigrette over it, and toss, using two forks, until all the cheese is moistened. Set aside, covered, for at least 1 hour, and up to 3 hours.

5. Meanwhile, remove the casings from the cervelas. Cut the sausages lengthwise in half and score the outside of each half with a sharp knife in a crosshatch pattern. (If you have large cervelas, cut them into thick rounds and score the rounds.) Lay the cervelas on a platter and pour the remaining vinaigrette over them. Turn the cervelas so they are moistened all over, then let them sit at room temperature for at least 1 hour, and up

2 tablespoons extra virgin olive oil

Fine sea salt

to 3 hours, turning them occasionally so they absorb the vinaigrette evenly.

6. To serve, in a large bowl, toss the salad greens with the olive oil and salt to taste, and divide among six small plates. Divide the cheese among the plates, mounding it slightly atop the salad greens. Place one half a cervelas (or an equal number of slices) next to the cheese, and serve immediately.

ASTUCES: The cheese and sausage are marinated at room temperature so they more easily absorb the flavors of the vinaigrette. Serve the salad at room temperature as well, for refrigeration mutes its flavor. This is good the day it is made, but it doesn't keep well even to the following day. ✤ I call for Batavia lettuce (what we call summer crisp or French crisp) because it has a lovely crunch but is more tender than Romaine.

Warm Green Salad with Sausages and Poached Eggs

Salade Tiède aux Saucisses et Aux Oeufs Pochés

❧ **Composed salads are a signature part of French cuisine. They take many forms, from this simple green salad with sausages and eggs to salade Niçoise to greens tossed with Roquefort, apples and walnuts. They are traditionally served as a first course, along with plenty of fresh bread and a cool Beaujolais.**

6 first-course servings

¼ cup (60 ml) white wine vinegar

4 to 8 large eggs (depending on the appetite of the eater)

Eight 1½ × 1½ × 1-inch (3.75 × 3.75 × 2.5-cm) slices sourdough bread

3 garlic cloves, green germ removed if necessary

1 pound (500 g) thin sausages, such as chorizo, cut into 1-inch (2.5-cm) lengths

¼ cup (60 ml) extra virgin olive oil, or as needed

10 cups (7 ounces; 210 g) loosely packed mixed winter greens such as escarole, curly endive, and arugula, rinsed, spun dry, and torn into bite-sized pieces

2 tablespoons red wine vinegar

Fine sea salt and freshly ground black pepper

1. Fill a medium to large saucepan with at least 4 inches (10 cm) water and bring to a boil over high heat. Add the white wine vinegar and return the water to a boil. Break an egg into a small bowl, then slide the egg into the boiling water right where it makes a whorl. Continue with some or all of the remaining eggs, adding as many to the pan as will easily fit and still allow the water to continue boiling gently, and poach the eggs until the whites are set and the yolks are pale yellow on top but still soft, 3 to 4 minutes.

2. While the eggs are poaching, fill a large bowl half-full with warm water. When the eggs are poached, with a slotted spoon or ladle, transfer them one at a time to the bowl of warm water. They should all fit easily in the bowl, and they will stay lukewarm in the water without continuing to cook.

3. Preheat the broiler. Place the bread on a baking sheet, place it about 3 inches (7.5 cm) from the heating element, and broil, turning once, until the toast is golden on both sides but not completely dry. Remove the toast from the broiler and as soon as you can handle it, rub each piece lightly on both sides with 1 of the garlic cloves.

4. Place the sausages and olive oil in a large, heavy skillet over medium heat stirring occasionally, and cook until the sausages are cooked through and golden, about 8 minutes. (If the sausages are already cooked just heat them until they are hot through.)

5. Meanwhile, dice the remaining 2 garlic cloves. Place the lettuces in a large heatproof salad bowl.

6. Add the diced garlic to the sausages, stir, and cook for 1 minute, then add the red wine vinegar and stir, standing back away from the pan so the steam doesn't irritate your eyes. Add the garlic croutons and stir until warmed through. Season the sausages and croutons with salt and pepper to taste and transfer them to the bowl of lettuces. Toss until everything is thoroughly combined, and adjust the seasoning. If the salad is at all dry, add a bit more olive oil to moisten it, keeping in mind that the egg yolks will provide moisture as well.

7. To serve, arrange the salad on four warmed dinner plates, spreading it out flat on the plates. One at a time, remove the poached eggs from the warm water with a slotted spoon, pat them dry, and trim off any unattractive edges of the whites with a pair of scissors. Place 1 or 2 eggs atop each salad, season lightly with salt and pepper, and serve.

LAST-MINUTE MINCING

Always mince herbs right before you use them, for the minute knife touches leaf, fragile aromatic oils are released. If you mince the herbs in advance, their oils—and the flavors they contain—are dispersed into the air, rather than into the food. So, mince at the last minute, then toss the minced herbs immediately into your dish, where their subtle flavors will be captured, ready for your palate.

Black Radish Salad
Salade de Radis Noir

❧ Snaky, fat black radishes begin appearing at the market in late summer and fall, replacing their tiny round red cousins. I consider them one of winter's finest treats, one of the few winter vegetables that gives a fresh, juicy snap to liven up a meal.

4 servings

4 teaspoons freshly squeezed lemon juice

½ teaspoon grainy mustard

3 tablespoons extra virgin olive oil

2 black radishes (about 8 ounces; 250 g each), trimmed and peeled

¼ cup flat-leaf parsley leaves

1 small shallot, sliced paper-thin

Fleur de sel

1. In a medium bowl, whisk together the lemon juice and mustard, then slowly whisk in the olive oil until the vinaigrette emulsifies and thickens. Reserve.

2. Grate the radishes on a grater with small holes. Mince the parsley.

3. Give the vinaigrette a quick whisk to re-emulsify it if it has separated, and add the radishes, shallot, and parsley. Toss so the ingredients are thoroughly combined. Season to taste with fleur de sel. Serve immediately.

> **ASTUCES:** In North America the most common black radish is the *Raphanus sativus*, usually available in Asian groceries. It has a similar flavor and texture to the black radish in France (*Raphanus sativus niger*).
> ❧ You'll notice there isn't an excess of dressing for this salad, but just enough to thoroughly moisten it. Do not be tempted to add more—it doesn't need it.

FISH,
THE BEAUTIFUL
SWIMMER

*Poisson,
le Beau Nageur*

In the hands of an able cook, fish can
become an inexhaustible source of
perpetual delight.

Jean-Anthelme Brillat-Savarin,
magistrate and gastronome (1755–1826)

Monkfish and Leeks for All Occasions

Lotte aux Poireaux pour Toute Occasion

❦ This looks like a simple family dish, but hidden inside it are ingredients fit for royalty: leeks, the sweetest and most elegant member of the vegetable family; monkfish, king of the sea; and that incomparable French balm of the gods, crème fraîche.

This dish is the brainchild of Arnaud Paulhe, a young man who considers himself a member of the "new" generation of French males, because unlike his father, his uncles, or any other man he knows, he often does the cooking at home for himself and his wife, Sophie, and occasionally when guests come for supper. This is the dish he makes most often. I mention Arnaud to credit him for this recipe, but also to call attention to a very fundamental shift in French society, for aside from professional chefs, who, in France, are mostly male, very few men cook at home. How sweet the winds of change!

Serve this with a lightly chilled white Beaujolais.

4 servings

1 pound (500 g) monkfish, bone and membrane removed, or other firm white fish fillets, skin and any bones removed

2½ pounds (about 1 kg) leeks, white part only, well rinsed and diced (save the green part for Leek and Bacon Quiche)

½ cup (125 ml) crème fraîche

1 tablespoon grainy mustard

10 dried green peppercorns, coarsely ground

Fine sea salt

Scant ¼ cup flat-leaf parsley leaves

1. Rinse the fish, pat dry, and cut it on the diagonal into 2-inch (5-cm)-thick slices. Refrigerate until ready to cook.

2. Bring about 3 cups (750 ml) water to a boil in the bottom of a steamer. Place the leeks in the top of the steamer, cover, and steam until they are tender, about 12 minutes. Transfer the leeks to a colander and let them drain for 30 minutes.

3. Preheat the oven to 400°F (200°C).

4. In a medium bowl whisk together the crème fraîche, mustard, half the green peppercorns, and salt to taste. Stir in the leeks. Spread half the mixture in a baking dish that measures about 12 × 8-inches (30 × 20-cm). Season the pieces of fish on one side with salt to taste and sprinkle them with the remaining green pepper. Place the pieces of fish, pepper side down, atop the leek mixture in a single layer. Season them generously with salt.

Dollop the remaining leek mixture over the fish, then carefully spread it out so the fish is completely covered.

5. Bake in the center of the oven until the leeks are hot and the fish is cooked through, 15 to 18 minutes. To test for doneness, remove the dish from the oven and check a piece of fish: it should be opaque through—if it is still very translucent, return it to the oven for another minute or two; if it is just slightly translucent, it will finish cooking in the heat of the leeks as you bring it to the table.

6. Just before serving mince the parsley. Sprinkle it over the fish in the baking dish, or divide the fish and leeks among four warmed plates and sprinkle with the parsley.

To Clean a Leek

Leeks are grown either in sand or in soil that is built up around them to keep as much of the vegetable as possible pure white, sweet, and tender. The downside is that grit often sifts right into the white part of the leek, and it must be removed.

There are several ways to do this. If you are going to dice, mince, or chop it, start by trimming off the tough outer leaves and the root end. Cut it lengthwise in quarters, leaving it attached at the root end, hold it under running water, and rinse it very thoroughly.

If you want to keep the leek whole, trim off all the tough outer leaves, right down to the white part, and the root end. Soak the leek in cool water for about 20 minutes. Lift it from the water with the cut end down so that the grit will drain out with the water. Let it sit, root end down, in a colander to drain for at least 10 minutes.

Curried Fish à la Meunière
Poisson à la Meunière au Curry

❧ Nine times out of ten fish in France is cooked *à la meunière,* in the style of the miller's wife, dredged in flour and sautéed in butter. The flour and butter provide texture and flavor contrasts to the fish, and help it stay moist and succulent. In addition, children will eat fish when it's prepared like this, which is no small consideration.

I have adapted the style by adding ground almonds and curry powder to the flour, which gives the fish a toasty, crisp dimension. And I sauté it in extra virgin olive oil instead of butter. I began doing this when our son, Joe, was small because it guaranteed that he would eat fish, and it has become a family favorite.

This goes beautifully with Tomatoes Provençal (page 186) or any gratin. I like a wonderful, lightly chilled Quercy with it.

4 servings

1 pound (500 g) perch, lingcod, salmon, or monkfish fillets, skin (or membranes) and any bones removed

⅓ cup (50 g) whole, unblanched almonds

⅓ cup (50 g) unbleached all-purpose flour

½ teaspoon curry powder, such as Madras

Heaping ½ teaspoon fine sea salt

Freshly ground white pepper

2 tablespoons extra virgin olive oil, or as needed

¼ cup (60 ml) milk

Lemon wedges and fresh herb leaves, such as lemon thyme, tarragon, mint, or chives

1. Rinse the fish and pat it dry. Refrigerate until just ready to cook it.

2. Place the almonds and flour in a food processor and process until the almonds are ground quite fine. Add the curry powder, salt, and white pepper to taste and process until combined. Transfer the almond mixture to a small platter, spreading it in an even layer.

3. Heat the oil in a large, heavy-bottomed skillet over medium heat.

4. Meanwhile, place the milk in a shallow dish. Cut the fillets into serving portions. Dip them in the milk, transfer to the almond and flour mixture, and gently press on the fillets so the mixture sticks to them, then flip them and gently press them into the mixture so they are completely covered.

5. When the oil is hot but not smoking, add the fillets, leaving plenty of room between them, and cook, turning

once, until golden on both sides, a total of 8 to 10 minutes. If the pan is dry, add additional oil as necessary.

6. To serve, place the fish on warmed plates and garnish the plates with lemon wedges and the herbs. Serve immediately.

Tuna with Ginger Yogurt Sauce and Cilantro Coulis

Thon Sauce Yaourt au Gingembre (Coulis de Coriandre)

Patrice Barbot of the tiny Parisian restaurant Astrance decided to make this one day after a visit to the market, where he had found all the ingredients. It was as simple as that. The dish is a perfect example of what is happening in French cuisine today, with influences from all over the globe. It is contemporary and light, and it makes use of ingredients that are widely available to everyone.

Be sure to include the flower petals (unsprayed, of course); they aren't an affectation but a vital part of the appeal of this dish.

6 servings

For the yogurt

1 cup (250 ml) plain full-fat yogurt

1 teaspoon minced lime zest

½ teaspoon grated ginger

For the tuna

1½ teaspoons powdered ginger

½ teaspoon fine sea salt

1¾ pounds (about 750 g) fresh tuna loin, with skin on one side if possible

¼ cup Cilantro Oil (page 273)

Fleur de sel

Begonia or geranium petals

1. The day before you plan to serve the tuna, start to drain the yogurt. Place the yogurt in a strainer lined with cheesecloth set over a bowl, and refrigerate for 6 hours.

2. Transfer the yogurt to a medium bowl (discard the liquid). Whisk the lime zest and ginger into the yogurt, cover, and refrigerate for at least 8 hours, or overnight.

3. In a small bowl, mix together the powdered ginger and salt. Put the tuna on a plate, rub the ginger mixture all over it, cover, and refrigerate for at least 2 hours, and up to overnight.

4. When the yogurt has drained, remove it from the refrigerator and strain it through a fine-mesh strainer to remove the lime and ginger. Set aside at room temperature.

5. Preheat the oven to 400°F (200°C).

6. Place the tuna skin side down in a baking dish and pour 1 cup (250 ml) water around it. Place the tuna in the center of the oven and roast just until it turns

opaque and slightly golden on the outside, 15 minutes (see Astuces). Remove the tuna from the oven and let it cool to room temperature, leaving it in the baking dish.

7. To serve the tuna, remove any skin, then, using a very sharp knife, slice the tuna into 6 even slices. Divide the yogurt evenly among six dinner plates, placing it in the center of each plate and flattening it into a round. Lay the slices of tuna atop the yogurt, and drizzle 2 teaspoons of the cilantro oil around each slice. Let sit for a few minutes to allow the cilantro oil to spread out and fill the remaining space on the plate.

8. Sprinkle the tuna with fleur de sel, garnish each plate with flower blossoms, and serve immediately.

ASTUCES: Impeccably fresh tuna is imperative for this recipe. It roasts just long enough to cook on the outside and remain rare and moist on the inside. Or, substitute any other firm, meaty fish, such as swordfish or mahi-mahi, but in that case, leave the fish in the oven for a good 15 to 20 minutes longer, so it is cooked all the way through. ❧ The tuna will be quite rare in the center. It is ideal cooked this way, but if you prefer your tuna cooked further, simply increase the cooking time to about 20 to 25 minutes. If you do cook the tuna for such a long time, be sure to cover it while it is roasting so the exterior will not dry out. ❧ Note that the yogurt needs to macerate overnight before serving. The skin on the tuna protects it from the intense heat of the pan. If you can't find tuna with the skin on, you will need to reduce the cooking time of the tuna by 2 to 3 minutes.

CARE AND FEEDING OF SEAFOOD

Ocean fish, shellfish, and crustaceans are fragile. They live in a rich salt ocean brine, which works to preserve their quality. Once removed from their environment, they begin to deteriorate in freshness and flavor. With that in mind, there are several things you can do to retard the deterioration of seafood, to make sure you get its best possible flavor and texture.

❧ Buy from a reputable seafood merchant—perhaps the most vital key to getting good-quality seafood if you aren't catching it yourself. You can identify a reputable merchant with your nose. No fish shop should smell fishy, because a fishy odor is a sign of spoilage. Of course, a fishy aroma can come from the paper seafood was wrapped in and not carefully disposed of, but the general rule is if you smell fishiness, change your plans and buy meat for supper. Before you buy fish, ask to smell it, too. A reputable merchant will be happy to acquiesce.

❧ You can judge good seafood with your eyes. Look for firmness, shiny skin, lovely fillets and steaks that look so fresh they make you want to eat them! Torn, bruised, dull, or otherwise damaged fish is to be avoided. Whole fish should be kept on ice. Skinless fillets or steaks shouldn't be in direct contact with the ice, but protected with something that is set on the ice—seaweed, lettuce or cabbage leaves, something that lets the cold through. Bright eyes in a fish are nice, but eyes can be deceptive because they can be damaged yet the fish can be perfect. Better indications in a whole fish are the gills, which should be bright red, and the cavity, which should smell sweet.

❧ Fish should be firm. A reputable merchant should let you touch fish, but when you do, touch gently. You don't need to poke and prod.

❧ If you are buying prepackaged seafood at a supermarket, look at it carefully. Pick up the container and run your hand underneath it, then smell your hand. If your hand smells fishy, don't buy the fish.

❧ Keep seafood cold! Seafood deteriorates rapidly, so travel with a cooler in the trunk of your car, and have the fish merchant pack your fish with ice. When you get home, rinse your fish, place ice in a dish, cover the ice with waxed or parchment paper or a towel, and set the fish on it. Cover the fish and place it in the coldest part of your refrigerator, usually the bottom. Cook the fish the day you buy it if possible. If not, change the ice under the fish at least once and cook it as soon as possible.

❖ Shellfish likes to be cool and moist. Clams and mussels don't keep well, so they should be cooked as soon as possible. To keep them for a day, place them in a colander set over a shallow dish, and lay a moist towel atop them, then place them in the bottom of the refrigerator.

❖ Crab and lobster should be purchased live and cooked immediately.

Spiced Fish Fillet in Parchment Paper

Filet de Poisson Épicé en Papillote

✦ Cooking in parchment is a perfect method for preparing fish because it respects its delicate nature, allowing it to braise in its own juices and steam in its own vapors so that when you open the parchment, aroma bursts forth and the texture of the fish is still intact.

Ideally, serve individual packets to each diner so they can enjoy the flood of aroma that escapes the minute it is open, even before the dish reveals what is inside.

I like to serve Braised Fennel (page 188) with this dish, and a lightly chilled, golden wine from the Jura, preferably from the Château de Persanges.

4 servings

Four 5-ounce (150-g) white fish fillets, such as lingcod, snapper, flounder, or halibut, any bones and skin removed

½ teaspoon coriander seeds

¼ teaspoon black peppercorns

Fine sea salt

12 fresh cilantro leaves, rinsed and patted dry

Fleur de sel

1. Preheat the oven to 450°F (230°C).

2. Rinse the fillets and pat them dry. Refrigerate until ready to assemble the dish.

3. Lightly toast the coriander seeds in a small heavy skillet over low heat, stirring and tossing them frequently, just until they turn golden, 2 to 3 minutes. Transfer them to a spice grinder or mortar and pestle, add the peppercorns, and grind to a medium-fine powder.

4. Cut four 12 × 8-inch (30 × 20-cm) sheets of parchment paper. Fold them horizontally in half, then unfold them. Lay one fillet on each piece of parchment paper, about 2 inches (5 cm) below the fold line. Lightly season the fillets with fine salt, then sprinkle an equal amount of ground spices evenly over each fillet. Lay 3 cilantro leaves atop each fillet.

5. Fold the upper half of the sheet of parchment down over the fillet so the edges of the paper meet. Brush the edges with water, then make a narrow fold all the way around to form a pocket, pressing firmly on the fold. Make another fold, this time crimping the edge as you

go to seal the packet well. Repeat with the remaining fillets. (The packets can be refrigerated for up to 2 hours at this point.)

6. Set the packets on a baking sheet and bake until they are puffed and golden, about 8 minutes. Remove from the oven.

7. Transfer the packets to serving plates and serve immediately. Each guest should cut into the paper, then either eat the fish directly from the paper, or carefully transfer the fish to their plate and discard the paper. Before eating, each guest should lightly season their fish with fleur de sel.

Mackerel with Dandelion Greens

Maquereaux aux Pissentits

❧ Both mackerel and dandelion greens are commonly eaten in France, and together they make beautiful music. Mackerel is available year-round; dandelion greens are a winter into spring offering. Here, they are paired in a lovely, hearty, satisfying dish that brightens up a cold winter evening. The first time I served this, friends were coming to dinner with their teenage children, schoolmates of Joe. I made a large vegetable gratin for the teenagers, thinking mackerel and dandelion greens might not be to their liking, but how wrong I was. The teenagers cleaned their plates and asked for more.

Serve this with a lovely Burgundy or a red Sancerre, from Domaine Reverdy.

4 servings

8 medium (about 2.5 ounces; 75 g each) mackerel fillets

¼ cup (60 ml) extra virgin olive oil

Six 4-inch (10-cm) fresh rosemary branches

Fine sea salt and freshly ground black pepper

½ teaspoon *quatre-épices* (page 268)

10 ounces (300 g) dandelion greens, trimmed and well rinsed

3 garlic cloves, green germ removed if necessary, coarsely chopped

Fresh chervil or flat-leaf parsley sprigs

1. Preheat the oven to 400°F (200°C).

2. Rinse the fillets and then check for bones by running your finger the length of each fillet from head to tail end. Remove any bones following the instructions in the Astuces. Place the fillets in the refrigerator until just before cooking.

3. Drizzle 2 tablespoons of the olive oil into a baking dish. Lay 4 of the rosemary branches in the dish, and place the fillets on top in one layer. Season the fillets with salt and pepper and the *quatre-épices* and lay the remaining 2 rosemary branches over them.

4. Bake in the center of the oven until the fillets are opaque through, about 8 minutes. Remove from the oven and set aside.

5. Prepare the dandelion greens. Shake most but not all the rinse water from the greens and chop them lengthwise in half. Heat the remaining 2 tablespoons olive oil in a large heavy-bottomed skillet over medium heat. When the oil is hot but not smoking, add the dandelion greens, which will sputter slightly from the water on

them, and stir so they are coated with oil. Season them with salt and a touch of pepper, cover, and cook until they are slightly wilted, about 4 minutes. Remove the cover, add the garlic, and cook, stirring frequently, until the greens and garlic are tender, an additional 4 to 5 minutes.

6. To serve, arrange one quarter of the dandelion greens on each of four warmed plates. Arrange 2 mackerel fillets atop the greens, crossing them at the tail end. Garnish the fillets with chervil sprigs, and serve immediately.

ASTUCES: Mackerel is an underused species in the United States, but it is one that offers gorgeously moist and flavorful meat. It rivals any of the more noble species like tuna, swordfish, and salmon and the French are well aware of its *richesse*, for they prepare it in dozens of ways. ❖ Generally mackerel is sold whole. Look for fish that is firm and has a fish aroma, but not a "fishy" one. Ask the fishmonger to fillet the fish if you don't care to do it yourself. Each fillet has a central line of pinbones running two-thirds of its length, beginning at the head end. To remove these, use a very sharp knife to make angled cuts (called V cuts) on either side of the row of bones, up to but not through the skin, then pull out the bones (and the strip of meat clinging to them). Check the belly area for bones too, and cut them away if necessary so the fillets are clean, tidy, and boneless. ❖ If you know of a field or garden where dandelions grow, go harvest them! Wild dandelions are the best, most tender, and most flavorful there are. Make sure no sheep have grazed around the dandelions, for they can leave disease in their wake. Otherwise, cut the plants at their base, wash and trim them, and prepare yourself for a delicacy. If you don't harvest them yourself, you can find them in the winter and early spring at any specialty grocery or farmers' market.

Skate with Potato Puree

Aile de Raie à la Purée de Pommes de Terre

❦ **Skate is one of the best fish that swims in the sea. Only the wings of the skate are sold at the fish market and they are large, oddly shaped, and covered with a viscous fluid. Don't let their appearance keep you from trying the tender, sweet meat, for it is elegant and very versatile. Skate like to munch on scallops, crab, and other sweet-fleshed delicacies, all of which give skate its own sweet dimension.**

Skate is available year-round, but this is a dish I make in late winter and early spring, for it fits cool weather evenings.

It merits an elegant, rich white wine such as a beautiful Saint-Véran.

6 servings

For the vinaigrette

2 teaspoons Dijon mustard

2 tablespoons red wine vinegar

Fine sea salt

1 shallot, minced

2 tablespoons almond oil

½ cup (125 ml) extra virgin olive oil

¼ cup (40 g) capers packed in salt, rinsed in warm water

To remove the skin of the skate

2 pounds (1 kg) fresh skate, with dark skin

Court Bouillon (page 262)

1. To make the vinaigrette, whisk together the mustard, vinegar, and about ¼ teaspoon of salt in a medium bowl. Whisk in the shallot, then slowly whisk in the oils. Add the capers, mix, and reserve.

2. If the skate has been skinned, simply rinse and refrigerate it. If you need to skin the skate, bring the court bouillon to a boil in a wide, heavy stockpot over medium-high heat and slip the skate into it. Reduce the heat to medium and simmer the skate until the skin begins to wrinkle, which will take very little time—about 5 minutes. If the skate isn't completely submerged in the poaching liquid, ladle the liquid over the skate as it cooks. The skate doesn't need to be cooked through, simply cooked enough so the skin is easy to remove. Transfer the skate to a large platter and carefully scrape off the skin with a sharp knife, using gentle sweeping motions. There may be some gristle to remove as well, a clear, jelly-like substance that scrapes easily away. There are also several nasty "hooks" embedded in the skate near its thickest part—these pry out very easily. Be careful not to disturb the striated pattern of the skate.

For the potatoes

2½ pounds (1 kg) starchy potatoes, such as russets, peeled and cut into 2-inch (5 cm) chunks

Fine sea salt

4 tablespoons (60 g) unsalted butter, or more if desired

½ cup (125 ml) whole milk

To cook the skate

½ cup (70 g) all-purpose flour

½ teaspoon fine sea salt

¼ to ½ teaspoon freshly ground blend of white, black, and green peppercorns

2 tablespoons (30 g) unsalted butter

3 tablespoons (45 ml) extra virgin olive oil

To finish the dish

¼ cup fennel fronds or 1 tablespoon fresh tarragon leaves

3. Place the potatoes in a heavy saucepan and cover them by 1½ inches (3.75 cm) with water. Add 1 scant tablespoon of salt and bring the water to a gentle boil over medium-high heat. Reduce the heat so the water simmers merrily and cook until the potatoes are just tender through, about 15 minutes. Keep the potatoes warm, in the water, over very low heat or a pilot light. Melt the butter with the milk over low heat and keep warm.

4. Place the flour, salt, and pepper on a large piece of parchment paper and mix it well, using your fingers. Dredge the skate, which should still be slightly moist, in the seasoned flour.

5. Heat the butter with the oil in a large, heavy skillet over medium heat until it is frothing. Place the skate gently into the pan, cover, and cook until it is golden, about 6 minutes, checking it occasionally to be sure it isn't cooking too quickly. Turn the skate, cover, and cook until it is golden on the other side, 3 to 4 minutes, or more or less depending on the thickness of the skate. To check for doneness, using a very sharp knife, cut into the meat at the thickest part of the skate, going all the way to the bone, then pull back on the knife blade — if the meat is still slightly pink and not opaque, it should cook for just a few minutes more.

6. Transfer the potatoes to a large bowl or the bowl of an electric mixer fitted with a whisk attachment, and whisk the potatoes until they break up. Alternatively, press the potatoes through a potato ricer. Whisk in the melted butter and the milk, and continue whisking until the puree is light and fluffy. Season it to taste. If you like

ASTUCES: Skate is usually sold with the skin on. It is simple to remove by poaching it briefly in a court bouillon, and I give the instructions here. Your fish merchant may remove the dark skin if requested. If you get skate that has been skinned, simply skip step number two. Skate is almost always served with an acidic sauce because its meat, though rich in flavor, is bland without such a foil. ✤ Once the potatoes are cooked they will keep perfectly in the hot water for up to two hours, so that you can prepare them in advance and puree them at the last minute. Do not make the puree in advance, as it quickly loses its freshness.

your puree with more butter, add it at this point. Keep the potatoes warm.

7. To serve, first mince the herbs and whisk them into the vinaigrette. Carefully remove the skate from its cartilaginous bone. First cut through the skate to the cartilage in serving-size portions then, using a spatula, carefully scrape off the meat so it keeps its shape. Place a small mound of mashed potatoes in the center of each of six very warm plates and flatten it slightly. Lay the piece of skate on the plates so that part of it rests on the potato puree. Pour equal amounts of the vinaigrette over the skate and get the plates to the table immediately.

Salmon à l'Unilatérale with Capers and Butter

Saumon à l'Unilatérale aux Câpres et au Beurre

⚜ **Salmon is universally available, and there exists no simpler preparation for it than this.**

4 servings

2 tablespoons (20 g) capers, preferably preserved in salt

2½ tablespoons (37 g) unsalted butter

One 16- to 20-ounce (500- to 600-mg) salmon fillet with skin and any bones removed and cut into 4 equal pieces

Fine sea salt and freshly ground black pepper

3 tablespoons freshly squeezed lemon juice

1 cup (10 g) loosely packed flat-leaf parsley leaves

Fleur de sel

1. If using capers preserved in salt, rinse the salt from them, place them in a bowl, and cover with cold water. Let stand for at least 30 minutes, then drain, rinse well, and pat dry. If using capers packed in brine, drain and cover them with water for 15 minutes, then rinse them well and pat dry.

2. Melt ½ tablespoon butter in a large heavy-bottomed skillet over medium heat. Add the salmon, skin side down, and season it lightly with salt and pepper. When it begins to sizzle, cover the pan and let the salmon cook until the skin is golden and crisp and the flesh is pale pink just about all the way through, about 7 minutes. Remove from the heat and leave the salmon in the pan, covered, to finish cooking while you make the sauce.

3. Melt the remaining 2 tablespoons butter in a saucepan over low heat. Add the lemon juice and keep warm. Mince the capers with the parsley.

4. Remove each piece of salmon from the pan by sliding a spatula between the meat and the skin. Place each piece in the center of a warmed dinner plate. Sprinkle one-quarter of the parsley and caper mixture over each piece, and drizzle the lemon and butter mixture over all. Rest a piece of golden, crisp salmon skin at an angle against each piece of salmon, and salt the skin. Serve immediately.

ASTUCES: *À l'unilatéral* means cooking on one side with the skin side down on the surface of the pan, for the entire cooking time. The skin protects the meat, allowing the heat to travel gently up through it. ⚜ The only salmon worth eating is wild-caught from the Pacific Northwest of the United States. Forgive me this prejudice, but it is based on many years of eating wild salmon, and too many years of having only insipid, flabby farmed salmon in its place. ⚜ I like to serve a rich Sauvignon Blanc with this, like one from L'Arpent du Vaudouns.

A Choice
of Poultry

*Un Choix
de Volailles*

If God grants me longer life,
I will see to it that no peasant in
my kingdom will lack the means to
have a chicken in the pot every Sunday.

Henri IV of France (1589–1610)

FREE-RANGE POULTRY

A chicken is considered free-range if it tries to walk out of its cage when the door is opened."

A joke? Not really. It is actually the logical interpretation of the USDA's definition of free-range poultry, which states that "poultry producers must demonstrate to the Agency that the poultry has been allowed access to the outside."

"Free-range" is intended to signify poultry raised out of doors with plenty of room to peck and scratch, and a shelter to return to at night. In France, the ultimate free-range poultry comes from the Bresse area in Burgundy. To merit the name *poulet de Bresse* each bird must have thirty square feet of land all to itself. A bird with that much space can run, develop muscle tone and strength, and peck and scratch at insects and seeds at will. Birds that have this kind of life, or even one approaching it, are much more flavorful and finer in texture than their penned cousins who spend their six to eight weeks of life in a cage.

To be sure that the poultry you are buying is free-range, try to get it from the producer at a farmers' market so that you can ask how it is raised. Barring that, buy organic poultry if possible, and always buy from a reputable supplier. You may pay more for free-range poultry, but it isn't really more expensive because it tastes so much better and is so much more satisfying.

Curried Chicken Wings

Ailes de Poulet au Curry

⚜ I was disconsolate when we first moved to France because I couldn't find chicken wings sold separately. When I asked my butcher about them, he looked at me as though I'd admitted to a cocaine addiction. "Madame," he said, "so few understand it is the best part of the chicken." He said he could get them for me easily, as each time a client ordered a chicken breast he had to dispose of the wings somehow. Usually he saved them for himself and his wife, but he was happy to share.

This is my favorite way to prepare them, which I shared with the butcher, and have shared with others since.

Serve this with a lovely micro-brewery beer, or a lightly chilled Riesling.

4 servings

4 pounds (2 kg) chicken wings, from a free-range or organic chicken

Fine sea salt

1 cup (250 ml) plain full-fat yogurt

2 tablespoons curry powder, preferably Madras

Hot paprika, optional

1. Preheat the oven to 475°F (245°C).

2. Place the chicken wings in a single layer in a baking dish. Season them on both sides with salt.

3. In a small bowl, whisk together the yogurt, curry powder, and paprika to taste, if using. Pour the mixture over the chicken wings and turn them so they are coated. Bake in the center of the oven until the wings are crisp and cooked through, about 50 minutes. The curry may darken at the edges of the pan; don't be concerned—it won't burn, and the high heat and long cooking time are both necessary for delicious wings.

4. Remove the chicken wings from the oven and let sit for 10 minutes, then serve.

ASTUCES: I use Madras curry powder, which is wonderfully spicy. If you use a milder curry powder, you may want to add some hot paprika to get the requisite heat. Make sure your curry powder is lively and fresh. The amount of curry powder called for here makes for flavorful but not overwhelmingly curry-flavored wings. If you're a real curry fan, you may want to increase the amount. ⚜ To be sure the wings cook evenly, tuck the tips under the fleshy "drumstick" part so they don't spring open during cooking.

Chicken with Artichokes

Poulet aux Poivrades

⚜ Come spring and summer, the market stalls in Provence are piled high with small, purple-hued artichokes that are sold for a song. Called *poivrade* or *violet de Provence*, they are known for their delicate proportions, meaty texture, and round, nutty flavor. The tender, pale-green flesh of the heart and inner leaves (the only part that is eaten) is as delicious raw as it is cooked.

Here, the artichokes elevate chicken to an ultimate state of goodness, for they are complementary to the full flavor of a good farm-raised, free-range bird. And though artichokes tend to be anathema to wine, you will see that they go well with a white Burgundy, such as a Pouilly-Vinzelles.

6 servings

½ lemon

18 small artichokes

3 tablespoons (45 ml) extra virgin olive oil

One 3½- to 4-pound (1.75- to 2-kg) free-range and/or organic chicken, cut into 6 serving pieces

Sea salt and freshly ground black pepper

18 small spring onions or pearl onions, trimmed and peeled

¼ cup (60 ml) red wine vinegar

2 bay leaves from the *Laurus nobilis*, or dried imported bay leaves

3 garlic cloves, green germ removed if necessary

½ cup (5 g) firmly packed fresh basil or flat-leaf parsley leaves

1. Fill a large bowl with water, and squeeze the lemon half into it. To prepare the artichokes, working with one at a time, trim off the end of the stem and remove all of the tough, outer leaves until you have just the pale yellow-to-green heart and tender leaves. Trim off the tip of these leaves, and add the artichoke to the lemon water. (The water will prevent the artichokes from turning brown and will eliminate their slightly bitter edge.)

2. Heat the oil in a large heavy-bottomed skillet over medium-high heat. Brown the chicken pieces on all sides, seasoning them lightly with salt and pepper as you do so, about 10 minutes. To avoid crowding the pan, you may need to do this in batches. Transfer the chicken to a plate and reserve.

3. Cut each artichoke heart lengthwise in half, and add them to the pan, along with the onions. Stir, season with salt, cover, and cook, shaking the pan several times, until the onions and artichokes turn golden and soften slightly, about 4 minutes. Add the vinegar, stir, and cook, uncovered, until the vinegar has completely evap-

orated. Pour ½ cup (125 ml) water over the vegetables and stir, scraping up any caramelized juices from the bottom of the pan.

4. Add the bay leaves and garlic, nestling them in among the vegetables, and arrange the chicken on top of the vegetables. Season with salt and pepper, cover, and cook until the chicken is just tender yet still moist and the artichokes and onions are tender through, about 25 minutes. Remove the pan from the heat, and adjust the seasoning.

5. Mince the basil immediately before you plan to serve the dish.

6. Transfer the chicken and vegetables, with their cooking juices, to a warmed platter and sprinkle with the minced herbs, or serve directly from the pan, garnished with the herbs.

Steamed Chicken with Cilantro Oil

Poulet à la Vapeur, l'Huile de Coriandre

❧ All I have to do is think of this dish and my mouth begins to water, it is so simple and delectable. I've adapted the recipe from one given to me by Guy Martin, chef at Le Grand Véfour in Paris, who cooks this for his family and friends on the weekends, when he's not in the restaurant kitchen.

The spices tucked under the skin of the chicken, along with the combination of steaming and sautéing used here, result in an uncanny depth of flavor that is set off by the deep green pool of cilantro oil.

I suggest a very fruity Sauvignon Blanc from Château Turcaud.

4 servings

One 3½-inch (9-cm) piece fresh ginger, peeled and coarsely chopped

The zest from 1 lime, minced

One 3½- to 4-pound (1.75- to 2-kg) free-range and/or organic chicken, cut into 8 serving pieces

1 tablespoon grapeseed oil

Fine sea salt and freshly ground black pepper

4 to 6 tablespoons Cilantro Oil (page 273)

Geranium blossoms (unsprayed)

1. Puree the ginger in a food processor; the puree won't be completely smooth, but that doesn't matter. Place the puree in a good-sized piece of cheesecloth and, working over a small bowl, twist it to extract as much juice as possible—you should get 2 teaspoons ginger juice. Discard the ginger pulp. Stir the lime zest into the ginger juice.

2. Gently peel back the skin on the pieces of chicken without detaching it and rub the ginger juice mixture over the meat, making sure that you divide the mixture evenly among the pieces of chicken, or dip the meat into the mixture. Bring the skin back up and over the meat and pat it into place. Tie the wings to the breast pieces with kitchen twine so that the wings are held close to the meat, which will prevent them from drying out in cooking. Let the chicken sit at room temperature for 30 minutes to 1 hour, so it can absorb the flavors of the ginger and lime.

3. Bring 4 cups (1 l) water to a boil in the bottom of a steamer. Place the chicken in the top, cover, and steam until the chicken is nearly cooked through, about 20 minutes. Remove the chicken from the steamer and

ASTUCES: During steaming, the fat drains away from the chicken yet the meat remains moist, and the flavors of the spices tucked under the skin permeate the meat. ✤ When you cut apart a chicken into serving pieces for a dish like this one, separate the thigh and the leg, then detach each side of the breast with the wing attached. Then cut each side of the breast meat in half on the bias to create good-sized, lozenge-shaped pieces, two of which have the wings attached.

pat it dry, or set it on a rack to dry at room temperature about 20 minutes.

4. Heat the grapeseed oil in a large heavy-bottomed skillet over medium heat until it is hot but not smoking. Brown the chicken on one side, then season it with salt and pepper, turn, and brown it on the other side, seasoning it again with salt and pepper; this will take a total of 8 to 10 minutes. Transfer the chicken to a plate lined with paper towels to drain and pat any excess fat from the chicken.

5. To serve, place the chicken in the center of four plates (preferably white ones). Surround each serving with 1½ tablespoons of the cilantro oil, garnish with the flower petals, and serve.

Syrian Chicken with Tahini, Lemon, and Yogurt Sauce

Tassqria

❧ According to our friend and neighbor Ziad Hatahet, this is the equivalent of fried chicken and potatoes in his native Syria. It is a typical family dish he ate when he was growing up, and he cooks this when he feels homesick.

Ziad is a perfectionist and the first time he made this dish for us he was so nervous he couldn't focus on the conversation. When he finally served it, he watched closely as we tasted it. The moment our delight became obvious, so did his.

I had to make this several times before Ziad was satisfied with my rendition, and now I make it often. "Now you can have fun with the flavorings," he said to me recently. By that he meant I could vary the amount of garlic and cumin, add a fresh herb like thyme or cilantro, strew the dish with pomegranate seeds. No matter what I do, this dish is always excellent, just a bit exotic and out of the ordinary.

It goes perfectly with a light Semillon.

4 servings

One 3½- to 4-pound (1.75- to 2-kg) free-range and/or organic chicken

2 large onions, cut into quarters

4 garlic cloves, green germ removed if necessary

1 tablespoon coarse sea salt

10 black peppercorns, preferably Vietnamese or Tellicherry, crushed

½ teaspoon cumin seeds, crushed

½ baguette, cut into 1-inch (2.5-cm) cubes (to 6 cups)

1. Preheat the oven to 350°F (180°C).

2. Place the chicken, onions, garlic, salt, pepper, and cumin seeds in a stockpot and cover with water by 2 inches (5 cm). Bring to a boil over high heat, reduce the heat to medium so the water is simmering merrily, and cook until the chicken is tender but not falling from the bone, about 1 hour. Remove the pot from the heat and remove the chicken from the broth. Let the chicken cool slightly. Set the broth aside.

3. While the chicken is cooking, toast the bread: Place the cubes of bread in a single layer on a baking sheet and bake in the center of the oven, turning them regularly, until they are golden on all sides, 8 to 10 minutes. Remove from the oven and let cool.

For the yogurt sauce

2 cups (500 ml) plain full-fat yogurt

2 tablespoons tahini (sesame paste)

2 garlic cloves, green germ removed if necessary, minced

2 tablespoons freshly squeezed lemon juice

Scant ¼ teaspoon cumin seeds, finely crushed

For the garnish

2 teaspoons unsalted butter

2 tablespoons pine nuts

½ cup (5 g) flat-leaf parsley leaves

10 fresh peppermint leaves

4. To make the sauce, in a medium bowl, combine the yogurt with the remaining ingredients. Adjust the seasoning with lemon juice and cumin, and set aside at room temperature.

5. Toast the pine nuts: Melt the butter in a small skillet over medium-low heat. Add the pine nuts and cook, stirring almost constantly so they don't burn, until they are golden, about 3 minutes. Remove from the heat and transfer to a plate so they won't continue to cook.

6. When the chicken is cool enough to handle, remove and discard the skin. Remove the meat from the bones and cut it into bite-sized pieces. Strain the broth, discarding the vegetables. Place the meat in a medium saucepan, with about ¾ cup (185 ml) of the chicken broth to keep it moist, and set over low heat to keep hot.

7. Immediately before serving, mince the parsley and mint leaves together.

8. To serve, place the chicken in an attractive shallow serving platter or serving dish. Top with a layer of the toasted bread cubes, and sprinkle with ½ cup (125 ml) of the warm broth. Pour the yogurt sauce over the bread, sprinkle with the minced herbs and toasted pine nuts, and serve immediately.

ASTUCE: The chicken is cooked through but not so long it falls from the bone, so the meat still has robust flavor. The resulting broth will be a light chicken broth. Use what you need here, then keep the rest to use in any recipe calling for chicken broth. The recipe calls for the yogurt sauce to be poured over all, but you may prefer to serve it alongside.

Chicken with Turmeric and Coconut Milk

Poulet au Curcuma et Noix de Coco

⚜ On the Ile de la Réunion, where this dish originated, the islanders grate and squeeze fresh coconut to get the milk, according to Claire Mutrelle, our neighbor's daughter, who lives on Réunion and gave me the recipe. Simple and straightforward, this dish brings forth images of coconut palms and lime trees, warm winds and hot sand.

Serve this with a very fruity chilled micro-brewery beer or a light white wine such as a Gaillac from Domaine Peyres-Roses.

4 to 6 servings

1 tablespoon grapeseed oil

One 4-pound (2-kg) free-range and/or organic chicken, cut into serving pieces

Fine sea salt and freshly ground black pepper

2 large onions, diced

1 tablespoon ground turmeric

3⅓ cups (two 13-ounce; 400-ml cans) coconut milk

1 cup (10 g) lightly packed fresh cilantro leaves, plus a few sprigs for garnish

1. Heat the oil in a large heavy-bottomed pot over medium heat. Lightly brown the chicken on all sides, seasoning it with salt and pepper as you turn the meat. Remove the chicken from the pot and drain away all but 1 tablespoon of fat.

2. Add the onions to the pot, stir, and cook until they have softened slightly, about 4 minutes. Return the chicken thighs and legs to the pot, nestling them into the onions. Season again with salt and pepper, then sprinkle the turmeric over all and stir. Add the coconut milk, stir so it is blended with the turmeric, and bring it to a gentle boil. Reduce the heat to medium-low so the milk is simmering and cook until the sauce has begun to thicken a bit, about 30 minutes.

3. Add the chicken breasts to the pot, pushing them down under the sauce, and continue cooking until all the chicken is cooked through and the sauce has reduced by about half, about 20 minutes. Remove from the heat and adjust the seasoning.

4. Coarsely chop the cilantro leaves and stir them into the chicken. Transfer it to a serving dish and serve, garnished with the additional cilantro sprigs and accompanied by rice.

PERFECT ROAST POULTRY

Here are several basic techniques to ensure the perfect roasted bird every time:

1. Bring the bird to room temperature before roasting to ensure that the heat evenly penetrates the meat.

2. Season the cavity with salt and pepper and stuff it with fresh herbs, citrus fruit, or several shallots to give it lovely flavor.

3. Pour about 1 cup (250 ml) liquid—water, wine, spirits—around the bird before roasting. Use whatever suits your fancy.

4. Roast in a hot, preheated oven—450°F (230°C) is ideal.

5. Once the bird is in the oven, turn it three times during roasting so it roasts evenly; start out a bird with its breast side up, turn it on each side, then back to a breast up position.

6. Pour vinegar over the bird 10 to 15 minutes before you will remove it from the oven, to crisp up the skin and add a tang to the sauce.

7. Once you've removed the bird from the oven, sprinkle it lightly with salt and pepper, then turn it onto its breast and shower it with more salt and pepper. Balance the bird so its feet are higher than its head and let it rest for at least 20 minutes, and up to 40 minutes. The juices will retreat into the meat, with most of them running into the breast meat to moisten it. The bird will retain its heat for up to 40 minutes.

Brined Roasted Chicken
Poulet Saumuré Rôti

❧ Brining poultry (marinating it in a flavorful, salty brine), a technique I learned about several years ago, infuses it with subtle flavor and major moisture. When I mentioned it to Mme. Breemersch, who sells her fresh chickens at the Louviers farmers' market, she nodded her head. "In France, cooks used to always simmer poultry in salted water before roasting it—it's the same idea." I was amused that I'd stumbled upon a time-honored French cooking technique, for I'd thought brining was something new. It just goes to show that when it comes to cooking not much is new, but there is always something to rediscover.

Serve this with a lightly chilled Pinot Gris from Alsace.

4 servings

1 cup (230 g) coarse sea salt

1 cup (220 g) packed dark brown sugar

5 bay leaves from the *Laurus nobilis*, or dried imported bay leaves

1 bunch fresh thyme

One 4-inch (10-cm) piece fresh ginger, peeled and cut into coins

10 allspice berries, crushed

10 black peppercorns, preferably Tellicherry or Vietnamese, crushed

3 dried bird's-eye peppers, crushed

2 star anise

5½ quarts (5½ l) water

One 3½- to 4-pound (1.75- to 2-kg) free-range and/or organic chicken

1. Place the salt, sugar, herbs, and spices in a medium saucepan, add 2 cups (500 ml) of the water, and bring to a boil. Cover, reduce the heat to medium, and simmer, stirring occasionally, for 10 minutes, or until the salt and sugar have dissolved. Remove from the heat and set aside to infuse and cool to room temperature.

2. Place the chicken in a bowl or nonreactive pot large enough to hold it and all of the water. Mix together the cooled spiced water and the remaining 5 quarts (5 l) water, then pour it over the chicken. To keep the chicken down in the brine, set a plate on top of it and weight the plate with at least 3 pounds (1.5 kg) of cans or similar weights. Refrigerate for 24 hours.

3. Remove the chicken from the brine and discard the brine. Set the chicken in a colander set in a bowl or shallow dish and refrigerate it, covered with a cotton towel, to drain overnight or for 8 hours.

4. An hour before you plan to roast the chicken, remove it from the refrigerator. Preheat the oven to 450°F (230°C).

5. Place the chicken in a roasting pan, breast up, and place in the center of the oven to roast for 20 minutes. Turn the chicken onto one side and roast for 10 minutes. Turn the chicken onto the other side and roast for 10 minutes. Finally, return the chicken to the breast-up position for an additional 20 minutes, or until it is golden and the juices run clear when the thigh and leg joint are pierced with a sharp knife. Remove the chicken from the oven and, using sturdy kitchen tongs or a poultry fork and tongs, immediately flip it over onto its breast, slightly angled so the juices run into the breast meat. Let it rest for 20 minutes before carving.

MAKE THE DEVIL GO AWAY!

Throughout history, sharing salt has signified hospitality, keeping one's word, fraternity, and a link with divinity. The only thing that can destroy any of these links is to deliberately spill salt. If you look closely at Leonardo da Vinci's *Last Supper*, you will notice an upset saltcellar near Judas's elbow ... If Jesus had only known to throw three pinches of salt over his shoulder in the direction of Judas, history might have been different.

In the French region of Brittany, the Devil is a particularly unwelcome fellow. The Bretons believe the Devil doesn't like salt, and that if he were to prepare a meal, it would be an unsalted one. To chase him away, they throw a fistful of salt into the fire, believing this will exorcise the house.

Champagne Chicken
Poularde au Champagne

❧ The Champagne region has a refined, elegant reputation and so it should, for its best-known export is the sparkling wine that has made it famous. But scratch the surface of Champagne, and you find a gutsy cuisine with a big personality whose cornerstones are hearty dishes like this one. This comes to the table as a rousing peasant dish with fancy ruffles under its skirt in the form of Champagne as the braising liquid, slices of truffle amidst the proletarian vegetables, and a sauce made velvety with egg yolks. Serve to company when you want something very, very French, something rich and lovely, something impressive.

Serve nothing other than Champagne with this dish.

4 to 6 servings

½ cup (70 g) all-purpose flour

Fine sea salt and freshly ground black pepper

One 3- to 4-pound (1.5- to 2-kg) young hen or free-range and/or organic chicken, cut into 8 serving pieces

2 tablespoons extra-virgin olive oil

1½ tablespoons (22 g) unsalted butter

2 shallots, minced

2 cups (500 ml) Champagne or other sparkling wine (see Astuces)

1 bay leaf

8 ounces (250 g) green beans, trimmed and cut lengthwise in half

1. Sift the flour with ½ teaspoon salt and ¼ teaspoon pepper onto a piece of parchment paper, then pour it into a small paper or plastic bag. Shake the pieces of chicken in the seasoned flour, working in batches, until each piece is evenly covered in flour. Let the chicken pieces sit on a cooling rack for 15 minutes, then dust them a second time with the seasoned flour.

2. Heat the oil and butter in a large deep skillet over medium heat until hot but not smoking. Working in batches to ensure that the pieces are evenly browned, brown the chicken on both sides until deep golden, about 7 minutes per batch. Transfer the chicken to a plate and reserve.

3. Add the shallots to the pan and cook, stirring constantly, until they are golden, about 2½ minutes. Return the chicken and any juices it has given up to the pan, and pour over the Champagne, which will froth up as it hits the hot pan. Stir, scraping up any browned juices on the bottom of the pan, add the bay leaf, then cover and cook until the chicken is cooked through, 20 to 25 minutes, turning the pieces once so they cook evenly. To test the

1 medium carrot, cut into julienne

8 ounces (250 g) celery root, cut into julienne

3 large egg yolks

1 small (½ ounce; 15 g) truffle, cut into julienne, optional

chicken for doneness, cut into the thickest part of the drumstick right down to the bone—if the juices and meat are still pink, continue cooking until the juices run clear.

4. While the chicken is cooking, blanch the vegetables: Bring a large saucepan of salted water to a boil over medium-high heat. Prepare a large bowl of ice water. Add the green beans to the boiling water and cook until they are tender-crisp, about 6 minutes. Transfer the beans to the ice water and leave them there until they are chilled through, then transfer them to a tea towel to drain. Meanwhile, return the water to the boil and add the carrots. As soon as the water has returned to a boil, remove the carrots and transfer them to the ice water, remove them once they are chilled. Return the water to a boil and add the celery root. As soon as the water returns to a boil, drain the celery root and transfer it to the ice water; remove it once it is chilled. Pat the vegetables dry.

5. In a small bowl, whisk the egg yolks with about 3 tablespoons chicken cooking juices.

6. When the chicken is cooked, transfer it to a warm platter, cover, and keep hot. Add the vegetables and truffle, if using, to the cooking juices and cook until the vegetables are hot through. Reduce the heat under the pan to medium-low, whisk in the egg yolk mixture, and cook just until it begins to thicken; be careful that the sauce doesn't boil, which would make it curdle.

7. Remove the vegetables from the sauce with a slotted spoon and arrange them around and over the chicken on the platter. Pour the sauce over all and serve immediately.

Rooster in Red Wine

Coq au Vin

⚜ A true *coq au vin* is made with the master of the farmyard, a rooster, whose meat is firm and full of texture. Long, slow cooking is the secret to unlocking its flavor and turning it into something sublime.

In researching *coq au vin,* I read dozens of recipes and spoke with dozens of poultry farmers, friends and neighbors, and other wonderful cooks to see how they made it. Using the information, hints, tricks, and techniques I gathered, I came up with this recipe, which incorporates the elements I think necessary to make the best, most complexly flavored coq au vin. The recipe isn't complicated, but it needs time and attention, then time to enjoy its rich and elegant flavor.

Coq au vin is a traditional Burgundian dish, so it must cook with a velvety Pinot Noir, which will complement it well at table too!

10 servings if using a rooster; 4 to 6 servings if using a chicken

One 4-pound (2-kg) chicken, free-range and/or organic, with its giblets

2 to 4 tablespoons (30 to 60 g) unsalted butter, or as needed

3 to 5 tablespoons mild cooking oil, such as grapeseed, or as needed

Fine sea salt

1 pound (500 g) small onions

12 ounces (360 g) slab bacon, rind removed, cut into 1-inch (2.5-cm) chunks (use 8 ounces; 250 g if cooking a chicken)

7 tablespoons (100 ml) Calvados, brandy, Poire Williams, or other liqueur (use ¼ cup; 60 ml if using a chicken)

1. Cut the rooster or the chicken into serving pieces, separating the legs and thighs. Mince the giblets.

2. Heat 2 tablespoons of the butter and ¼ cup (60 ml) of the oil in a large heavy pot over medium heat. When the fats are hot, brown the rooster on all sides, seasoning it lightly with salt before removing it from the pot and placing it on a platter. You may need to brown it in batches, and you may need to add the additional oil to the pot to brown the rooster. If using a hen, begin browning it with half the amount of fat, adding additional butter and oil if necessary.

3. Drain all but ¼ cup (60 ml) of fat from the pot. Add the onions and cook, stirring until they are golden and beginning to turn translucent, about 5 minutes. Transfer the onions to a bowl and add the bacon to the pot. Cook until it is golden on all sides, about 3 minutes, then transfer it to the bowl; reserve. Drain all but ¼ cup (60 ml) fat from the pot (2 tablespoons if using a chicken).

¼ cup (35 g) all-purpose flour

Fine sea salt and freshly ground black pepper

2 bottles hearty red wine, such as a good Pinot Noir

4 cups (1 l) chicken stock (see recipe, page 252)

1 bouquet garni—thyme sprigs, bay leaves, and parsley sprigs, tied together

2 garlic cloves, green germ removed if necessary

1 pound (500 g) button mushrooms, trimmed, brushed clean, and cut into quarters

½ cup (5 g) flat-leaf parsley leaves, for garnish

4. Return all of the pieces of the rooster to the pot, along with any juices that have drained from them. Stir the pieces around in the pot so they heat up slightly, then, standing back (make sure your hair is tied back and your sleeves are not over the heat), add ⅓ cup (80 ml) of the liquor and flambé it by lighting a match and holding it just above the pot (see "Flambéing," page 132). The liqueur will catch fire and flames will leap into the air and burn out within 1 minute.

5. Sprinkle the flour over the pieces of rooster and stir them around to cook the flour, then add the wine and enough of the chicken stock to cover the rooster. Add the bouquet garni and garlic, push them down into the liquid, and bring to a boil over medium-high heat. Reduce the heat to medium-low so the liquid is simmering and simmer, partially covered, for 1½ hours.

6. Add the onions and bacon to the pot, stir them into the liquid, and return it to a simmer, increasing the heat briefly if necessary. Continue simmering the rooster until it is tender but not falling from the bone, about another 1½ hours, to make 3 hours total. Check the rooster while it is cooking to be sure that it isn't drying out, and add the remaining chicken stock if necessary. If cooking a chicken, it should be cooked after 1½ to 2 hours.

7. About 20 minutes before serving, heat the remaining 2 tablespoons butter in a medium heavy-bottomed skillet over medium heat. When the butter is foaming, add the mushrooms and cook, stirring, until they have given up their liquid and are golden at the edges and tender

through, about 5 minutes. Add the remaining 2 tablespoons liquor and, standing back (and being careful as above), flame it by lighting a match and holding it just above the pan. Shake the mushrooms in the pan until the flames die down, then season them lightly with salt and pepper and add them to the simmering rooster, stirring them down into the liquid.

8. Just before serving, mince the parsley.

9. To serve, taste the sauce for seasoning and adjust it if necessary. Arrange the pieces of rooster on a large warmed serving platter, and top with the mushrooms, onions, and bacon. Pour enough of the sauce over all to moisten it and sprinkle the parsley over the top. Serve the remaining sauce alongside.

Flambéing

Flambéing refers to dousing a preparation with an alcohol such as brandy or Calvados, then igniting it with a match. It bursts into dramatic flames, which gradually die down. According to scientists who conducted a study on the effects of cooking on alcohol, flambéing burns off about twenty percent of the alcohol. The beauty of flambéing is the way it caramelizes sugars in the alcohol as well as concentrating its flavor, and thus deepening the flavors in the dish.

When you flambé, follow these safety precautions:

❧ Tie back your hair.

❧ Roll up your sleeves and tuck in any loose clothing.

❧ Make sure everyone is standing away from you.

❧ Make sure there are no flammable items near you.

❧ Use a long kitchen match.

Braised Guinea Hen with Savoy Cabbage
Pintade au Chou Braisé

❧ Come winter and the season of huge, gorgeous, waffle-leafed Savoy cabbages, and people all over France are preparing succulent braises like this. While pork in all its forms is the most typical partner to cabbage, here the full-flavored meat of a *pintade,* or guinea hen, provides the centerpiece to this hearty dish.

The *pintade* is a perky little bird that must run wild to thrive — no cages or batteries will keep it happy. Because it must be free-ranging to survive, pecking for its sustenance, its meat has body and texture, personality, and verve. Substitute chicken if you cannot find guinea hen.

Serve a lightly chilled white wine with plenty of personality, like a Côteaux du Tricastin from Domaine Montine.

6 servings

1 large or 2 smaller Savoy cabbages (about 2½ pounds; 1 kg 250 g total), cored and cut into 6 wedges if using a large cabbage, into quarters if small ones

2 teaspoons extra virgin olive oil or goose or duck fat

2 teaspoons grapeseed oil

One 3½- to 4-pound (1.75- to 2-kg) guinea hen or free-range and/or organic chicken, cut into serving pieces

Fine sea salt

6 ounces (180 g) slab bacon, rind removed, cut into 1½ × ¼ × ¼-inch (3.75 × 0.6 × 0.6-cm) pieces

3 medium carrots, peeled and diced

2 medium onions, diced

1. Bring a large pot of salted water to a boil. Prepare a large bowl of ice water. Add only as many wedges of cabbage to the boiling water as will easily fit, pushing them under the surface. Return the water to a boil, and cook until the wedges begin to turn very bright green, about 1 minute. Transfer the cabbage wedges to the ice water, and repeat with the remaining cabbage. Drain the cabbage and reserve.

2. Preheat the oven to 400°F (200°C).

3. Heat the oils (or the fat and oil) in a large heavy-bottomed flameproof Dutch oven over medium-high heat. Brown the pieces of guinea hen on both sides, seasoning each side with salt after it has browned. Remove the guinea hen and reserve.

4. Add the bacon and vegetables to the Dutch oven and cook, stirring frequently, until the onions are translucent and turning golden at the edges and the bacon is golden, about 8 minutes. Drain all but 1 tablespoon of fat from the Dutch oven and season the bacon and veg-

Freshly ground black pepper

1 cup (250 ml) aromatic white wine, such as Sauvignon Blanc

Large bunch of fresh thyme

4 bay leaves

2 dried bird's-eye peppers

Flat-leaf parsley leaves, optional

etables with salt and pepper. Pour the wine and ¾ cup (185 ml) water into the pan and stir, scraping up any golden cooking juices from the bottom. Place the pieces of guinea hen in the pan, nestling them among the bacon and onions, then tuck the thyme, bay leaves, and peppers in among the pieces of guinea hen. Arrange the cabbage on top so that it completely covers the guinea hen, season with salt and pepper, and bring the liquid to a boil over medium-high heat.

5. Cover and place on the center rack in the oven to braise until the guinea hen is thoroughly cooked and the cabbage has melted into a sweet tenderness, about 1½ hours.

6. To serve, discard the herbs and the bird's-eye peppers. Arrange the guinea hen and vegetables on a platter and garnish with parsley leaves, if desired.

ASTUCES: There are several different techniques used in this recipe: blanching, or cooking in boiling, usually salted, water, for the cabbage; browning, which is often done as here with two fats, one to impart flavor, the other with a high smoke point so the food browns without burning; and braising, or simmering in liquid, which gently coaxes flavors from ingredients. The combination of these techniques makes this a perfect example of how a simple dish is made extraordinary when it passes through the hands of a French cook. The combination of techniques encourages the innate flavors from each ingredient, which together make a harmonious whole. ❧ A guinea hen has more meat on it than a chicken because its frame is more delicate.

Roasted Lemon and Orange Guinea Hen

Pintade aux Agrumes

⚜ Lemons and oranges are at their finest and juiciest during the winter. Winter days in Normandy are short, the evenings long, so we need every reminder of warmth we can get. We cocoon, often eating near the fireplace in the kitchen to stay cozy and warm. Eating this little bit of sunshine on a plate further warms and satisfies us.

This calls for a rich Sauvignon Blanc, like the Arpent de Vaudons from J. Mérieau.

4 to 6 servings

One 3½- to 4-pound (1.75- to 2-kg) guinea hen, at room temperature

Fine sea salt and freshly ground black pepper

2 teaspoons fragrant dried oregano

1 lemon, cut in half

1 small orange, cut in half

1 tablespoon (15 g) unsalted butter, softened

1. Preheat the oven to 450°F (230°C).

2. Season the cavity of the guinea hen with salt and pepper, then sprinkle the cavity with 1 teaspoon of the oregano. Stuff the lemon and orange inside the cavity—don't hesitate to use force!

3. Mix the butter with the remaining teaspoon of oregano. Carefully loosen the skin from the breast meat of the guinea hen, and pat the meat dry with a paper towel. Rub the meat with the butter and oregano.

4. Truss the guinea hen, place it in a roasting pan breast-side up, and pour ½ cup (125 ml) water around it. Roast the guinea hen for 20 minutes, then check to be sure the pan isn't dry. If necessary, add another ½ cup (125 ml) water to the pan. Turn the guinea hen on one side and roast for 10 minutes. Turn the guinea hen on the other side and roast for 10 minutes. Return the guinea hen to the breast-up position and roast until the guinea hen is golden and cooked through, for an additional 20 minutes. To test for doneness, pierce the thigh joint with a sharp knife—the juices should run clear.

5. Remove the guinea hen from the oven and sprinkle it lightly with salt. Transfer it to a cutting board and turn it over onto its breast, angling it so the feet are above the head. Sprinkle it with salt, and let it rest for at least 20 and up to 40 minutes.

6. Meanwhile place the roasting pan over low heat and reduce the cooking juices until they are almost syrupy. Season to taste and keep warm.

7. Removed the citrus fruits from the cavity of the guinea hen, and reserve. Cut the hen into serving pieces and arrange on individual dinner plates or a warmed platter. Squeeze the lemon and orange over the hen, drizzle with the cooking juices, and serve.

ASTUCES: When you loosen the skin from the breast of the guinea hen, do so with care, as it tears easily. First pat the meat dry with a paper towel so you can rub the butter mixture over the meat more easily. The butter may clump—just even it out the best you can. ❖ The secret to this dish is squeezing the lemon and orange over the guinea hen right before serving. The fruit absorbs some of the guinea hen's juices during roasting, so what squeezes forth is a lightly herbal, slightly tart, ready-made sauce. ❖ There are trussing techniques that turn out a bird looking as though it were wrapped for Christmas. I'm not concerned about that—what does concern me is making sure the bird is a tight bundle so that it roasts evenly. To that end, I suggest you truss any way you can. You can simply tie each end of the bird together. Alternatively, wrap the string around the legs, pushing in the tail so that the cavity is closed, then cross the string over the breast and firmly tie it together near the neck, tucking the neck inside the string alongside the body.

Roast Duck with Stuffed Apricots

Canard Rôti aux Abricots Farcis

This idea came to me during apricot season. There I was making jam, feeding apricots to everyone who came near me, completely surrounded by their sweet aroma. I got to thinking about how delicious they might be stuffed, and what best they might accompany. Duck seemed the obvious choice, and, sure enough, the combination is heavenly.

Serve this with a rich and lovely Clos d'Anhel from the Languedoc.

4 servings

One 3½- to 4-pound (1.75- to 2-kg) free-range and/or organic duck, giblets reserved, fat trimmed

Fine sea salt and freshly ground black pepper

4 to 6 bay leaves

¼ cup (35 g) whole, unblanched almonds, lightly toasted

1 garlic clove, green germ removed if necessary, coarsely chopped

1 tablespoon lavender or other aromatic honey

Fleur de sel

12 medium apricots (14 ounces; 420 g total weight), pits carefully removed, leaving the fruits whole

2 tablespoons red wine vinegar

1. Preheat the oven to 450°F (230°C).

2. Prick the duck all over, through the skin but not into the flesh, so that excess fat can drain away. Season the cavity evenly with salt and pepper. Place the bay leaves in the cavity, along with the giblets, and truss the duck.

3. Set the duck in a roasting pan, pour 1 cup (250 ml) water around it, and place it in the center of the oven breast-side up to roast for 20 minutes. Turn the duck on one side and roast for 10 minutes. Turn the duck on the other side and roast for 10 minutes. Return the duck to the breast-up position, and roast for 10 minutes.

4. While the duck is roasting, prepare the apricots: Mince together the almonds and garlic. Transfer them to a small bowl and stir in the honey until thoroughly combined. Season lightly with fleur de sel. Divide the stuffing evenly among the apricots, pushing it down into the hollows left by the pits. You can use short skewers to hold the apricots together, if desired, though this will not prevent some of the stuffing from leaking out.

5. When the duck is golden brown and nearly cooked, after 50 minutes, pour the vinegar over it, and continue to roast it until it is cooked through and the skin is crisp and golden, about 10 minutes longer. Remove the duck

The apricots must be slightly underripe so they hold their shape. When you extract the pits, make the smallest slit possible in the fruit. During roasting, the apricots will deflate and some of the stuffing will leak out to blend with the succulent juices of the duck. ✿ Trim off as much fat as you can before roasting the duck, and prick it all over with a fork so that any remaining fat will drip out as the bird roasts. To save the juices without all that fat, pour them into a gravy separator (a pitcher with a spout that pours from the bottom rather than the top, allowing just the juices and none of the fat to flow out). ✿ To prevent the duck fat from spattering the oven, line the edge of the pan with a 6-inch (15-cm) wide strip of aluminum foil so it sticks well above the edge. Bend the foil out, like a flange, so it will catch the worst of the fat.

from the oven, shower it with salt and pepper, and turn it on its breast so the juices will run into the breast meat. Let rest for at least 20 minutes or up to 40 minutes.

6. Place the apricots on their sides in the roasting pan, turn them once so they are coated with the fat and juices, and place the pan in the oven. Roast the apricots until they are golden on one side and beginning to soften, about 10 minutes, then turn them and roast until they are tender through but still hold their shape, 5 to 7 more minutes. Remove the pan from the oven.

7. Transfer the duck to a cutting board, and carve it. Arrange the duck on a warmed serving platter. Carefully transfer the apricots to the platter, arranging them attractively on and around the duck. Place an aluminum foil tent over the duck and apricots to keep them warm.

8. Place the roasting pan over medium heat and cook, scraping up the caramelized juices from the bottom of the pan and until the juices are steaming hot. Season the juices to taste and pour them into a gravy separator (if you don't have one, do your best to skim off the excess fat from the cooking juices). Serve the juices in a sauceboat alongside the duck and apricots.

Duck Breast with Apple Sherry
Magret de Canard au Pommeau

❧ Magret is the choice breast meat from a duck or goose that has been specially fattened to produce foie gras. Delicate like poultry, yet rich and savory like red meat, its texture is butter-tender.

In France, magret is reserved for a special occasion, a *fête*. I often make it for guests, because as Normandy has become a region vaunted for its foie gras, so magret has become a local specialty. Pommeau, what I like to think of as the sherry of Normandy, is a rich and appley counterpart. Made with two parts fresh apple juice and one part aged Calvados, aged in an oak barrel, it gives a sweet tartness to the rich and savory meat.

Serve a wonderful, rich red Burgundy with this dish, such as a Marsannay.

4 servings

Two 13-ounce (390-g) magret (fattened duck breasts)

Fleur de sel or fine sea salt

Freshly ground black pepper

2 tablespoons apple cider vinegar

½ cup (125 ml) pommeau, tawny port, or semi-dry sherry

1 tablespoon unsalted butter, cut into 4 pieces, chilled

1. Heat a large heavy-bottomed skillet over medium heat. When it is hot but not smoking, place the duck breasts in it skin side down, cover, and cook until the skin is deep golden, about 8 minutes. Turn the duck and cook it for 2 to 3 minutes on the flesh side, then remove it from the pan. Drain off all of the fat and return the duck to the pan, skin side down. Reduce the heat to low, cover, and cook just until the meat is done on the outside but is still very rare inside, 5 to 6 minutes. Transfer the duck breasts to a plate and season with fleur de sel and pepper.

2. Add the vinegar and Pommeau to the pan, scrape up any browned bits from the bottom, and reduce the pommeau until it is slightly syrupy, 5 to 7 minutes. Remove the pan from the heat and add the butter. Swirl the sauce in the pan until the butter is melted and the sauce is glossy, 2 to 3 minutes.

ASTUCE: Because the magret has a thick layer of flavorful fat under the skin, it requires no additional fat for cooking. You will have to pour off some fat partway through the cooking. The meat is so rich, four or five slices make a satisfying serving. Do not overcook the magret, for it toughens mercilessly beyond the rare stage.

3. Cut the duck breasts on the bias into thin slices and fan them out on a warmed platter or on four warmed plates. Drizzle with the sauce and serve immediately.

Turkey Roast with Shallots

Rôti de Dinde à l'Échalote

❧ Turkey has always struck me as a bland and listless meat, but it is hugely popular in France and the tidy little turkey roasts at my butchers always look so tasty that one day I overcame my prejudice and tried one. I followed the butcher's wife's instructions for cooking it, and I'm a convert now. This is an excellent way to prepare turkey, for the shallots and onions add their sweetness to the natural juices of the turkey, and the barding fat creates richly flavored juices.

Serve a chilled white Beaujolais from Domaine Moulin Blanc along with this.

6 servings

2 tablespoons extra virgin olive oil

One 2½-pound (1k 250-g) breast from a wild (free-range and/or organic) turkey boneless roast

7 shallots, peeled and halved

3 Italian frying peppers, cored, seeded, and cut into ½-inch (1.3-cm) rings (you may use one red and/or yellow bell pepper)

2 medium red onions, cut in 8 wedges each

Fine sea salt and freshly ground black pepper

2 bay leaves from the *Laurus nobilis,* or dried imported bay leaves

1 tablespoon fresh thyme leaves

1. Preheat the oven to 400°F (200°C).

2. Heat the olive oil in a flameproof baking dish or Dutch oven over medium heat. When it is hot but not smoking, brown the turkey roast on all sides, which will take about 8 minutes. Remove the pan from the heat. Add the shallots, peppers, and onions to the pan and season the roast and vegetables with salt and pepper to taste. Crush the bay leaves and sprinkle over the turkey roast, along with the thyme leaves.

3. Cover the pan and place on the center rack in the oven. Roast until the meat is firm to the touch and cooked through, about 1 hour and 10 minutes, checking it occasionally to be sure the vegetables aren't sticking to the bottom of the pan; if they are, simply add a tablespoon or two of water to the pan. Remove the turkey from the oven, uncover it, and let rest for at least 15 minutes.

4. Slice, the roast and place the slices on a warmed platter, or six warmed dinner plates, with the vegetables alongside.

ALL THE FLAVORS OF MEAT

Toutes les Saveurs de la Viande

You may be exasperated at the mention of "a little thyme," "a trickle of lemon juice," or "a few onions," and protest that it isn't specific. But Clémentine will counter with, "How big is an onion?" and it is admittedly difficult to answer her. Discretion is indeed one of the vital ingredients to a good French recipe.

Clementine in the Kitchen,
Phineas Beck (alias Samuel Chamberlain) (1943)

The Vintner's Wife's Pork Chops

Côtelettes de Porc Vigneronnes

⚜ It could only be in Burgundy, with its rolling fields and their backdrop of sharp slopes so welcoming to the vines, that the vintner's signature dish would be dressed with a tart and savory sauce seasoned at the last minute with the sprightly mustard of Dijon, the capital city of the region.

Historically, during the fall when time was spent either watching over the vines or hastily harvesting them, the grape grower's wife—for she is the author of this Burgundian specialty—prepared dishes that were quick and simple yet substantial, to nourish the workers. This recipe is a perfect example, with its blend of substance yet subtlety, its contrasting flavors and textures, its simple goodness. Serve it, of course, with a well-aerated Burgundy!

6 servings

1 tablespoon mild cooking oil, such as grapeseed

1 tablespoon (15 g) unsalted butter

6 thick-cut (about 1½ inches; 3.75 cm) bone-in pork loin chops

Fine sea salt and freshly ground black pepper

½ cup (125 ml) water

1 large shallot, peeled and minced

1 garlic clove, green germ removed if necessary, finely chopped

½ cup (5 g) flat-leaf parsley leaves

4 cornichons, homemade (page 296) or store-bought, finely diced

1 tablespoon Dijon mustard

1. Heat the oil and butter in a large heavy-bottomed skillet over medium heat. When the fats are hot but not smoking, add the pork chops, season generously with salt and pepper, and brown them on the first side, 3 to 4 minutes. Turn the chops, season again, and brown on the other side, for another 3 to 4 minutes. Cover the pan and cook until the pork chops are cooked through, about 7 minutes. Check the pan once, and if the chops are sticking, add a tablespoon or two of water to the pan. Transfer the chops to a serving platter, cover loosely with aluminum foil, and keep them warm.

2. Add the water to the pan, and then the shallot and garlic, and scrape up the browned juices from the bottom of the pan. Cook, stirring almost constantly, until the shallot and garlic soften, 3 to 4 minutes. Pour any juices from the pork chops into the pan, then cook the liquid until it is reduced by about half and slightly thickened, about 3 minutes.

3. Meanwhile, mince the parsley.

4. Add the cornichons to the pan and stir, then add the mustard, stirring constantly until it is thoroughly incorporated. Taste for seasoning—the sauce will be quite acidic—then pour it over the pork chops. Sprinkle the parsley over all, and serve immediately.

Aromatic Braised Pork Shoulder

Échine de Porc aux Arômates

❧ Though this is a simple preparation, its flavor is elegant. It is also a bit surprising, for pork shoulder (Boston butt) is considered a humble cut of meat, yet it is so flavorful and the texture is so satisfying that it is an unexpected treat; in fact, it is the best piece of the animal in my opinion.

Two techniques go to work here to produce a succulent roast of pork shoulder that is both golden and slightly crisp on the outside and moist and tender inside. I do qualify the use of the word *tender* here, because pork shoulder isn't tender in the classic sense. It is laced with gelatin and the meat is actually firm, which gives it enormous, toothsome appeal.

I like to serve a Saint-Véran with this because for me, pork is a white wine sort of meat.

6 servings

2 tablespoons extra virgin olive oil

One 2-pound (1 kg) pork shoulder roast (with bone)

2 medium carrots, peeled, trimmed, and sliced on the diagonal

2 medium onions, peeled and thinly sliced

1 large fennel bulb, trimmed and thinly sliced

3 cups (750 ml) spring or filtered water, or as needed

3 bay leaves from the *Laurus nobilis*, or dried imported bay leaves

A handful of fresh lemon thyme sprigs

2 unpeeled coins fresh ginger

1. Preheat the oven to 400°F (200°C).

2. In a medium heavy-bottomed flameproof baking dish or Dutch oven, heat the oil over medium heat until it is hot but not smoking. Brown the pork on all sides, about 6 minutes total. Remove the pork from the dish and set aside. Add the carrots, onions, and fennel to it, stir so they are coated with the oil, and cook just until they begin to soften, about 5 minutes.

3. Return the pork to the pan, nestling it into the vegetables, and pour the water around it. Push the herbs and garlic down into the water, sprinkle the salt over all, cover, and bring to a boil. Reduce the heat so the liquid is simmering and cook for 10 minutes more.

4. Remove the cover from the pork, and place the dish in the center of the oven. Cook for about 1 hour, turning the pork every 20 minutes so it cooks evenly. If all the water evaporates, add up to ½ cup (125 ml) more so the dish stays moist.

4 garlic cloves, green germ removed if necessary

1 tablespoon coarse sea salt

Freshly ground black pepper, preferably Tellicherry or Vietnamese

Flat-leaf parsley leaves

Fleur de sel

5. When the pork is cooked through (it should register about 140°F; 60°C on an instant-read thermometer), remove it from the oven and season it all over with pepper. Remove the herbs and discard, and let the pork rest for about 15 minutes.

6. To serve, transfer the pork from the dish to a cutting board. Return the vegetables to low heat and heat until they are steaming, stirring very gently once or twice so they heat evenly but don't break up. Slice the pork into 6 thick slices, and place a slice in the center of each of six warmed dinner plates. Arrange an equal amount of vegetables over and around each slice and drizzle the pork slices with the cooking juices. Garnish the plates with parsley leaves, sprinkle the pork lightly with fleur de sel, and serve immediately.

ASTUCES: I recommend using spring water as a cooking liquid because so often tap water has the flavor of chlorine, which can adversely affect the flavor of the dish. ✤ I specify either Tellicherry black peppercorns, from India, or black pepper from Vietnam for this recipe. Tellicherry black pepper, which has long been considered the best quality because of its large size and robust flavor, is most likely easier to obtain than black pepper from Vietnam, though this country is now one of the main exporters of gorgeously aromatic black peppercorns. Both types are delicious, and interchangeable in any recipe.

Savory Stuffed Tomatoes

Tomates Farcies Savoureuses

❧ There is something about the stuffed tomato that brings a look of hunger to the French eye, for practically no other dish speaks so much of home, comfort, satisfaction. There are a million recipes for the dish, and in my opinion this is head and shoulders above all the rest for it tastes fresh, bright, and lively.

I serve these throughout tomato season, which, in Normandy, begins in late July and lasts well into September. In a typical French household these would be served as a first course, but I generally serve them as a main course because they are substantial and satisfying.

Serve a chilled rosé along with these, from Domaine Turcaud.

4 servings

3 thin slices baguette

3 tablespoons milk

8 medium tomatoes (about 2½ pounds; 1 kg 120 g total)

Fine sea salt

1 tablespoon extra virgin olive oil

1 large onion, minced

3 garlic cloves, green germ removed if necessary, minced

½ cup (5 g) flat-leaf parsley leaves, plus parsley sprigs for garnish

½ cup (5 g) fresh basil leaves, plus basil sprigs for garnish

8 ounces (250 g) lean ground pork

1 large egg

Freshly ground black pepper

1 tablespoon unsalted butter, cut into 8 pieces

1. Place the baguette slices and milk in a bowl. Push the bread down so it is completely covered, and let it sit until it has absorbed all the milk, about 30 minutes.

2. Slice the top off each tomato and reserve the tops. Remove and discard the seeds and the hard core from the tomatoes. Reserve any other pulp, separating it from any remaining seeds. Sprinkle the cavity of the tomatoes evenly with about ½ teaspoon salt and turn them upside down on a nonreactive cooling rack, set over a baking sheet to drain for 20 minutes.

3. Preheat the oven to 425°F(220°C).

4. Place the oil, onion, and garlic in a medium skillet and cook over medium heat, stirring, until the onions and garlic are translucent, about 5 minutes. Remove from the heat and let cool to room temperature.

5. Mince the herbs. In a medium bowl, mix the pork with the tomato pulp, if there is any, the onion and garlic, the egg, the soaked bread, and minced herbs. Season to taste with salt and pepper. Cook about 1 teaspoon of the mixture in a skillet over medium heat, and taste it

ASTUCES: Salting and letting the tomatoes drain concentrates their flavor and makes them just a bit sturdier for containing the filling.
✤ You can use any fresh herbs you like to flavor the filling. I've called for equal amounts of parsley and basil, but you can use all of one or the other, or sage, fennel, or sweet cicely, depending on what is best and freshest in your garden or at your market.

for seasoning when it is cool enough. Season the stuffing again if necessary, and divide it evenly among the tomatoes, mounding it slightly above the top edges of the tomatoes.

6. Place the tomatoes in a baking pan and place a piece of butter on top of each one. Balance the tops on the tomatoes. Bake in the center of the oven until the stuffing is golden and cooked through and the tomatoes are completely tender, about 1 hour.

7. Remove the tomatoes from the oven and place 2 in the center of each of four warmed plates. Drizzle the tomatoes with any cooking juices from the pan, garnish the plates with the herb sprigs, and serve.

Stuffed Cabbage for After the Hunt
Chou Farci Pour Retour de Chasse

This dish may just be the reason Jean-Claude Martin, market gardener, married his wife, Monique. It is certainly one that brings a glint to his eye the minute he hears that Monique is going to make it.

The Martins sell their produce at the Louviers market, and we have become friends over the years. Monique had often talked with me about this dish and I finally asked one day if she would show me how to make it. We settled on a date, and I arrived at the enormous double wooden door of their handsome farm.

The first step of our cooking morning together was a walk through the beautiful farmyard surrounded by timbered buildings to "go shopping" in the barn, where we chose a fat cabbage for each of us, carrots, shallots, and bundles of parsley, all freshly harvested. Then we went to the butcher next door to the farm to buy meat for the stuffing.

Monique was the chef as we began our *mise-en-place* in her efficient little kitchen, and I was the assistant as we chopped and diced ingredients for this delicious and beautiful peasant dish.

We began the satisfying task of patting and spreading the stuffing between the tender cabbage leaves. Jean-Claude drove the tractor into the yard and came to see us, breaking open his morning beer as he leaned against the kitchen wall. His bright blue eyes sparkled. "Oh, we'll eat well tonight, Suzanne. It's a good thing you wanted to make this, otherwise Monique might never have made it again and it's my favorite," he said, then was off back to the fields.

"He's happy today," Monique said. "*La terre est amoureuse* (the soil is in love), which means that it will accept tilling or planting, or whatever he needs to do to it. It is never easier to work."

We patted our respective cabbages into shape, and I prepared to take mine home to cook, according to Monique's instructions. When I served the cabbage, an impressive and imposing green ball surrounded by bright carrots and golden onions, my family was awestruck. It was flavorful and delicious, and I hastened to let Monique know. "We loved it too," she said, "but I'm going to make it again—I think it needs more Armagnac." Between us we made six or seven stuffed cabages over a two-week period getting the recipe just right, and the results are here for you.

Serve a with a lightly chilled Pouilly-Vinzelles or Macon.

10 servings

One large (2 pounds 10 ounces; 1.75 kg) Savoy cabbage, trimmed of any torn or brown leaves

1 cup (60 g) fresh bread crumbs

½ cup (125 ml) milk

2 cups (20 g) flat-leaf parsley leaves

1½ pounds (750 g) ground lean and fatty pork (ask the butcher for about one-third fatty and two-thirds lean)

2 large shallots, minced

1 medium carrot, peeled and minced

1 large garlic clove, green germ removed if necessary, minced

¼ teaspoon ground allspice

Fine sea salt and freshly ground black pepper

2 large eggs

2 tablespoons (30 ml) Armagnac or Calvados

5½ quarts (5.5 l) chicken stock or 3 quarts (3 l) chicken stock plus 2½ quarts (2.5 l) water

2 ounces (60 g) caul fat, optional

1. With a sharp knife, cut an X about 2 inches (5 cm) deep in the base of the cabbage, to help it cook evenly.

2. Bring a large pot of heavily salted water (¼ cup; 60 g of coarse or kosher salt to 8 quarts; 8 l water) to a boil. Plunge the cabbage into the water, and return the water to a boil. Once the water is boiling again, cook the cabbage for 5 minutes, then remove it from the water and let it drain, upside down in a colander for 1 hour.

3. While the cabbage is draining, make the stuffing: Place the bread crumbs and milk in a bowl and set aside until the bread has absorbed all the milk, about 5 minutes.

4. Mince the parsley. In a large bowl, combine the soaked bread, minced parsley, ground pork, shallots, carrot, garlic, and allspice and mix well. Season generously with salt and pepper. Add the eggs one at a time, then add the Armagnac and mix well. To test the flavor, cook 1 teaspoon of the stuffing in a small skillet over medium heat. Taste it and adjust the seasoning if necessary.

5. The cabbage is left whole for stuffing. Gently press the leaves out from the core, without breaking them off, until you get to the very center of the cabbage, where you will find its heart, a small bunch of tightly closed, pale yellow leaves. Moisten your hands with cold water to prevent the stuffing from sticking to them, and mound a bit of stuffing over the heart of the cabbage, then bring the next layer of leaves up and around the stuffing and press them firmly but gently against it. Press a layer of stuffing evenly over the outside of those

For the accompaniment

2 tablespoons (30 g) unsalted butter

20 small fat carrots (about 2 pounds; 1 kg), peeled and trimmed

24 small white onions slightly larger than pearl onions; (11 ounces; 310 g) an X cut in the root end of each one

leaves, then bring the next layer of leaves completely up and around that stuffing, pressing firmly but gently on them so they stay sealed over the stuffing. The leaves are supple and won't easily tear, so be sure to press on them firmly. Continue this way, using a generous amount of stuffing between each layer of cabbage leaves, and pressing the leaves firmly over it, until you've used up all the stuffing and the cabbage is reconstructed. If you happen to run out of stuffing when you still have two layers of leaves to go, don't be concerned. Simply bring those leaves up and around the final layer of stuffing and press on them firmly so they completely enclose the stuffing. Wrap the cabbage in caul fat or a large square of doubled cheesecloth.

6. Bring the chicken stock to a boil in a large stockpot over high heat. Season to taste with salt—it should be nicely flavored, as well as salted as though it were to be served as soup. Gently lower the cabbage into the stock, return it to the boil, and then lower the heat so the stock is simmering. Weight the cabbage, using a plate weighted down with a heavy bowl or a can, so it stays submerged, and simmer for 1 hour.

7. Meanwhile, melt the butter in a large skillet over medium heat. When it is foaming, working in batches brown the carrots and onions on all sides. Remove from the heat and reserve.

8. When the cabbage has simmered for 1 hour, add the carrots and onions to the pot, gently pushing them down around the cabbage so they are submerged in the cooking liquid. Cook until the cabbage is tender through and the stuffing is cooked, about 2 additional hours.

9. Using a slotted ladle or spoon, transfer the carrots and onions to a platter, and keep them warm. Transfer the cabbage to another large platter and let drain for 10 minutes.

10. To serve, pour off any liquid the cabbage has given up. If you used cheesecloth to wrap the cabbage, remove it, and resettle the cabbage on the platter. Using a slotted spoon, transfer the carrots and onions to the same platter, arranging them around the cabbage. Pour about 2 cups (500 ml) of the cooking liquid into a serving dish.

11. Cut the cabbage into 10 wedges and serve a wedge to each person, accompanied by vegetables and enough broth to moisten the cabbage.

ASTUCES: The carrots will be cooked through, tender, and very delicious when the cabbage is cooked. I prefer them this way, but if you prefer your carrots slightly al dente, you should add them later in the recipe. Large cabbages like those we have in France may be hard to find in North America. If you can't get such a large cabbage, adjust the amount of stuffing accordingly. You may also need to reduce the cooking time just slightly. ✣ Try to find caul fat for wrapping the cabbage at a specialty butcher, as it melts away during cooking, keeping it moist. If you have caul fat and it isn't in water, soak it in a bit of cold water, which will help you flatten it out to use for wrapping.

Tender White Beans and Air-Cured Ham
Mojhettes au Jambon

✦ The Vendée is a mostly agricultural region south of Brittany and east of Bordeaux, whose culinary foundation rests on dried white beans. Called *mojhettes,* these satisfying, nourishing beans have a pure, nutty flavor and incomparable tenderness.

I first tasted *mojhettes* at, of all places, the world-renowned theme park of Puy du Fou, near the town of Les Herbiers, which is dedicated to the history of the Vendée. There are several restaurants in the theme park, and *mojhettes au jambon* is on the menu at each one—and is delicious at each one!

It was at L'Hermitage, a nearby hotel, however, where I truly understood why this simple fare has become vaunted in gastronomic circles. Seasoned simply with garlic and butter, the beans I tasted there were like silk, and the ham, which is rubbed with eau-de-vie, herbs, and salt and pepper, then aged in a jute bag, is a perfect salty-sweet accompaniment. My appreciation for the dish was so apparent that when I checked out of the hotel, Chef Jean-Yves Jaulin handed me a bag of dried *mojhettes* and a foil-wrapped package. "It's our ham," he said. "Share this with your family so they'll know what they've missed." I did, and we all loved it!

Try this simple but sumptuous dish with a full-bodied Minervois.

4 servings

1 pound (500 g) dried white beans—*mojhettes* if you can find them, or Great Northern

2 shallots, minced

4 tablespoons (60 g) unsalted butter

2 large garlic cloves, green germ removed if necessary, diced

Coarse sea salt

Four ¼-inch (0.6-cm) thick slices cured or top-quality boiled ham

1. Place the beans in a large pot and cover them with cold water. Cover and bring the water to a boil over medium-high heat, then remove the pot from the heat and let sit for 1 hour. Drain the beans and reserve.

2. Place the shallots and 3 tablespoons of the butter in a large heavy-bottomed saucepan over medium heat and cook, stirring, until the butter has melted and the shallots have begun to sizzle, then continue to cook, stirring often so they don't brown, until the shallots begin to turn translucent. Add the beans and garlic, stir, and add water to cover, about 4 cups (1l). Increase the heat to medium-high and bring to a boil. Reduce the heat again so the water is simmering very gently, cover, and cook until the beans are soft and some are beginning to fall

apart, about 1½ hours. Season with salt to taste, remove from the heat, and keep warm.

3. About 10 minutes before serving, heat a large cast-iron or other heavy-bottomed skillet over medium heat until it is hot but not smoking. Add the ham slices and cook until they are golden on both sides, about 4 minutes per side.

4. Stir the remaining tablespoon of butter into the beans, adjust the seasoning, and divide them among four plates. Lay the slices of ham next to the beans and serve, with the pepper mill alongside.

ASTUCES: The ham of the Vendée is virtually impossible to get anywhere else, even in other regions of France. I recommend using a good air-cured ham such as prosciutto San Daniele, cut in fairly thick slices, or a good ham that has been boiled on the bone. ✿ The recipe calls for the ham to be browned in a dry pan. You could also grill it over a hot, but not scorching, fire or on a stove-top grill. ✿ When you buy dried beans, make sure they were harvested in the year that you are buying them. Get them from a store where they are sold in bulk so that you can ask when they were harvested. Otherwise, buy from a store where there is high turnover, and where you trust the quality of the products. Dried beans keep a long time but not forever, and when they are old, they aren't as tender.

THE BROTHERHOOD OF *MOJHETTES*

There are many exquisite bean varieties cultivated in France, and the *mojhette* is among the nuttiest and most tender. Cultivated in the Vallée de l'Arnout in the Vendée which is north of La Rochelle and south of Nantes, on marshy coastal land near the oyster capital of Marennes, this pearly white kidney-shaped bean is the basis of the region's culinary wealth.

Like so many French specialties, the *mojhette* has remained best known in its own locality. In order to encourage consumption (and thereby support production), *mojhette* producers have applied for various quality labels, hoping for an AOC, or pedigree for their beans. In 2001, they created La Confrérie de la Mojhette, a brotherhood whose members dress in dramatic green capes and red-tinged caps, and whose sole goal is to spread the word about the tender, succulent *mojhette*. A version of their favorite recipe can be found on page 154.

Many-Layered Eggplant
Feuilleté d'Aubergines à la Bolognaise

❧ The word *feuilleté* literally means "laminated," but in cooking terms it has come to mean "many layered." It generally refers to light, flaky pastry, but here it describes layers of eggplant with a robust tomato sauce.

Serve this with a Touraine from Domaine des Corbillières.

8 to 10 servings

½ cup (70 g) all-purpose flour

½ teaspoon fine sea salt

3 large eggplant (about 2 pounds; 1 kg), cut into slices slightly less than ½ inch (1.3 cm) thick

About ⅔ cup (160 ml) extra virgin olive oil

Bolognaise Sauce (page 283)

¼ cup (from about ½ ounce; 15 g piece) finely grated Parmigiano-Reggiano

---

ASTUCE: Eggplant absorbs a great deal of oil as it fries, so try brushing the slices on each side with oil and bake them in a hot 425°F (210°C) oven for 10 to 15 minutes, or until they are translucent, then proceed with the recipe. You will end up using much less oil but the dish will be less moist as a result. Many eggplant recipes call for lightly salting the eggplant before cooking to remove bitterness. If your eggplant are firm and garden-fresh, they don't need salting.

---

1. Place the flour and salt on a piece of parchment paper and mix well with your fingers. Dredge the eggplant slices on both sides in the flour.

2. Heat 3 tablespoons of the oil in a large heavy-bottomed skillet over medium heat. When the oil is hot, add only enough slices of eggplant to just cover the bottom of the pan and cook until the eggplant is golden on the first side. Turn and continue cooking until the eggplant is translucent and soft through, about 4 minutes total. Transfer the eggplant to a platter. Add enough oil to the pan to cover the bottom again, and continue cooking the eggplant in batches, adding more oil as necessary. Set the eggplant aside.

3. Preheat the oven to 450°F (230°C).

4. To assemble the feuilleté, cover the bottom of a 12 × 9-inch (30 × 22.5-cm) lightly oiled baking dish with one third of the eggplant. Cover the eggplant with about one-third of the sauce then repeat with the remaining eggplant and sauce, ending with the sauce. Sprinkle with the cheese.

5. Bake in the center of the oven just until the feuilleté is hot through, about 15 minutes. Serve immediately.

Rib-eye Steak with Bordelaise Sauce

Entrecôte Sauce Bordelaise

❧ **The French love steak, and this classic dish from Bordeaux is a national favorite. In France, steak is served either *bleu*, very, very rare, or *saignant*, rare, which guarantees moistness and flavor. Serve this with a Côtes de Blaye.**

4 servings

1 cup (250 ml) beef stock or water

One 2-ounce (60-g) marrow bone

8 tablespoons (1 stick; 120 g) unsalted butter

Four 6- to 8-ounce (180- to 250-g) sirloin steaks, about ½ inch (1.3 cm) thick

Fine sea salt and freshly ground black pepper

4 shallots, minced (to give about 3 tablespoons minced)

1 cup (250 ml) Bordeaux, such as a Côtes de Blaye

½ cup (5 g) flat-leaf parsley leaves

ASTUCE: For butter to emulsify into a sauce, the sauce must not be too hot, the butter must be cold and cut into small pieces, and the sauce must never boil. If the sauce seems to be getting too hot as you whisk in the butter, simply move the pan off the heat to cool it, then move it back over the flame when it needs to be heated back up.

1. Bring the stock to a boil in a small saucepan. Reduce the heat so it is simmering, add the marrow bone, and cook just until the marrow is slightly translucent, about 5 minutes. Remove the bone from the stock and cool. When the marrow is cool, cut around it to loosen it then gently push it out of the bone and dice it into ⅛-inch (0.3-cm) cubes. Reserve.

2. Melt 1 tablespoon of the butter in a large heavy-bottomed skillet over medium heat. When the butter is foamy and sizzling but not smoking, brown the steaks until they are deep golden on the first side, then flip them, season them with salt and pepper, and brown them on the other side, a total of about 6 minutes. Transfer the steaks to a platter and keep warm, covered, in a low oven.

3. Reduce the heat under the pan slightly and add the shallots. Cook, stirring constantly, until they turn translucent, about 5 minutes. Add the wine and stir, scraping up the bottom of the pan, then reduce the wine by three-quarters. Whisk the remaining 7 tablespoons (105 g) butter into the sauce, working on and off the heat so that the butter doesn't melt but emulsifies into the sauce. Remove the sauce from the heat and stir in the marrow.

4. Just before serving, mince the parsley.

5. To serve, arrange a steak in the center of each warmed dinner plate, and pour one-quarter of the sauce over each one. Sprinkle the steaks with the parsley and serve.

U.S. Beef Cuts for Braising

Beef for braising should be marbled with a certain amount of fat and gelatinous gristle. The fat gives flavor and tenderness and the gristle softens into a wonderful, gelatinous toothsomeness.

Rump pot roast   Bottom round

Chuck pot roast   Eye of round

There Is Nothing like a Little Bit of Tradition

Though French cooking is evolving with the speed of light, simple, traditional dishes haven't lost their cachet.

Not long ago, three thousand French chefs were asked what was their favorite dish. Every one of them, without exception, mentioned *pot-au-feu* as their second choice. (Their first? Foie gras . . . who can blame them?) One finds *pot-au-feu,* a dish that is almost a synonym for the French *petite bourgeoisie,* or middle class, on the menu in the country's finest restaurants as well as its most simple bistros, a perennial favorite.

Why? It's simple. *Pot-au-feu* endures because it is uncomplicated and pure. Based on simple, common ingredients cooked long and slowly together to emerge succulent and full of flavor, there is little mystery to *pot-au-feu*—it is simply what it appears to be.

It is also a dish rife with memories that serve as an emotional reference point. What French person doesn't remember sitting at Mamie's table and eating her succulent *pot-au-feu*? What French cook doesn't count pot-au-feu as one of his or her specialties, and compare it with another, claiming their own as the best?

One of the things that makes France such a wonderful place to live is the French loyalty to traditional dishes, even as they embrace a whole world of new ones.

Savory Beef Stew
Pot-au-Feu

✣ André Taverne, who was the florist across the street from us, didn't look as if he loved to cook, for he was tall, thin, and angular. Yet it turned out that many of the delicious aromas issuing from the apartment where he lived with his wife, Marie-Odile, came from his cooking. He gave me his very detailed recipe for *pot-au-feu* one morning as we stood outside the shop. He then directed me to the butcher where he bought the meat for his *pot-au-feu*. "You can't go wrong if you go there," were his words of advice.

Serve a Beaujolais with this, and enjoy!

6 to 8 servings

6 pounds (3 kg) beef—including top or bottom round, beef cheeks, pot roast, and oxtails

1 tablespoon coarse sea salt

1 pound (500 g) small onions

6 whole cloves

1½ pounds (750 g) carrots, peeled and cut crosswise in half, then lengthwise into quarters

1 medium rutabaga, peeled and cut in 8 wedges

6 small turnips (about 1 pound; 500 g), peeled and quartered

2 pounds (1 kg) celery root, peeled and cut in 4 × ½ × ¼-inch (10 × 1.3 × 0.6-cm) sticks

12 medium leeks (about 2 pounds; 1 kg), trimmed, well rinsed, and tied into 2 bundles of 6 each

1. Tie the top or bottom round, beef cheeks, and pot roast (separately) into compact bundles so they don't fall apart during cooking. Place them, with the oxtails, in a large deep pot. Add the salt, cover with water by at least 2 inches (5 cm), and bring just to a boil, then reduce the heat so the liquid is simmering. When impurities (in the form of grayish white foam) begin to rise to the surface of the water, skim them off, and continue skimming until you no longer see any impurities, about 20 minutes.

2. Pierce the onions with the cloves and cut the onions in half.

3. Add half the onions, carrots, rutabaga, turnips, celery root, and leeks, the bouquet garni, and 1 of the garlic cloves to the meat, and make sure all the ingredients are covered by at least 1 inch (2.5 cm) of water. Add half the peppercorns, cover, and bring just to a boil. Adjust the heat so the liquid is simmering: it shouldn't boil, or the meat will be tough. Cook, partially covered, for 3 to 3½ hours.

1 bouquet garni—parsley stems, bay leaf, leek greens, fresh thyme sprigs, tied together

2 garlic cloves, green germ removed if necessary

10 black peppercorns, preferably Tellicherry

2 bay leaves

1 marrow bone, cut into six 2-inch (5-cm) pieces (have the butcher do this)

For the croutons

6 slices day-old bread, roughly 4 inches (10 cm) square

2 garlic cloves, green germ removed if necessary

For the condiments

Coarse sea salt

Cornichons

Pickled onions

Horseradish

A variety of mustards

4. Remove the meat from the broth. Strain the broth and discard the vegetables. Return the broth to the pot, add the bay leaves, and bring just to a boil. Add the remaining carrots and rutabaga and cook until they are beginning to turn tender, about 10 minutes. Add the remaining turnips and onions and cook until they are beginning to turn tender, about 10 minutes. Add the remaining celery root, leeks, and garlic and cook until all the vegetables are tender through, about 15 minutes.

5. Remove the vegetables from the broth and place them in a shallow bowl. Moisten with some of the broth, cover, and keep them warm. Return the meat to the broth, along with the marrow bones, and simmer for 15 minutes. Transfer the meat and marrow bones to a platter, drizzle with a ladle or two of broth, and keep it warm in a low oven.

6. Rub the pieces of bread with the garlic and place in the bottom of six shallow bowls. Pouring an equal amount of broth over each, and serve as the first course.

7. Remove the strings from the meat and cut the pieces into thick slices or into chunks. Arrange the meat on a warmed platter, surrounded by the vegetables. Serve with the condiments alongside.

> **ASTUCES:** The humble nature of pot-au-feu is its glory. It uses all the best, though least vaunted, cuts of meat, which give it flavor, texture, and personality. By skimming off the impurities and replacing the vegetables partway through cooking, you ensure a pure, clean-flavored, satisfying stew, which is served in two courses. The first course is the flavorful broth, the second course is the meat and vegetables. ♣ *Pot-au-feu* is succulent the day it is made, and almost better the day after. Then, serve it cold, dressed with a Basic Vinaigrette (page 265).

Beef Braised with Carrots, Onions, and Dried Plums

Boeuf Mode aux Pruneaux

❧ *Boeuf mode* is to France what pot roast is to the United States, a homey dish that evokes fond memories of Grandmère supervising its long, slow cooking. *Boeuf mode* doesn't stay at home, though, for it is often on the menu in a café or bistro noted for its good home cooking.

This version is from Anne Lemarchant, a lovely young woman who left her job as a social worker in the city of Caen to return to the family farm near Mont St. Michel where she receives paying guests, cooking dishes for them based on recipes passed down from her mother. When I tasted this dish I loved it, for the meat was tender and flavorful, set off beautifully by the prunes.

I make this for a casual weekend supper, either just for the family or when we have friends coming to join us. I love this the first day, then I love it for two days afterwards when the flavors have mellowed into smoothness.

Try this with a wonderful, deep Côtes du Rhône, like a Vacquéras from Domaine Sang de Cailloux.

6 servings

1½ tablespoons grapeseed oil or extra virgin olive oil

One 2 pound 6-ounce (1 kg 180-g) boneless chuck pot roast, tied

Coarse sea salt and freshly ground black pepper

12 ounces (360 g) onions, thinly sliced

4 cups (1 l) warm water

2 sprigs fresh rosemary

1 large bunch fresh thyme

6 fresh sage leaves, plus a few leaves for garnish

1. Preheat the oven to 350°F (180°C).

2. Heat the oil in a large heavy-bottomed Dutch oven or flameproof baking dish over medium heat. When it is hot but not smoking, add the beef and brown it well on all sides, about 9 minutes total; as you turn the roast, season it generously with salt and pepper. Transfer the roast to a plate or platter that will catch any juices.

3. Add the onions to the pan and stir, then reduce the heat and cook until they are wilted and beginning to turn translucent, about 5 minutes, stirring frequently so they don't stick to the pan.

4. Return the beef and any juices to the pan, nestling it in the onions. Pour in the water and increase the heat to

3 bay leaves from the *Laurus nobilis*, or dried imported bay leaves

1 pound (500 g) carrots, peeled and cut on the bias into thick slices

9 ounces (270 g) dried plums (prunes) with pits

bring it to a gentle boil. Shift the onions and beef around in the pan so you can scrape up any browned juices on the bottom. Tie the herbs together using kitchen string. Add the herbs and more salt to taste to the pan, stir, and reduce the heat so the water is simmering.

5. Cover the pan and place it on the center rack in the oven to cook for 1 hour. Remove the pan from the oven and turn the beef, return to the oven, cover, and continue cooking for 30 minutes.

6. Remove the pan from the oven and add the carrots, pushing them down into the cooking juices. Cover and return to the oven to cook for 1 hour.

7. Remove the pan from the oven, turn the beef, and add the prunes. Return the pan to the oven, uncovered, and cook until the beef is tender but not dried out, 20 to 30 minutes. The liquid should be reduced by about one-third. If the beef is cooked through before the juices have reduced, transfer the beef to a cutting board, place the pan over medium-high heat, bring to a boil, and cook until the juices have reduced by one-third and are richly flavorful and slightly thickened. Transfer the beef to a cutting board if you have not already done so, and taste the sauce for seasoning. Keep it warm.

ASTUCES: The beef cooks for about 3 hours, and it needs every single minute of that time. You don't have to hover over it, but you do need to be in the vicinity as it cooks, for it requires regular turning to cook evenly. As it nears completion, check the meat often to make sure it doesn't dry out. ✣ I often use grape-seed oil for browning meat, as its smoke point is higher than that of most other cooking oils. ✣ Freshly cooked pasta is the typical accompaniment to *boeuf mode*.

8. To serve, cut the beef into 6 slices. If it breaks up a bit and the slices aren't perfectly symmetrical, don't be concerned. Arrange the slices (and the pieces) attractively on a platter. Remove and discard the herbs from the cooking juices and pour the juices, with the carrots, onions, and prunes, over the meat. Serve immediately, garnished with sage leaves.

Pan Fried Steak with Leek Coulis

Biftech Poêlé au Coulis de Poireaux

❧ Leeks are a vegetable dear to the French palate, and each winter, when they are in full season, the year is judged by their price. If it is high, faces are downcast and troubled; if it is low, happiness reigns.

Franck Pecqueux, who helps out in our garden, is a good old-fashioned cook who abides by his mother's, grandmother's, and grandfather's recipes. He and I share a love for leeks and he gave me this recipe one day when he described how he makes it for special occasions or Sunday lunch. I tried it and have been making the coulis ever since, though I don't confine its use as a sauce for steak. It makes a fine filling for filo triangles and a wonderful warm dip for blanched vegetables, too.

Serve with a full, rich red Burgundy.

6 servings

For the leek coulis

2½ tablespoons (37 g) unsalted butter

2 pounds (1 kg) leeks, white part only, well rinsed and cut into very thin rounds

¾ cup plus 1 tablespoon (200 ml) crème fraîche or heavy cream, preferably not ultra-pasteurized

Fine sea salt and freshly ground black pepper

Freshly grated nutmeg

1 tablespoon unsalted butter

Six 6-ounce (180-g) steaks, such as New York cut

Fine sea salt and freshly ground black pepper

Fresh flat-leaf parsley, chervil, or sage leaves, or chives

1. To make the coulis, place the butter in a heavy skillet over medium heat and once it is beginning to melt, add the leeks and stir. Cook until the butter sizzles, then reduce the heat to medium-low, cover, and cook until the leeks are tender through, stirring occasionally to be sure they don't stick, about 20 minutes.

2. Remove the leeks from the heat and transfer them to a food processor. Add half the cream and puree the leeks, slowly adding the remaining cream. Season to taste with salt and pepper, then with nutmeg. Transfer the coulis to a small saucepan and keep warm over low heat.

3. Melt the butter in a large heavy-bottomed skillet over medium heat. When the butter is very hot but not smoking, add the steaks and cook until they are golden on the first side, about 5 minutes. Turn the steaks, season them generously with salt and pepper, and cook until they are done to your liking; for a rare steak, the way steak is eaten in France, another 2 minutes will suffice.

4. To serve, place an equal amount of the leek coulis in the center of each of six warmed dinner plates, then place a steak atop each pool of coulis. Garnish with the herbs and serve.

> **ASTUCES:** Only the white part of the leek is used here, because it is the sweetest part. Use the green parts, trimmed of any tough leaves, in the Leek and Bacon Quiche (page 72). ✤ *Coulis* is a term generally used to describe a sauce that has been strained through a fine-mesh strainer. In this case, the term is used loosely.

Lamb and Dried Plum Tagine with Toasted Almonds

Tagine d'Agneau aux Pruneaux, et aux Amandes Grillées

❧ The aroma of spices always swirls around Fatna Loutfi and her shop in Louviers, a small grocery that I refer to as our local 7-Eleven. When the aromas are intensely fresh and lively, it means Fatna is upstairs cooking while her daughter, son, or husband is at the register in the store. She not only makes this tagine, a North African dish that has become part of the French culinary repertoire, but she sells all the ingredients for it to the many North Africans who live in and around Louviers.

Fatna is Moroccan and her tagine is more delicate, more refined, more lovely in flavor and aspect than tagines I've eaten that come from other North African countries. It may be that it reflects the cooking of her country or simply that she is a marvelous cook. Whatever it is, I've included it in my repertoire, reserving it for special occasions as Fatna does, for its subtle exotic flavors and textures are worthy of particular attention.

I like to serve a hearty red wine with this, such as a Gaillac from Domaine Peyres-Roses.

6 servings

1 cup (10 g) gently packed fresh cilantro leaves

1 tablespoon extra virgin olive oil

1 tablespoon grapeseed or mild vegetable oil

2 large onions, diced

4 garlic cloves, green germ removed if necessary, minced

1 teaspoon powdered ginger

½ teaspoon freshly ground white pepper

½ teaspoon freshly ground black pepper

1. Mince the cilantro and place it in a medium bowl. Add the oils, onions, garlic, spices, lemon juice, and 1 cup (250 ml) of the water and mix very thoroughly. Turn the mixture out into a 10½-inch (26.5-cm) tagine or a Dutch oven or heavy-bottomed stockpot. Set the pieces of lamb on top and push them slightly into the onions, then turn them so the lamb is imbued with the mixture. Macerate the lamb for 1 hour at room temperature, turning it once.

2. If using an earthenware tagine, place it in a heavy-bottomed skillet that will keep it off the direct heat or use a heat diffuser, set the skillet or pot over medium-high heat, add the remaining ½ cup (125 ml) water, stir well, and bring to a boil. Cover the lamb, reduce the heat

Large pinch saffron threads

1 scant tablespoon coarse sea salt, or to taste

1 tablespoon freshly squeezed lemon juice

1½ cups (750 ml) water

One (3½-pound; 1.75-kg) bone-in lamb shoulder, cut into 6 pieces

For the dried plums

24 large dried plums, with pits

¼ cup (50 g) vanilla sugar

4 cups (1 l) mineral or filtered water

1 tablespoon orange flower water

4 cinnamon sticks

For the garnish

1 teaspoon extra virgin olive oil

1 scant cup (about 140 g) blanched whole almonds

1 tablespoon raw sesame seeds

to low, and cook, stirring occasionally and turning the lamb at least four to five times, until the meat is almost falling from the bone, about 1 hour and 45 minutes. The dish should remain at a definite though gentle simmer.

3. While the meat is cooking, prepare the dried plums: Place them in a small bowl and cover them with tap water; let them sit for about 20 minutes, then drain. Place the sugar in a medium saucepan along with the mineral water, orange flower water, and cinnamon sticks and bring to a boil over medium-high heat. Reduce the heat slightly so the mixture is boiling merrily and cook, uncovered, until it has reduced by about two-thirds. Add the dried plums, stir, and cook, stirring from time to time, until all but about 1 tablespoon of the syrup has evaporated and the dried plums are beginning to caramelize on the outside, about 20 minutes. Once the cooking liquid begins to caramelize, be sure to turn the dried plums often so they become evenly caramelized. When the caramel becomes almost too thick to stir, remove the pan from the heat and set aside. (Do not keep the dried plums over low heat, or the caramel will become too thick.)

4. To prepare the almonds, heat the oil in a heavy-bottomed skillet over medium heat. When the oil is hot but not smoking, add the almonds and cook, stirring constantly, until they are golden, 7 to 10 minutes. Transfer the almonds to a bowl to cool.

5. Rinse the sesame seeds in a fine sieve under cold running water, then pat them dry. Place the seeds in a small cast-iron skillet or a wok and set it over medium heat.

When the sesame seeds begin to pop and crackle, stir them constantly until they are golden, 2 to 3 minutes. Immediately transfer to a bowl to cool.

6. When the lamb is tender, remove the heat diffuser if you used it, and increase the heat to medium so the dish bubbles merrily. Cook, turning the meat and stirring the onions, until both are golden. Remove from the heat, and set aside, covered.

7. To serve, adjust the seasonings, place the pan of caramelized dried plums over medium heat. When the caramel in the bottom of the pan and on the dried plums begins to heat and loosen up, remove and discard the cinnamon sticks and transfer the dried plums to the tagine, arranging them individually on top of the meat. If there is extra caramel in the bottom of the pan, you may drizzle this atop the dried plums (though it isn't easy to do). Sprinkle the almonds over the dried plums, then sprinkle the sesame seeds over all. Serve immediately.

ASTUCES: The lamb is cooked on the bone, which gives it much more flavor. Ask the butcher to cut a lamb shoulder into pieces. ❧ The dish *tagine* takes its name from the flat round earthenware vessel with a cone-shaped earthenware cover, known as a tagine, that was originally used as a portable oven by North African nomads. While the dish can be cooked in a conventional pot, earthenware tagines are inexpensive and easy to come by in Middle Eastern/Moroccan markets. They are built to withstand heat and encourage slow cooking—that said, I don't trust mine over a flame but set it on a heat diffuser or inside an old cast-iron skillet that takes the brunt of the flame, conducting the less-intense heat to the tagine. ❧ Serving the tagine in the traditional cooking vessel makes for a dramatic, exotic presentation. According to Fatna, no bread or starch is served with this dish, but I often make Steamed Couscous (page 278) to serve alongside anyway. Begin this meal with the Khlat (Beet Mix-up) (page 79), and follow it with a light dessert such as Red Currant Sorbet (page 246) or Lychee, Lime, and Candied Ginger Salad (page 246).

Roasted Leg of Lamb with Herbs and Mustard

Gigot d'Agneau Rôti aux Aromates et à la Moutarde

❧ When you slather lamb with mustard, you both flavor it and begin the slow, gentle process of tenderizing it. The slight bit of vinegar in the mustard slowly, slowly seeps into the meat and relaxes it so that when you put it in the oven, it is prepared to receive the heat and cook evenly and gently. When it emerges, the mustard has created a sort of tender crust around it, allowing the juices to remain inside the meat. After the meat has rested, you'll find the mingling of mustard and lamb spectacular.

This roast is simple to prepare and impressive to serve. Accompany it with a dish of Tomatoes Provençal (page 186) and a Pouilly-Fumé from Domaine Maltaverne, or a Marsannay Clos du Roy from Domaine Bouvier.

6 to 8 servings

1 large garlic clove, green germ removed if necessary

2 tablespoons fresh thyme leaves

1 bay leaf from the *Laurus nobilis*, or dried imported bay leaf

One 4- to 4½-pound (2- to 2.25-kg) leg of lamb, bone-in, fat trimmed if desired

Fine sea salt and freshly ground black pepper

⅓ cup (80 ml) Dijon mustard

6 fresh rosemary sprigs

1 cup (250 ml) water

1. At least 2 hours before you plan to roast the leg of lamb, mince the garlic, thyme, and bay leaf together. Make 10 slits in the lamb that are about ½ inch (1.3 cm) deep and ½ inch (1.3 cm) wide, and divide the minced herbs among the slits, pushing them right down into the meat. Lightly season the lamb with salt and pepper, then slather it all over with the mustard. Cover and marinate at room temperature for 2 hours, or refrigerate for up to 12 hours. If you refrigerate the lamb, remove it from the refrigerator at least 2 hours before you plan to roast it, so it can come to room temperature.

2. Preheat the oven to 425°F (220°C).

3. Lay 3 of the rosemary sprigs in a roasting pan large enough to accommodate the leg of lamb. Set the lamb in the pan, and lay the remaining rosemary sprigs over it. Place the lamb in the center of the oven and roast until the meat is golden on the outside and the interior temperature registers about 137°F (58°C) on an instant-

read thermometer, about 50 minutes; this results in a leg of lamb that offers something for everyone, from rosy to rare. Remove the lamb from the oven, transfer it to a cutting board, and let it sit for at least 20 minutes, and up to 40 minutes. Reserve the roasting pan.

4. Just before carving the leg of lamb, remove and discard the rosemary sprigs from the roasting pan (and from the lamb). Place the pan over low heat, add the 1 cup (250 ml) water, and heat the water to a boil, stirring and scraping up the caramelized juices from the bottom of the pan. Cook until the liquid is reduced by about one-third. Taste for seasoning. If the juices don't have quite enough flavor, continue reducing until their flavor is concentrated to your taste. Adjust the seasoning and strain the sauce.

5. Carve the leg of lamb and pour the sauce over it, or serve it alongside.

Marinated Lamb Shoulder Grilled over the Coals
Épaule d'Agneau à la Braise

❧ Lamb is my favorite red meat, and I love just about any cut prepared just about any way at all. But I think that lamb shoulder is my favorite cut because its texture is so firm, its flavor so hearty. When it is marinated with herbs and oil, then grilled, the meat emerges moist, lightly crisp, rich with herb flavor, and subtle with smoke.

Served with Aromatic Quinoa alongside (page 189), and a lovely Chinian from Domaine Navarre, this is an elegant dish.

Serves 6

One 4-pound (2-kg) (3 pound; 1.5 kg without bone) lamb shoulder, boned and butterflied (you can have the butcher do this)

⅓ cup fresh rosemary leaves

2 garlic cloves, green germ removed if necessary, each cut into 6 thin slivers

Coarsely chopped zest of 1 lemon

2 tablespoons extra-virgin olive oil

About 2 teaspoons coarse sea salt

About 1 teaspoon coarsely ground blend of green, white, and black peppercorns

1. Make 6 slits about ½ inch (1.3 cm) in the lamb shoulder, and put it on a plate. Mince together the rosemary, garlic, and lemon zest and transfer to a small bowl. Add the olive oil and stir, then add the salt and pepper and mix well. Insert about ½ teaspoon of this mixture into each slit in the lamb, and rub the remaining mixture all over the surface of the lamb. Refrigerate it, covered with parchment paper and aluminum foil, for at least 12 hours, or overnight.

2. About 2 hours before you plan to cook the lamb, remove it from the refrigerator so it can come to room temperature.

3. About 45 minutes before you plan to cook the lamb shoulder, build a good-sized fire in the grill. You will need quite a thick bed of coals to sustain the heat, which needs to remain intense for 25 to 30 minutes. When the coals are red and dusted with ash, spread them out and place the grill rack about 4 inches (10 cm) above them.

4. Place the lamb shoulder on the grill and cook until it is well browned but not at all burned on the first side. Turn the shoulder and cook until the other side is

browned, then continue to cook, turning the shoulder regularly so its color stays evenly golden, until the shoulder is cooked according to your liking: for medium-rare, the interior temperature should be about 150°F (65°C) on an instant-read thermometer.

5. Transfer the lamb to a warmed platter and let it rest, loosely covered with a tent of aluminum foil, for 20 minutes before slicing and serving.

A SELECTION
OF VEGETABLES

Éventail de Légumes

By burning the garden weeds, I didn't
forget to roast the potatoes underneath, for
this was a treat of my childhood, I know
nothing better. They smell of burning, of
smoke, of grasses, of wildness. After eating
them there is nothing for it but to go to the
river and drink the clear water of our
fountains from the palm of your hand, and
talk comfortably of the end of the world,
for we are one with the beginning of time.

Magaridou,
a Book of Reminiscences of an Auvergnat Cook,
Suzanne Robaglia (1992)

Potato Gratin with Cauliflower

Gratin de Pommes de Terre au Chou-Fleur

❧ The potato gratin is one of France's greatest culinary gifts to the world. No one can resist the aroma as it bakes, nor its golden bubbling crust when it is set on the table. Over the years I've experimented by adding different vegetables to potato gratins, and I've decided that cauliflower is my favorite. It becomes elegantly smooth and adds its light, nutty flavor to the potatoes.

Gratins make a wonderful main course served with a salad, or served as a side dish with grilled or roasted meat, poultry, or fish.

6 side-dish servings

1½ cups (325 ml) whole milk

¾ cup (150 ml) half-and-half, preferably not ultra-pasteurized

¾ cup (150 ml) crème fraîche or heavy cream, preferably not ultra-pasteurized

1½ pounds (750 g) russet potatoes, peeled

The florets from one 1¾ pound (875 g) cauliflower

Fine sea salt and freshly ground black pepper

2 shallots, minced

ASTUCE: A traditional gratin is made exclusively with crème fraîche. I lighten a gratin by using a combination of milk, half-and-half, and crème fraîche (or heavy cream). It remains rich and satisfying but is not in the least bit heavy.

1. Preheat the oven to 375°F (190°C).

2. In a large bowl, whisk together the milk, half-and-half, and crème fraîche.

3. Cut the potatoes and cauliflower florets into very thin slices. Arrange half of the potato and cauliflower slices in an even layer in the bottom of a medium gratin dish. Season with salt and pepper and sprinkle evenly with half of the shallots. Top with the remaining potatoes and cauliflower, then season with salt and pepper and sprinkle with the remaining shallots. Pour the crème fraîche mixture over the vegetables, lifting and moving them as necessary so they are thoroughly coated.

4. Bake in the center of the oven for 15 minutes. Using a spatula or wooden spoon, stir the vegetables gently in the baking dish, and bake for 20 minutes. Stir the vegetables again, and bake until the vegetables are tender through and the gratin is bubbling and golden on top, about another 20 minutes.

5. Remove from the oven, let cool for 10 minutes as it will be blistering hot, then serve.

Fennel Gratin

Gratin de Fenouil

✤ Agnès Gaudrat-Pourcel writes and edits children's books for Bayard Presse in Paris. I've known her for twenty years (she loaned me the frilly slip I wore for my wedding, which hung a seductive little inch below the hem of my silk dress), and we trade publishing stories and books whenever we get together. Agnès claims not to be a good cook, but from the earliest days of our friendship, she has exhibited a flair with foods, flavors, colors, and presentation.

This dish is a perfect example of Agnès's cooking, something she once served us as an accompaniment to salmon. Lamb is another favorite accompaniment to this dish.

6 servings

3 pounds (1.5 kg) fennel bulbs, trimmed and cut into quarters

1 garlic clove, green germ removed if necessary, minced

Fine sea salt and freshly ground black pepper

1½ ounces (45 g) Parmigiano-Reggiano, finely grated

1 tablespoon (15 g) unsalted butter

ASTUCES: Reserve some of the blanching liquid to pour over the fennel to moisten the gratin in a light way. ✤ The fennel can be blanched in the morning, then the dish can be put together quickly and easily in the evening.

1. Bring a large pot of salted water to a boil over high heat. Add the fennel and return the water to a boil, then reduce the heat so the water is boiling gently and cook until the fennel is nearly tender through, about 8 minutes. Prepare a big bowl of ice water, and when the fennel is cooked, transfer it to the ice water; reserve the fennel blanching liquid. When the fennel is cool, remove it from the ice water and let it drain on cotton towels.

2. Preheat the oven to 425°F (220°C).

3. Place the fennel in a gratin dish and pour ¼ cup (60 ml) of the blanching liquid over it. Add the garlic, salt and pepper to taste, and the grated cheese and mix well with your hands, making sure the ingredients are thoroughly combined. Dot with the butter.

4. Bake in the center of the oven until the tips of the fennel are golden and it is hot through, about 25 minutes. Remove from the oven and serve immediately.

Belgian Endive and Leek Gratin

Gratin d'Endives et Poireaux

❧ The French repertoire is replete with gratins, for the gratin is the mainstay of the French home cook. This one is unconventional, and surprisingly popular with children, given its ingredients. I say surprising—it's not surprising to me because I love everything in it, but it is surprising that children love this dish enough to gobble up the first serving and ask for seconds.

You can make this family-style as described here, or make individual portions—which immediately become elegant—by using small gratin dishes. Reduce the cooking time to about 20 minutes. While most gratins are served as a side dish to roasted meat or poultry, this gratin makes a substantial main dish, best followed by a large green salad.

Serve with a simple red Gaillac.

6 servings

4 fresh bay leaves from the *Laurus nobilis*, or dried imported bay leaves

2 pounds (1 kg) Belgian endive, trimmed

1½ pounds (750 g) leeks, trimmed, well rinsed, cut into ½-inch (1.3-cm) rounds

For the sauce

3 tablespoons (45 g) unsalted butter

¼ cup (35 g) unbleached all-purpose flour

2½ cups (625 ml) whole milk

½ cup (125 ml) heavy cream, preferably not ultra-pasteurized

4 ounces (120 g) Gruyère, grated

1. Bring a large pot of salted water to a boil over medium-high heat. Add the bay leaves, then add the whole endives and cook until they are tender through, 10 minutes. Transfer the endive to a strainer set in a bowl or in the sink and let them drain for 1½ hours.

2. Meanwhile, return the water to a boil and add the leeks. Boil just until they soften, about 4 minutes. Transfer the leeks to another strainer set in a bowl or in the sink and let drain for 1½ hours.

3. To make the sauce, melt the butter in a medium heavy-bottomed saucepan over medium heat. Whisk in the flour and cook until the mixture foams, for at least 2 minutes, to cook out the raw taste of the flour. Whisk in the milk and cream and cook, whisking until the mixture has thickened. Whisk in all but ½ cup of the grated cheese and the nutmeg, then stir in the ham. Adjust the seasoning, remove from the heat, and reserve.

4. Preheat the oven to 375°F (190°C).

Fine salt

Scant ¼ teaspoon freshly grated nutmeg

8 ounces (250 g) ham, trimmed of excess fat and cut into ¼-inch (0.6-cm) cubes

6 ounces (180 g) slab bacon, rind removed, cut into 1 × ¼ × ¼-inch (2.5 × 0.6 × 0.6-cm) strips

5. Cook the bacon in a heavy skillet over medium heat, stirring occasionally, until it is golden all over, about 5 minutes. Remove from the pan with a slotted spoon and drain on a plate covered with a paper towel.

6. Spread ¼ cup (60 ml) of the sauce over the bottom of a medium gratin dish or other baking dish. Add the endive and leeks, arranging them evenly in the dish, and interspersing them regularly. Sprinkle the bacon evenly over the vegetables. Pour the remaining sauce over the top of the vegetables, spreading it out evenly, and urging it down among them. Sprinkle the remaining ¼ cup cheese over the top of the gratin.

7. Bake in the center of the oven until the gratin is deep golden on top and bubbling, about 25 minutes. Remove from the heat and let cool for about 10 minutes before serving. (Alternatively, take it to the table immediately, but warn your guests that it is blistering hot.)

ASTUCES: The endives and leeks are blanched and then left to drain for what sounds like a very long time. This is vital to the quality of the dish, for if you don't drain the vegetables, they will add too much liquid to it and make it watery and unappetizing. ♣ A good, fresh Belgian endive doesn't require much trimming. Once it is harvested, cut from its root, the cut surface turns rusty brown. Cut a thin layer off the exposed surface layer. Aside from a good rinse, that should take care of it. If the endive has been damaged in transport, you may need to peel away some of the outer leaves.

Provençal Vegetable Gratin

Tian aux Artichauts et aux Épinards

❧ *Tian* is the Provençal name for a gratin. Unlike in northern France where cream is the natural moistening and flavor agent in a gratin, in Provence it is extra virgin olive oil. The choice of vegetables is regional too, and this particular combination is as Provençal as the lavender that blooms there in early summer.

This tian combines two of my favorite vegetables, artichokes and spinach, whose flavors and textures are magical together. I like to serve this as a side dish with Marinated Lamb Shoulder Grilled over the Coals (page 172) or other hearty meat or fish dish, or as a first course.

Try this with a Côtes du Rhône, such as a Sablet from Domaine des Gouberts.

6 servings

2¼ pounds (1 kg 125 g) spinach, stems trimmed and well rinsed

1 lemon, cut in half

12 small artichokes or 8 large ones, stems removed

2 teaspoons extra virgin olive oil

Fine sea salt and freshly ground black pepper

2 garlic cloves, green germ removed if necessary, minced

5 ounces (150 g) Gruyère, finely grated (to give 1¼ cups)

1. Place the spinach in a large nonstick skillet over medium heat and cook, stirring frequently, until it wilts and has given up a great deal of liquid but is still a lovely deep green, about 5 minutes. Transfer it to a colander set in a bowl or the sink and let it drain for at least 30 minutes; it should be neither wet nor dry, but pleasantly moist.

2. Fill a large bowl with water. Squeeze the lemon juice into the water, and add the squeezed halves. Remove the outer leaves from the artichokes, leaving the inner, golden leaves and hearts. Trim any green parts from the stems. If you have small artichokes, simply slice them lengthwise into thin (just less than ¼ inch; 0.6 cm) slices, and place them in the lemon water. If you are using large artichokes, working with one artichoke at a time, remove all of the leaves and the prickly choke, leaving just the bowl-shaped heart. Cut the heart into thin (just less than ¼ inch; 0.6 cm) slices and add the lemon water.

3. Preheat the oven to 375°F (190°C).

4. Brush a heavy, preferably earthenware, medium baking dish with the olive oil. Drain the artichokes and pat them dry. Line the bottom of the dish with an even layer of artichokes. Season lightly with salt and pepper. Add a layer of spinach, and sprinkle with half of the minced garlic. Season with salt and pepper and sprinkle with one-third of the grated cheese. Repeat, using up all the garlic on the second layer, and ending with spinach and cheese.

5. Place the gratin in the center of the oven and bake until the vegetables are tender through and the cheese on top has melted, about 55 minutes. Remove from the oven and serve immediately.

Red Peppers, Tomatoes, and Garlic in Pastry

Tourte de Frita

⚜ Given the opportunity, I could easily eat half of this tart all by myself. Buttery pastry encases a sweet, meaty sort of red pepper, tomato, and garlic marmalade in this French-Algerian dish. Isabelle Guillot, the daughter of a *Pied Noir*, a French-man born in Algeria and repatriated when France gave up its colonial hold in the 1960s, grew up eating her father's Algerian specialties. *Frita,* the one she makes most often, is the traditional name given to the red pepper and tomato filling, which, in Algeria, is served as a vegetable side dish, or a sort of "dip" for fresh bread. Is-abelle, whose very French idea it was to put the filling inside tender pastry, applies the name to the entire tart.

Though I like this as a side dish—try it alongside roasted lamb—I often serve it as a main course with a salad and call it dinner. Frita also makes a lovely first course, with each slice set on a plate and garnished with a small sprig of fresh sage or flat-leaf parsley.

6 servings

Pâte Briseé (page 256)

2 tablespoons extra virgin olive oil

2 pounds (1 kg) red bell peppers, cored, seeds and white pith removed, and cut into narrow strips

4 medium (about 1½ pounds; 700 g) ripe tomatoes, peeled, cored, and diced

2 garlic cloves, green germ removed if necessary, coarsely chopped

Fine sea salt

1. Divide the pastry in half. On a lightly floured sur-face, roll out one half to an 11-inch (27.5-cm) round. Fit it into a 9½-inch (24-cm) tart pan with a removable bot-tom, leaving the pastry hanging over the edges of the pan. Roll out the remaining pastry to a 9½-inch (24-cm) round. Refrigerate the tart pan and the round of pastry.

2. Place the olive oil in a large heavy-bottomed skillet over medium heat, add the pepper strips, tossing so they are coated with oil, and cook until the peppers are tender and the liquid they exude has almost all evapo-rated, 15 to 17 minutes.

3. Add the tomatoes and garlic to the pan, season lightly with salt, stir, and cook, partially covered, until the tomatoes have melted into the peppers and the peppers

are completely tender, about 50 minutes. Adjust the seasoning, remove from the heat, and let cool to room temperature.

4. Preheat the oven to 425°F (220°C).

5. Remove the prepared tart pan and the round of pastry from the refrigerator. Turn the pepper and tomato mixture into the tart shell, smoothing it into an even layer. Place the round of pastry atop the pepper and tomato mixture, and bring the edges of the bottom pastry over the edges of the top pastry. Gently press the edges together, then crimp them attractively. Poke several steam holes in the top of the pastry and place the tart on a baking sheet.

6. Bake the tart in the center of the oven until the pastry is golden and cooked through, 30 to 35 minutes. Remove the tart from the oven, remove the ring from the tart pan, and let the tart cool on a wire rack for at least 10 minutes.

7. Transfer the tart to a serving platter, and serve, warm or at room temperature.

Frosty Lentils
Lentilles au Givre

❧ The inspiration for this dish came from Pascal Barbot, chef of l'Astrance, a tiny restaurant in the 16th arrondissement of Paris. We were talking about favorite dishes we cook at home, and this was one of his. "I cook it for my staff," he said. "That's about the only home cooking I do!"

The lentils are cooked to a crisp tenderness with Asian spices and dressed with a nut oil. A celadon snow of pureed cucumbers and cornichons, which has been frozen in an ice cube tray, is quickly grated atop the warm lentils just before serving. Yes, you have to move to get it to the table before the tart ice melts into the lentils, but that is a small sacrifice for such a stunning dish.

10 servings

For the granité

½ cup cornichons, homemade (page 296) or store-bought, or baby dill pickles

One 1½ × 1½-inch (3.75 × 3.75-cm) piece cucumber, seeds removed and diced

For the lentils

1 pound (2 cups; 500 g) lentils, preferably lentils de Puy

3 coins unpeeled fresh ginger

3 small star anise

1 bouquet garni—parsley stems, fresh thyme sprig, bay leaf, leek greens, tied together

1 medium carrot, peeled and cut into 4 chunks

1 small onion, cut into quarters

1. To make the granité, place the cornichons and cucumber in a food processor and blend until the mixture is very finely chopped (it won't be a puree). Place the mixture into an ice cube tray—it will fill about 6 spaces—and freeze until solid, which will take several hours.

2. Place the lentils, ginger, star anise, bouquet garni, carrot, and onion in a large saucepan and cover with water by about 3 inches (7.5 cm). Bring to a boil over medium-high heat, reduce the heat so the water is simmering merrily, partially cover, and cook until the lentils are tender but still slightly crisp, about 35 minutes. The cooking time for lentils can vary enormously, depending on their freshness. Begin checking their texture after 20 minutes. Drain the lentils, reserving the cooking liquid. Remove and discard the carrots and onions.

3. While the lentils are cooking, prepare the shallots: Place the shallots and vinegar in a small heavy-bottomed saucepan over medium-high heat. When the vinegar begins to boil, reduce the heat to medium low,

For the shallots

2 shallots, sliced paper-thin

3 tablespoons sherry vinegar

For the vinaigrette

½ cup (5 g) flat-leaf parsley leaves

2 tablespoons sherry vinegar

Fine sea salt and freshly ground black pepper

6 tablespoons (90 ml) hazelnut oil or walnut oil

1 small young spring onion, preferably red, thinly sliced

so the vinegar is simmering, and cook, stirring occasionally, until the shallots are translucent and the vinegar has evaporated, about 7 minutes. Remove from the heat.

4. To make the dressing: Mince the parsley. In a large bowl, whisk together the vinegar, parsley, and salt and pepper to taste. Slowly add the oil, whisking constantly until the vinaigrette is emulsified and thickened. Whisk in the onion and shallots.

5. Fold the cooked lentils into the dressing until they are completely coated. Let stand at room temperature for at least 2 hours and up to 4 hours.

6. Just before serving, remove the pieces of ginger, all the star anise from the lentils, and the bouquet garni. Adjust the seasoning. If the lentils seem dry, stir in a bit of the lentil cooking liquid. Divide the lentils among ten plates, mounding them in the center. Using a fine-holed grater, grate an equal amount of the cornichon granité over each lentil salad so that it looks like a mound of green/white snow. Serve immediately.

ASTUCE: Properly cooked lentils are al dente, that is, cooked to a tender crispness rather than soft. The most flavorful lentils are the slate-gray *lentilles de Puy*, from the flinty soil of the Auvergne. Ordinary flat brown lentils don't work well for this dish.

Tomatoes Provençal

Tomates Provençales

❧ Whenever I visit the Côte d'Azur in southern France, this dish is served at every meal but breakfast. I never tire of it, though, because it is such a fleeting seasonal specialty. Make it in summer with local vine-ripened tomatoes that have the flavor of liquid sun.

Although these are typically served as an accompaniment to grilled meat or fish, I sometimes offer them as a first course, and I often make a double recipe so there are leftovers. I serve them at room temperature, either by themselves or on freshly toasted bread rubbed with garlic and drizzled with olive oil.

A lightly chilled rosé from the Lubéron is perfect here.

4 to 6 servings

2 generous pounds (1 kg) ripe tomatoes, cored

Fine sea salt and freshly ground black pepper

3 garlic cloves, green germ removed if necessary, minced

1 cup (10 g) loosely packed flat-leaf parsley leaves

½ cup (5 g) loosely packed fresh basil leaves

¼ cup (30 g) fresh bread crumbs

2 tablespoons extra virgin olive oil

1. Preheat the oven to 450°F (230°C).

2. Cut the tomatoes horizontally in half. Heat a large dry nonreactive skillet over medium-high heat. When it is hot, place the tomatoes in it, cut side down; the tomatoes will spit and sizzle, so be careful to avoid getting burned. Cook the tomatoes until they are golden at the edges and the juices in the pan are deep golden, about 5 minutes. Remove the pan from the heat, and let the tomatoes cool slightly in the pan.

3. Transfer the tomatoes to a 9½ × 6-inch (24 × 15-cm) baking dish, fitting them in a single layer—the tomatoes will be squeezed tight in the pan, and if you have any that are very small, you can layer these if necessary. Scrape any caramelized juices from the skillet into the tomatoes. Sprinkle the tomatoes evenly with salt and pepper to taste, and the garlic.

4. Mince the parsley and basil and sprinkle half the herbs over the tomatoes. In a small bowl, combine the remaining herbs with the bread crumbs, and sprinkle

these over the tomatoes. Drizzle the tomatoes with the olive oil.

5. Bake in the center of the oven until the tomatoes are sizzling and the bread crumbs are golden, about 40 minutes. Remove the tomatoes from the oven and let them sit for at least 10 minutes before serving, as they will be blistering hot. They can also be served at room temperature.

Braised Fennel
Fenouil Braisé

⚜ Here, fennel caramelizes to a glistening golden color on the outside, while tender and almost pureed inside, and all in a mere twenty minutes. Prepare this dish up to two hours before you plan to serve it, and then reheat. Try it as a side dish with the Marinated Lamb Shoulder Grilled over the Coals (page 172), or any other grilled or roasted meat or poultry.

6 servings

3 pounds (1.5 kg) fennel bulbs, trimmed

2 tablespoons (30 g) unsalted butter

2 tablespoons cooking oil, such as grapeseed, or extra virgin olive oil

¼ to ⅓ cup (60 to 75 ml) mineral or filtered water

Fine sea salt and freshly ground pepper

1. Cut large fennel bulbs into sixths, small bulbs into quarters.

2. Melt the butter with oil in a large heavy-bottomed skillet over medium-high heat. Add the fennel and stir until all the pieces are coated with the oil, then stir and turn the fennel until golden on all sides, about 5 minutes.

3. Add the water to the pan, and season the fennel lightly with salt and pepper. Reduce the heat to medium, cover, and cook, stirring and turning the fennel occasionally, until it is completely tender and a gorgeous golden color, about 20 to 25 minutes. Remove from the heat. If you are not going to serve the fennel immediately, keep it off the heat, partially covered, so it stays warm but doesn't continue to cook and soften; just before serving, reheat it gently over low heat. Correct the seasoning and serve.

ASTUCE: Fennel is at its best from early fall through late spring. When you buy it, be sure it is firm and very crisp, that its outer layer isn't brown or wrinkled, and that the fluffy green fronds are still attached. If there are slight bruises on the exterior but the bulb is otherwise in perfect condition, you can simply peel or trim away the brown areas. If you get fennel bulbs with an outer layer that is slightly dried out, they are just this side of perfectly fresh; the interior should still be firm and good. Trim the root ends and pull off the entire outer layer, which is fibrous and tough.

Aromatic Quinoa

Quinoa Aromatique

❖ Quinoa is an ancient grain that sustained the Incas and other ancient South American peoples. Noted for its high protein content, nutty flavor, and crisp, slightly crunchy texture, it is chic and exotic in France, and often served in high-profile restaurants.

I include quinoa in my repertoire because I love its flavor and texture, which is so subtle yet hearty that it defies description. It makes a tasty, nutritious alternative to rice, too. I love to fold herbs and flavored oils into it, but don't stop there, as quinoa is eminently versatile.

6 servings

1 cup (6.5 ounces; 190 g) quinoa

2 cups (500 ml) spring water

1 bay leaf from the *Laurus nobilis*, or dried imported bay leaf

¼ cup fresh tarragon, sweet cicely, fresh thyme, and fennel fronds

¼ teaspoon fleur de sel, or to taste

2 teaspoons pine nut oil

Sprigs fresh tarragon as garnish

ASTUCE: Quinoa holds together very well and I often mold it before serving. My favorite is to mold it in heart-shaped cheese molds—yes, it's a little corny!—for the heart shape on a plate always brings a smile. If you don't have pine nut oil, use your favorite nut oil here.

1. Rinse the quinoa under cold running water until the water runs clear. Place the quinoa in a medium-sized pan and add the water and the bay leaf. Cover, bring the water to a boil over medium-high heat, reduce the heat so the water is simmering merrily, and cook until the quinoa is tender, about 12 minutes. Remove the quinoa from the heat and let it sit, covered, to "plump" and absorb any remaining water, for at least 10 minutes and up to 40 minutes.

2. Just before serving, mince the herbs and fold them, with the salt, into the quinoa. Drizzle 1 teaspoon of the pine nut oil over the quinoa and toss it, using two forks, or fold it lightly using a rubber spatula, until it is thoroughly combined with the quinoa. Adjust the seasoning, but do not add too much pine nut oil as it can be overpowering.

3. To serve, fill a ½ cup (125 ml) mold (such as a ramekin), gently but firmly with quinoa, then turn it out with a small rap onto a very warm dinner plate. Alternatively, simply serve it by the spoonful. Drizzle each serving with a bit of pine nut oil, garnish with the fresh herbs, if desired, and serve.

BREADS AND PASTRIES

Pains et Pâtisseries

Crêpes . . . sprinkled with sugar and eaten
hot, they form an exquisite dish. They have
a golden hue and are tempting to eat. Thin
and transparent like muslin, their edges are
trimmed to resemble fine lace. They are so
light that after a good dinner, a man from
Agen is still willing to sample three or four
dozen of them! Crêpes form an integral
part of every family celebration. Served
with white wine, they take pride of place
on all joyful occasions.

Le Temps,
Anatole France (1844–1924)

Light Whole Wheat and Flaxseed Bread

Pain Demi-Complet aux Graines de Lin

❧ **No longer is the baguette the queen of the French boulangerie. Now there are oceans of "specialty breads," any number of them made with dark flours and combinations of seeds. While good, they lack the density I prefer, so I often make my own. I serve a variety of breads with a cheese course, and this is one of my frequent choices.**

One 2-pound (1-kg) loaf

3 cups (750 ml) lukewarm water

1 teaspoon active dry yeast

4 to 6 cups (540 to 870 g) whole wheat pastry flour

1 scant tablespoon fine sea salt

2 tablespoons flaxseed, coarsely ground

1 tablespoon whole flaxseed

1. Place the water in a large bowl or the bowl of an electric mixer fitted with a paddle attachment. Add the yeast and stir, then add 1 cup (135 g) of the flour and stir. Wait until bubbles or foam drift to the surface, which will take about 5 minutes.

2. Add the salt and ground and whole flaxseeds and stir to blend, then add as much flour as you need to make a soft dough. Mix or knead the dough until it is elastic and no longer sticks to your hand or to the paddle attachment, 5 to 8 minutes in a mixer, 10 to 12 minutes by hand.

3. Sprinkle the dough with flour, cover with a damp towel, and let it sit in a warm spot (68° to 70°F; 20° to 22°C) until it doubles in bulk and develops a lovely yeasty aroma, about 2 hours.

4. Punch down the dough and shape it into a round. Transfer it to a heavily floured pan and let it sit, lightly covered with a very slightly damp towel, until it rises by one-third, for 45 minutes to 1 hour.

5. Preheat the oven to 425°F (220°C).

6. Slash the bread several times on top with a sharp knife or razor blade, or snip it with scissors. Bake in the bottom third of the oven until it is golden and sounds hollow when tapped on the bottom, about 40 minutes. Remove from the oven and turn out onto a wire cooling rack to cool to room temperature before slicing.

ASTUCES: When making bread, never add the salt to the water with the yeast, because salt retards yeast action. First dilute the yeast in the water and add some of the flour to get the yeast activated—bubbles or little patches of foam will rise to the surface to let you know it is alive and kicking. Once you are assured, add the salt, stir well to dissolve it, then continue adding flour until you get the texture you are looking for. ❧ How do you determine the correct texture? You want the dough stickier than you might think you do. A hard, dense dough will give a very dry loaf, whereas a slightly softer dough will give a lighter, moist loaf. Ambient humidity will make a difference in how much flour you will use. If the atmosphere is humid, you will need more flour than if it is dry. As with any bread dough, add the flour 1 cup (140 g) at a time so you don't add more than the liquid can absorb. When making bread in an electric mixer don't use the dough hook, which is inefficient, but the paddle attachment. ❧ You can find whole wheat pastry flour at markets or co-ops specializing in organic ingredients.

A SEED FIT FOR A KING

Legend has it that Charlemagne, often referred to by historians as the greatest of medieval kings, was one of the first to champion the use of flaxseed, to the point where he mandated his subjects eat it to enhance their health. He would certainly be happy in France today, where flaxseed is kneaded into breads in nearly every bakery in the country.

Adding 2 to 3 tablespoons flaxseed to dough gives the bread an earthy, toasty flavor. Once I discovered its considerable nutritional attributes—flax contains fiber, phytonutrients, omega-3 fatty acids, and many vitamins and minerals—I started using it more often, grinding the seeds to make the nutrients more available. Now I add both whole and ground flaxseed to many of the breads I bake.

I prefer to grind my own whole flaxseed in a coffee grinder reserved for seeds and grains, for once it is ground, its potency quickly diminishes. Keep whole flaxseed in an airtight container in the refrigerator to maintain its freshness. Use it and you, too, may become strong of body and courageous of spirit, like King Charlemagne.

Savory Lemon and Rosemary Bread
Pain au Citron et au Romarin

⚜ The French call this a *pain fantaisie,* or a fantasy bread, delicious to serve along with a meal, with the cheese course, or with an apéritif with a bit of olive oil drizzled on it.

  I bake this as called for in the recipe, but the dough can also be shaped into two round loaves.

Two 8 × 12-inch (20 × 30-cm) loaves

1 teaspoon active dry yeast

3 cups (750 ml) warm water

5 cups (875 g) semolina flour

2 cups (280 g) unbleached all-purpose flour

1 heaping tablespoon coarse sea salt

¼ cup Lemon Oil (page 272)

Minced zest of 2 lemons

3 tablespoons fresh rosemary leaves

1. Place the yeast and water in a large bowl or the bowl of an electric mixer and stir. Add 1 cup (160 g) of the semolina flour, stir well, and let stir until little patches of bubbles rise to the surface of the water, about 5 minutes.

2. Add the salt and stir, then add the remaining 4 cups (700) of the semolina flour 1 cup (175 g) at a time. Add 3 tablespoons of the oil and stir until well mixed, then add 1 cup (140 g) of the all-purpose flour. Turn the dough out onto a well-floured work surface.

3. Mince the lemon zest and rosemary together, then gradually knead them into the dough. Continue kneading the dough, adding enough of the remaining 1 cup (140 g) all-purpose flour as necessary, until the dough no longer readily sticks to your fingers or the work surface and is smooth and satiny, about 10 minutes. The dough may feel sticky if you pinch it hard, but if you handle it gently, it shouldn't stick to your hands. Return the dough to the bowl, cover with a towel, and let it rise until it is doubled in bulk, about 2 hours.

4. Sprinkle two baking sheets with an even layer of semolina flour. Turn the dough out onto a lightly floured work surface and remove the air from it by kneading it for about 5 minutes. Divide the dough in half. Roll out

each piece into a rectangle that measures 8 × 12 inches (20 × 30 cm). To transfer each dough rectangle to a baking sheet, set the rolling pin across the dough about 2 inches (5 cm) from one short end, bring the end of the dough loosely up around the rolling pin, and then quickly roll the pin down the length of the dough so that all the dough is around the rolling pin. Quickly unroll the dough onto the baking sheet, pulling and patting the dough back into an even shape if necessary. Make several 3-inch (7.5-cm)-long slits in each piece of dough in an attractive pattern such as parallel rows of diagonal slashes, cutting right down to the baking sheet. Gently pull apart the slits in the dough so they are obvious — they will help the dough rise and will remain as the dough bakes, allowing it to bake evenly. Lay a dry towel over the dough and let it rise until it is doubled in bulk, about 30 minutes.

5. Preheat the oven to 425°F (220°C).

6. Bake the breads in the center of the oven until they are golden brown and puffed, 25 to 30 minutes. Remove from the oven and transfer them to wire cooling racks. Brush the breads all over with the remaining 1 tablespoon lemon oil. Let the loaves cool for at least 10 minutes, then either present them whole, or cut them into thick strips.

Flat Semolina Bread for Couscous

Galette de Pain Plat Pour Couscous

❦ A traditional couscous meal wouldn't be complete without flat semolina bread, which is served warm before and during the meal. Before the meal, the bread is dipped in olive oil or eaten as is; during the meal it is used for sopping up juices. It may seem like overkill to serve bread with couscous, but this bread is so tender and delicate that you'll find it enhances the couscous experience. You can make this at other times, too, for it is truly delicious, and quick and simple to assemble and cook.

Traditionally the bread is cooked on the floor of a wood-fired oven. In a contemporary household, it is cooked atop the stove in an ungreased cast-iron skillet. The dough is patted out to a flat round, the pan is heated until blistering hot, and then the dough goes into the pan; the cook courageously spins it around, pokes it with a knife or a matchstick to let air escape, turns it, and generally keeps it moving for the approximately ten minutes it takes for it to cook through. It emerges very dark and smoky tasting, absolutely delicious.

The bread can also be baked in the oven, which I prefer because it is equally delicious and there are no burned fingers!

10 small flat loaves

3 cups (750 ml) very warm water

2 teaspoons active dry yeast

5 to 6 cups (875 g to 1 kg 50 g) semolina flour, or as needed

2 teaspoons coarse sea salt

1. Place the water in a large bowl or the bowl of an electric mixer and stir in the yeast. Add 1 cup (175 g) of the semolina, stir well, and let the mixture stand until it bubbles, 10 to 15 minutes. Add the salt, then continue adding some or all of the remaining semolina until you have a soft, but not sticky, dough.

2. Turn the dough out onto a heavily floured surface and knead it for about 10 minutes. Alternatively, let the machine do the kneading. The dough should be quite soft but no longer sticky. Cover with a towel and let it rise until it is doubled in bulk, about 30 minutes.

3. Strew two heavy baking sheets thickly with semolina.

4. To form the breads, turn the dough out onto a lightly floured surface. Divide the dough into 10 equal pieces.

Roll each piece into a ball, then flatten it so that it is ¼-inch (0.6-cm) thick. Transfer the pieces of dough to the prepared baking sheets and let rise for about 30 minutes, preferably on top of the stove, so they are quite warm.

5. Preheat the oven to 450°F (230°C).

6. To bake, place the baking sheets in the bottom third of the oven or right on the oven floor, and bake until they are gold and the semolina on the baking sheet is a very deep brown, about 20 minutes. Flip the breads and continue baking until they are a pale golden on the other side and sound hollow when you tap them, about 10 more minutes. You may need to bake the bread in batches.

7. Remove the breads from the oven and transfer them to an unlined basket to prevent them from steaming. Serve immediately.

Crêpes for "La Chandeleur" and Fat Tuesday
Crêpes pour la Chandeleur et le Mardi Gras

⚜ One day there was a knock on our front door and we opened it to find Miche, a neighbor who stops by regularly, bearing a willow basket. When she removed the lace towel that covered it, a yeasty aroma emerged from a plate inside that was stacked with still-warm crêpes.

Miche didn't stay. "You enjoy these, we'll talk later," she said as she hurried away.

It was La Chandeleur, the festival of light celebrated in February. The name refers to the large candles that were carried in processions to honor, among other things, the presentation of Jesus at the temple and the purification of the Virgin Mary. While processions still take place in many French churches, most religious significance has been removed from La Chandeleur. Crêpes are also a tradition on Mardi Gras, or Fat Tuesday.

Traditionally when white flour crêpes are served as the main course, usually at dinner, they have sweet fillings—jam, sugar and lemon juice, Nutella, honey. I often fill them with cheese, eggs, ham, mushrooms, or shallots sautéed in butter as a main course, then revert to sweet fillings for dessert.

About 12 crêpes

3 large eggs

1 to 1½ cups (250 to 375 ml) whole milk

1 cup (250 ml) golden beer, such as Amstel

1¾ cups (245 g) all-purpose flour

Pinch of fine sea salt

2 tablespoons (30 g) unsalted butter, melted

2 tablespoons (30 ml) clarified butter (see below)

1. In a large bowl, whisk the eggs until they are combined, then whisk in 1 cup (250 ml) of the milk and the beer. Shower the flour over the mixture, whisking as you do so to prevent lumps. Whisk in the salt and melted butter, then whisk the batter vigorously for 3 to 5 minutes. Let the batter sit for 1 hour at room temperature. The batter will thicken slightly as it sits.

2. Just before you begin to make the crêpes, whisk the batter quickly—it should be like thin pancake batter. If it has thickened appreciably, gently whisk in all of the additional milk.

3. Heat a 10-inch (25-cm) skillet, preferably nonstick, over medium heat. Gently stir the batter once or twice in case it has separated. Brush the skillet with clarified butter and when it is hot but not smoking, pour a scant

ASTUCE: The resting
time for the crêpe batter is
essential, as it allows the
gluten in the flour to relax
and the flour and liquids to
combine thoroughly and
thicken. The first crêpe or
two are throwaways—it
takes time for the pan to
reach the optimum heat
and for the cook to get the
right heat/oil balance to
keep them from sticking!

⅓ cup (85 ml) of batter into the center of the skillet. Rotate the skillet so the batter covers the bottom of the pan in a thin layer, and pour any excess batter back into the bowl. Cook the crêpe just until it is golden on the first side, 1 to 2 minutes, then turn and cook it until it is golden on the other side, about 30 seconds. (If you want to flip the crêpe, jerk back firmly on the pan to loosen the crêpe, then flip the crêpe up into the air and catch it in the pan.)

4. Serve the crêpe immediately or transfer it to a warmed plate and cover with foil to keep warm. Continue until all of the batter is used.

CLARIFIED BUTTER

Clarified butter means that the fatty part of butter has separated from its milk proteins. The advantages of cooking with clarified butter are its purity of flavor and the fact that it can be heated to a much higher temperature than unclarified butter because there are no milk solids to burn.

To clarify butter, place it in a heavy pan over low heat to melt. When it is melted, let it cool, then refrigerate until it is solid. Scrape away the pale yellow froth on top; this is caseine, which has much butter flavor. Toss it with cooked grains or vegetables, or use it in an omelet. The thick yellow layer under the caseine is the clarified butter. You can easily remove it from the white milk proteins under it; discard the milk proteins.

Belgian Waffles

Gaufres

❦ I have a good repertoire of recipes up my sleeve for *le goûter*, afternoon snack, because my children come home from school hungry enough to eat the house. I like them to eat something nutritious, and quickly made *gaufres* are one of their favorites; they're nourishing, too, giving them the energy to get through their homework.

When making *gaufres*, we often all join in, slathering the hot waffles with salted butter and strawberry jam or red currant jelly. Sometimes I make them savory by adding grated Parmigiano-Reggiano to the batter instead of the sugar, which makes them extra-crisp and toasty. Then we eat them as an early dinner, with a green salad alongside.

About ten 4 × 4-inch (10 × 10-cm) waffles

5 large eggs, separated

¼ cup (50 g) vanilla or regular sugar

1 cup (250 ml) whole milk

Fine sea salt

2 cups (280 g) cake flour

4 tablespoons (60 g) unsalted butter, melted and cooled

¾ cup (70 g) finely grated Parmigiano-Reggiano, optional

1. In a large bowl, whisk together the egg yolks, and sugar if using, just until they are combined, then whisk in the milk and ½ teaspoon salt. Shower the flour over the batter, whisking it in quickly, to make a smooth batter, then quickly whisk in the melted butter. If using grated cheese, fold it in at this point.

2. In a separate large bowl or the bowl of an electric mixer, whisk the egg whites with a pinch of salt until they form soft peaks, and fold them into the batter. Let the batter sit for 1 hour before making the waffles as directed by the maker of your waffle iron.

ASTUCES: The batter rests for an hour so the gluten in the flour can relax and the flour can absorb the milk, making the batter smooth. ❦ Adding a pinch of salt to the egg whites helps break down the albumin so the whites whip up easily and uniformly. Whisk the egg whites just to the soft peak stage; any stiffer, and the *gaufres* will be dry.

Alsatian Butter Cookies
Butterbredel

❧ **Alsace is France's sparkling, cinnamon-scented, beribboned heart, and these tender, buttery cookies are its perfect symbol. Unlike in other French regions, homemade Christmas cookies are a tradition there, and each baker has a huge variety in his or her repertoire. They are varied, handed down through generations in each family so that no two are alike. Every visit with friends and acquaintances in Alsace around Christmas includes a cup of coffee and a plate heaped with cookies.**

Butterbredel **is the most common cut-out cookie in Alsace. This recipe is the best I've ever used, for it is simple and basic, but makes a dough that is a joy to work with, and cookies that melt in your mouth.**

About 90 small (1½-inch; 3.75-cm) cookies

3¾ cups (525 g) all-purpose flour

Pinch fine sea salt

½ pound (2 sticks; 250 g) unsalted butter, softened

1¼ cups (250 g) vanilla sugar

4 large egg yolks

1 large egg

For the glaze

1 large egg yolk

1 teaspoon water

6 tablespoons (75 g) vanilla sugar

½ teaspoon ground cinnamon

1. Sift together the flour and salt onto a piece of parchment paper.

2. In a large bowl or the bowl of an electric mixer, beat the butter and sugar until pale yellow and smooth. Add the egg yolks one at a time, mixing until thoroughly combined, then add the whole egg and mix until thoroughly combined. Mix in the flour and the salt until the dough is smooth. Divide the dough into quarters, form each one into a disk, and wrap them in parchment, then in aluminum foil. Refrigerate for at least 8 hours, or overnight. (The dough can be refrigerated for up to several days.)

3. To make the glaze, whisk together the egg yolk and water in a small bowl. In another small bowl, mix the sugar and cinnamon.

4. Preheat the oven to 350°F (180°C). Remove the dough from the refrigerator. Prepare baking sheets by lining them with parchment paper.

5. Roll out one-quarter of the dough on a lightly floured surface until it is about ⅛ inch (0.3 cm) thick and cut into shapes with cookie cutters. Paint the cookies with the glaze and sprinkle with the cinnamon sugar. Bake until the cookies are pale gold, about 15 minutes. Repeat with the remaining dough, glaze, and cinnamon sugar. Transfer the cookies to cooling racks and let cool to room temperature before serving.

ASTUCE: The dough is chilled so it is easier to work with, and to relax the gluten so the cookies are tender and melting. Remove the dough from the refrigerator at least one hour before rolling it out for easy handling.

Spice Cookies

Gâteaux aux Épices

❧ **Alsace is the only region in France where cookies are made both in pastry shops and in homes, and they are served after nearly every meal throughout the month of December.**

About 34 cookies

¾ cup (150 g) sugar

A knife point of ground cloves

½ teaspoon ground cinnamon

10 tablespoons (1¼ sticks; 150 g) unsalted butter, softened

Minced zest of 1 lemon

1 large egg separated

1 large egg yolk

1¾ cups cake flour or all-purpose flour (245 g)

½ cup (70 g) unblanched whole almonds, cut lengthwise in half

1. Preheat the oven to 350°F (180°C). Line two baking sheets with parchment paper.

2. In a small bowl, mix together the sugar and spices. In a large bowl or the bowl of an electric mixer, beat the butter until it is pale yellow and very soft. Beat in the sugar and spices and the lemon zest until combined, then beat in the egg yolks one at a time, until thoroughly combined.

3. Using a wooden spoon or the paddle attachment of the mixer, mix in the flour; the dough will be firm but sticky.

4. In a small bowl, whisk the egg white just until it is foamy. Reserve.

5. On a lightly floured surface, roll out the dough until it is about ⅜ inch (0.9 cm) thick, working lightly and quickly so the dough doesn't stick to the surface. Cut the dough into strips that measure about 2¾ × 1¼ inches (7 × 3 cm). Brush them with the egg white, and place a half almond in each corner of each strip, pointing toward the center of the cookies. Bake until the cookies are pale golden, about 17 minutes. Transfer them to a wire rack to cool.

ASTUCES: These cookies are most tender and light when made with cake flour. The dough is very soft, though, and a bit difficult to manage because it can be quite sticky and requires frequent flouring. Strew a fine, even layer of flour over the work surface and the dough. ❧ A "knife point" is a very specific measurement in France. Stick the point of a sharp knife into the ingredient—here, ground cloves—and what the knife comes out with on the tip of the blade is the correct measurement.

Normandy Sand Cookies
Sablés de Normandie

⚜ Though native to Normandy, *sablés* are found in pastry shops throughout France. They are usually the size of a large coffee can lid, striated with the tines of a fork, and glazed with egg so they bake up golden, shiny, and tempting. Sweet and crisp, they make a satisfying afternoon snack, particularly when dipped into a cup of coffee.

These cookies are atypical; vanilla and chocolate doughs are rolled together to create a spiral design. I roll the dough into logs, chill the logs, and then cut them into rounds, resulting in a light and crumbly cookie.

This recipe was inspired by Nicholas Gosselin, whose pastry shop on the rue du Quai in Louviers supplied us with many a *sablé*—and baguettes, quiches, and sandwiches—while we worked to make our house habitable. I have lovely memories of sitting upstairs in our freezing house when it was still in ruins, sipping coffee and nibbling on these delicate, buttery cookies.

About 84 cookies

For the vanilla dough

1¾ cups (245 g) cake flour

¼ teaspoon fine sea salt

14 tablespoons (1¾ sticks; 210 g) unsalted butter, softened

¾ cup (90 g) vanilla confectioners' sugar

1 large egg yolk

¼ teaspoon vanilla extract

For the chocolate dough

1½ cups (210 g) cake flour

⅓ cup (30 g) unsweetened cocoa powder

¼ teaspoon fine sea salt

1. To make the vanilla dough, sift the flour and salt onto a piece of parchment paper.

2. In a large bowl or the bowl of an electric mixer, beat the butter until it is pale yellow and soft. Add the confectioners' sugar and mix well. Add the egg yolk and mix until it is blended, then mix in the vanilla extract.

3. Add the flour and mix well. Turn the dough out onto a lightly floured surface and pat it into a rectangle that is about 1 inch (2.5 cm) thick. Wrap well and refrigerate for at least 2 hours, and up to 24 hours.

4. To make the chocolate dough, sift together the flour, cocoa, and salt onto a piece of parchment paper.

5. In a large bowl or the bowl of an electric mixer, beat the butter until it is pale yellow and soft. Add the confectioners' sugar and mix well. Add the egg yolk and mix until it is blended, then mix in the vanilla extract.

14 tablespoons (1¾ sticks; 210 g) unsalted butter, softened

¾ cup (90 g) confectioners' sugar

1 large egg yolk

¼ teaspoon vanilla extract

For coating the dough

½ cup (100 g) vanilla sugar

6. Add the flour and cocoa mixture and mix well. Turn the dough out onto a lightly floured surface and pat it into a rectangle that is about 1 inch (2.5 cm) thick. Refrigerate the chocolate dough for at least 2 hours, and up to 24 hours.

7. About 20 minutes before you plan to roll them out, remove the doughs from the refrigerator so they aren't too stiff to work with.

8. To roll out the cookies, place two 12 × 17-inch (30 × 42.5-cm) pieces of parchment paper on a work surface and lightly flour them. Place the vanilla dough on one piece of the parchment, lightly flour it, and roll it out to a 10 × 15-inch (25 × 37.5-cm) rectangle. Repeat with the chocolate dough. Brush any excess flour from the doughs with a pastry brush, then gently flip the chocolate dough atop the vanilla dough, leaving the parchment paper on the chocolate dough. Gently but firmly press the doughs together by rolling over them with the rolling pin until they adhere to each other. Remove the top piece of parchment paper and trim the edges of the doughs to make an even rectangle. Reserve the scraps of dough.

9. Turn a long edge of the dough towards you. Gently pinch together the two doughs and roll them into a long tight roll, using the parchment paper to help you by pulling on the edge of it to encourage the dough to roll, then pulling down on it to encourage the dough to roll tightly. This will take a bit of care and time, but persist. Sprinkle the sugar on the work surface and roll the log in the sugar to coat it evenly. Refrigerate for at least 2 hours, and up to 24 hours. Gently press the scraps together and roll them into a tight roll. Roll it in the sugar, wrap in parchment paper, and refrigerate for at least 1 hour.

10. Preheat the oven to 400°F (200°C). Line two baking sheets with parchment paper.

11. Cut the dough into ¼-inch (0.6-cm)-thick rounds and place them about ½ inch (1.3 cm) apart on the prepared baking sheets. Bake in the center of the oven until the *sablés* are golden on the edges and slightly puffed, about 12 minutes. Transfer to a cooling rack to cool. (The *sablés* will keep for about 3 days in an airtight container.)

ASTUCE: This recipe makes a large quantity of dough, which freezes well. Bake what you need and freeze the logs, so you'll have *sablés* at a moment's notice. ❦ To make vanilla confectioners' sugar, simply grind vanilla sugar to a fine powder.

Lemon Verbena Madeleines
Madeleines à la Verveine

❧ **What would the French be without these wonderful little cakes? Madeleines can be found at every pâtisserie and most boulangeries throughout the country, but the truth is they are always best when freshly made at home. This recipe, which has been lovingly tested over a period of at least twenty years, makes madeleines that are tender and buttery, as close to perfect as madeleines can be!**

Here I've flavored them with lemon verbena. You may substitute lemon zest — a traditional flavoring — vanilla, diced candied ginger, allspice, or a tablespoon or two of very finely ground nuts.

A perfect madeleine has a bulb that forms on top, and a tenderness so seductive you'll have a hard time not eating every single one.

About 36 madeleines

1¾ cups (245 g) all-purpose flour

Pinch of fine sea salt

4 large eggs

1 cup (200 g) vanilla sugar

12 tablespoons (1½ sticks; 180 g) unsalted butter, melted and cooled

¼ cup (10 g) firmly packed, dried lemon verbena (or 1 tablespoon diced candied ginger, ½ teaspoon ground allspice, minced zest of 1 lemon, or 2 tablespoons finely ground nuts)

1. Butter and flour two madeleine tins. Refrigerate them.

2. Sift together the flour and salt.

3. Place the eggs and sugar in a large bowl or the bowl of an electric mixer and whisk or beat until very thick and pale yellow. Fold in the flour, then the melted butter. Crumble the lemon verbena leaves over the batter so they are in small pieces (not powdered), then fold them in, or add any other flavoring of your choice.

4. Spoon a generous tablespoon of batter into each mold, so it is filled about three-quarters full. Refrigerate the filled madeleine pans (and the remaining batter) for at least 1 hour.

5. Preheat the oven to 425°F (220°C).

6. Bake the madeleines in the center of the oven just until they are firm and puffed, about 8 minutes. Immediately turn them out unto a rack. Wipe out one of the tins and let cool, then brush with butter and fill it with the remaining batter. It isn't necessary to refrigerate the batter in the pans at this point, as it is already chilled. Bake as directed. The madeleines are best slightly warm or at room temperature the same day they are made.

ASTUCES: Here is a tip for buttering the madeleine tins: When I am going to butter the madeleine tins I gingerly stick a pastry brush into the butter I've melted for the madeleines and use that tiny amount to butter them. It uses about 1 teaspoon of the butter, which makes no difference to the quality of the finished cakes. ✣ Use dried lemon verbena rather than fresh because it crumbles and permeates the batter better. ✣ To get the signature bulb on top of the madeleines, don't do what most pastry shops do and add baking powder, which can leave an unpleasant burning sensation on your tongue. Instead, make sure the batter and the pans are very cold and the oven is very hot. I butter and flour the pans and fill them with batter, then refrigerate them for at least 1 hour before baking. Refrigerate the remaining batter as well, which keeps well in an airtight container for at least 3 days.

Tile Cookies
Tuiles

❧ Tuiles are cookies that resemble the curved roof tiles found throughout France. The still-hot-from-the-oven cookie is placed over a curved object to get its shape. Crisp and lacy, buttery and sweet, they are irresistible.

No tuile I've ever had is better than one of these, for they are crisp, not too sweet, and rich with almonds. I owe the recipe to Odile Engel, chef and owner of Le Beffroy, a restaurant in the heart of Rouen, who bakes fresh batches to serve to satisfied diners at the end of lunch and dinner service.

About 24 tuiles

6 large egg whites

Pinch fine sea salt

8 ounces (250 g) sliced almonds

½ cup plus 2 tablespoons (125 g) vanilla sugar

7 tablespoons (105 g) clarified butter (page 199)

ASTUCE: I use empty wine bottles with their labels removed to form the tuiles; the glass surface is perfect. These cookies have a very short shelf life, particularly in humid climates, because they quickly turn limp. If you have leftovers and they are soft, put them in a 350°F (180°C) oven for 5 minutes and they will crisp right up. That said, these really are best the day they are made. The batter will keep for 3 to 4 days in an airtight container in the refrigerator.

1. In a small bowl, stir the egg whites with the pinch of salt just to break them up. In a medium bowl, mix together the almonds and sugar, then stir in the egg whites. Stir in the clarified butter and mix until the batter is homogeneous. Refrigerate, covered, for 1 hour.

2. Preheat the oven to 350°F (180°C). Oil a baking sheet; if you use a nonstick baking sheet, you still need to lightly oil it. Set out a clean broomstick, several wine bottles, or one or more rolling pins for shaping the tuiles.

3. Place about 1 tablespoon of batter on the baking sheet and spread it into a 4-inch (10-cm) round. Repeat with the remaining batter, leaving ½ inch (1.3 cm) between each round. Bake in the center of the oven until the tuiles are deep golden on the edges and pale gold in the center, about 12 minutes.

4. Remove the tuiles from the oven. Working quickly, remove them from the baking sheet and lay them over the broomstick, wine bottles, or rolling pins, pressing them very gently to give them a rounded shape. Let the tuiles cool, then arrange them on a serving plate. (The tuiles stay fresh and crisp for about 4 hours.)

THE CHEESE COURSE

As my husband, Michael, says, "Just when you can't eat another bite, it's time for cheese." Which is actually the point of cheese in a meal, for aside from it being a delight on the palate, cheese acts as a *digéstif*, making room for what follows.

In a French meal, cheese comes after the main course. During a casual meal, it is served with the green salad; for a more formal occasion cheese is served afterwards. A well-balanced cheese tray features a selection of different flavors and textures, from creamy and soft, to buttery and firm, to sharp. A classic tray includes cheeses made from cow's, goat's or sheep's milk, a double or triple cream cheese, such as a Gratte-Paille from Normandy or Grand Vatel from Burgundy; a soft cheese like Camembert, Livarot, or Brie; a mountain cheese like Comté, Beaufort, or Ardi Gasna (Ossau Iraty) from the Pyrenées; and a blue, such as Roquefort or Bleu d'Auvergne.

I sometimes depart from the traditional presentation by offering a trio of Roqueforts from different producers, or a selection of mountain cheeses from the Alps (Beaufort, Comté, Gruyère) or from the Auvergne (St. Nectaire, Cantal, Salers). Sometimes I serve goat cheeses ranging from three days to six months in age, or exclusively Norman cheeses (Neufchâtel, Camembert, Livarot, Pont l'Evêque). When I find an absolutely perfect cheese, like a Vacherin Mont d'Or, which is so creamy when ripe that it requires a spoon, I serve it by itself.

Advise your guests to begin with the youngest cheeses and move on to those that are more aged, always saving blue cheeses for last.

In France, there is rarely anything else on the cheese tray but cheese. Occasionally a pat of unsalted butter might be slipped onto a tray, intended for the blue cheeses, to soften their saltiness. This is a country habit, though, and true blue lovers would never do this. Although grapes, nuts, dried fruits, and other garnishes aren't usually found on a French cheese tray, I often add them as a counterpoint, more for aesthetic appeal than anything else. A bunch of grapes draped on the tray is gorgeous, as is a mound of dried apricots (nonsulphured), or a small dish of lightly toasted nuts. Don't crowd the tray, however, and if you've gone to the effort to obtain top-notch cheeses, the tray doesn't need any garnishes at all. Do, though, provide a separate knife to cut each cheese, so flavors don't blend.

A Well-Aged Cheese

The ideal way to get a well-aged cheese is to purchase it either directly from the producer or from a respected cheese *affineur,* or cheese ager. Of course, that isn't possible for many people, so here are some other tips.

No matter where you live, patronize a reputable cheese merchant who knows the cheeses he or she is selling. Buy locally made cheeses when you can, and raw-milk cheeses whenever possible, for they offer the most exciting flavors and textures.

Why raw-milk cheeses? Because pasteurization removes bacteria from milk, and it is bacteria that develops flavor in cheese. If you are a true French cheese enthusiast, don't bother with French pasteurized-milk cheeses because they are pale, ersatz versions of themselves. Instead, buy the aged cheeses that are available. Or, go to www.fromages.com, which offers a stunning array of perfectly aged, small-production raw-milk cheeses that will be shipped to your doorstep within three days of your order. How can this be? This website has a special dispensation from the FDA to sell raw-milk cheeses of any age because they are shipped directly to the consumer and are not for resale.

Hints for Serving Cheese

Most cheeses are best at room temperature, as long as the room isn't any warmer than 68°F (20°C). A cheese that is too warm won't impart the full delicacy of its flavor. That said, in France it is generally considered heretical to refrigerate cheese, particularly if you plan to serve it the day you buy it. Keep it in a cool place, then bring it to warm room temperature a couple of hours before serving.

What is a cool place? Well, keep it in the wine cellar if you have one (50° to 55°F; 10° to 12°C), although wine aficionados will shake their heads at this, as they, rightfully, fear the aroma of cheese will affect the wines—in truth, a day or two in the wine cellar won't have any adverse affect on the wine. If you don't have a wine cellar, identify the coolest place in your house outside your refrigerator and store your cheese there.

Wrap cheese in parchment or waxed paper and then loosely in aluminum foil to keep it, and serve it as soon as you can.

If you buy a quantity of cheese to eat over a period of time, it will have to be refrigerated. For cheeses other than goat and blue, you want to create a moist environment inside your refrigerator. Line a large plastic container with a damp—not wet—kitchen towel. Leave the cheese wrapped in the breathable paper from the cheese shop—not plastic wrap, which can transfer its flavor to cheese and seal it off from moisture—and place it in the container. Lay another damp towel over the cheese and top with a lid. Set the container in the warmest part of the refrigerator. Keep the towels moist, and use the cheese as quickly as you can. Be sure to remove the cheese from the refrigerator one to two hours before serving. For goat and blue cheeses, wrap in the breathable paper from the cheese shop and store in a separate box.

THE RIND

To eat or not to eat the rind of the cheese? It depends upon you and the rind. The most intense flavor of a cheese is in the rind, so if you love intensity, go for it. I usually eat the rind except in certain cases like Livarot, whose rind smells like a barnyard and interior tastes like heaven, because its rind is grainy and almost soapy, or St. Nectaire, that most ethereal of cheeses (made from the milk of the Salers cow, who will only release her milk if a calf begins to suckle), because of its toughness and earthy flavor. The rinds on mountain cheeses (the Cantal family excepted) that taste of spring and summer flowers in the pastures where the cows graze are generally too hard to eat.

HOW TO CUT CHEESE

When confronted with virgin cheeses on a tray, some people aren't sure about where to begin and tremble at the thought of erring with their first cut. For a wedge of cheese, the rule of thumb is to cut a piece of cheese in the direction in which it has already been cut.

For a whole round cheese like Camembert, cut it as you would a pie, in wedge-shaped pieces. Cut a square cheese along the length of one side. Cut a heart-shaped cheese (Neufchâtel) however you think it should be cut; there is no rule. It is considered bad form to cut off the tip of a wedge.

Spelt

When I mentioned how much I like spelt flour to a friend, he wrinkled his nose and called it hippie food. His reaction to spelt resembled my mother's reaction to a carob cake I once made while in college. Although my mother was right about the heavy and dull carob cake, a similar reaction to spelt is misplaced. Spelt, a red wheat, is sweet and fruity, and when ground into flour and combined with water and yeast, it reacts quickly, rises well, and emerges from the oven as a bread with a cake-like texture that makes it hard not to serve it as dessert.

My passion for spelt flour began several years ago, when I first used it to make a loaf of walnut bread. From the minute I began to knead the dough, which felt positively jumpy beneath my hands, I knew this flour was far from the usual white flour I used. When I washed the dough off my hands, it melted away instead of turning stringy and gluey the way regular flour does. When baked, the bread tasted purely and sweetly of wheat, and its crumb was tender.

This makes sense in considering the origin of spelt, which is thought to be the precursor of wheat. It is the result of a cross-pollination of two ancient grains, emmer (*Triticum dicoccoides*) and goat grass (*Aegilips sqarrosa*), and it hasn't been further hybridized. Spelt is loaded with protein and vitamin B and is highly water soluble, so the body can easily access its nutrients. Because the gluten in spelt is fragile, it is easier to digest than some other grains.

Spelt has a hard husk that doesn't separate from the kernel during harvest, which became the grain's downfall in the 1800s when mechanical harvesting and milling processes for softer hulled wheats were introduced. The only places spelt survived were in remote pockets of southeastern Europe and Iran, until it was "rediscovered" in the 1990s and returned to cultivation. While spelt hardly competes with contemporary wheat varieties, it is now a major cereal crop in areas of Germany and Switzerland, in the Haute Provence region of France, and in the American Midwest. Now its tough husk is an advantage, for it makes spelt insect-resistant and thus a perfect candidate for organic cultivation.

Spelt flour is a dream to bake with. When I use spelt by itself for making bread, I find that the dough requires less kneading than other flours, and it rises more quickly. If you're new to using spelt, start by substituting about 2 cups to any recipe that calls for other flours.

Walnut Bread

Pain aux Noix

❧ This simple dough makes a sweetly nutty bread that goes well with cheese. Use the dough as a base for adding mixed grains, other nuts, herbs, or spices. I call for spelt flour here because it is the naturally sweetest and nuttiest of all the wheat flours, and it makes a full, richly flavored loaf. Spelt's nutritional benefits are a bonus as far as I'm concerned; what appeals most to me is its sweet flavor that turns a loaf of bread into something close to cake. This loaf is delicious fresh, and even better when toasted, with the thinnest sheen of butter and a sprinkling of fleur de sel.

2 medium loaves

1 teaspoon active dry yeast

3 cups (750 ml) warm water

2 cups (280 g) unbleached all-purpose flour

1 heaping tablespoon coarse sea salt

7 cups (1 kg 50 g) spelt flour, or as needed

2 cups (300 g) walnuts, lightly toasted and coarsely chopped

1. Place the yeast and water in a large bowl or the bowl of an electric mixer and stir. Add 1 cup (140 g) of the all-purpose flour, stir well, and let sit until little patches of bubbles rise to the surface of the water, about 5 minutes.

2. Add the remaining 1 cup all-purpose flour, stir, add the salt, and stir again. Add the spelt flour 1 cup (150 g) at a time until 5 cups are incorporated. Cover the bowl and let the dough rise for 1 hour.

3. Add 1 cup more spelt flour to the dough and gently mix it in. Sprinkle half the remaining cup of spelt flour on a work surface and turn out the dough onto the flour. Dust the dough with a bit more spelt flour and gently knead the dough as you incorporate the flour. Press the dough out into a thick round.

4. Pour the walnuts atop the dough and gently fold the dough in around them, then begin to knead the dough to incorporate the walnuts. Add the remaining spelt flour a bit at a time to keep the dough from sticking to your hands and to the work surface. When the walnuts are incorporated into the dough and the dough is sticky but keeps its shape when you form it into a round, divide it in half and form each half into a round.

5. Thickly dust an even layer of all-purpose flour into two 9½-inch (24-cm) round cake pans. Dust the loaves all over with flour, then transfer them to the pans. Cover them loosely with a towel and let rise until they have nearly doubled in bulk, about 1½ hours.

6. Preheat the oven to 425°F (220°C).

7. Snip the tops of the loaves in several places with scissors, or slash them to a depth of about ½ inch (1.3 cm) with a sharp knife. Immediately place them in the center of the oven and bake until they are golden brown and sound hollow when you tap them on the bottom, about 30 minutes. Remove from the oven and turn out onto a wire rack to cool.

Apple Streusel Tart

Tarte Streusel

❧ Apple tarts are a standard dessert in France, but this one is head and shoulders above any other I've had. Inspired by my friend Guy Untereiner, a former pastry chef turned illustrator, it is so rich and appley, so creamy and delicious, so gorgeous.

It reheats well too, as I learned one evening when we had supper with Guy at his home near Strasbourg. He handed me a streusel tart all wrapped up. "Take this home to your children. It will heat up just fine," he said.

Serve a glass of *vieilles vignes* (old-growth) Riesling with this wonderful tart.

6 to 8 servings

For the cream

1 large egg

¾ cup (185 ml) crème fraîche, or heavy cream, preferably not ultra-pasteurized

½ cup (100 g) vanilla sugar

¼ teaspoon ground cinnamon

For the streusel

¾ cup (105 g) all-purpose flour

½ teaspoon fine sea salt

½ cup (110 g) packed light brown sugar

¾ teaspoons ground cinnamon

7 tablespoons (105 g) unsalted butter, softened

1 tablespoon finely ground almonds or almond powder

Pâte Sucrée (page 260)

1. To make the cream, in a medium bowl, whisk together the egg, crème fraîche, sugar, and the cinnamon. Reserve.

2. To make the streusel, place the flour and salt in a food processor and process to blend. Add the brown sugar and cinnamon and process to blend, then add the butter and ground almonds and process until the mixture is thoroughly combined and homogeneous. Transfer to a small bowl and reserve.

3. Roll out the pastry to about 14 inches (35 cm) and fit it into a 10½-inch (26.5-cm) tart pan with a removable bottom by pushing it gently against the sides, and leave the edges hanging over. Refrigerate for at least 30 minutes.

4. Preheat the oven to 375°F (190°C).

5. Distribute the apples evenly in the tart shell. Bake in the center of the oven until the apples begin to turn tender and the pastry begins to bake but doesn't color, 10 to 15 minutes.

2 pounds (1 kg) tart apples, such as Winesaps, Melroses, or Cox Orange Pippins, peeled, cored, cut vertically in half, and then each half cut in 8 wedges

6. Remove from the oven and pour the cream evenly over the apples. Working very carefully, fold the edges of the pastry up over the apples. Distribute the streusel topping evenly over the exposed apples, and bake until the streusel and pastry are golden and crisp, about 1 hour.

7. Remove from the oven and let cool for 15 minutes, then remove the ring from the tart pan and serve.

ASTUCE: Yes, the recipe is correct, the pastry for the tart is partially baked, then folded up and over the apples, giving it a wonderful, rustic look and delicious crispness. It isn't difficult, but you must work quickly and be careful not to burn yourself.

Mascarpone and Peach Tart

Tarte à la Pêche et au Mascarpone

⚜ **The French fruit tart is an object of beauty, with its creamy filling and lovely fresh fruit topping. The bed for the fruit is typically a layer of pastry cream on top of pastry. Here, a layer of mascarpone mixed with *fromage blanc* is delightfully fresh and light, perfect on a hot summer day!**

8 servings

Pâte Sablée (page 258)

For the filling

2/3 cup (180 ml) Fromage Blanc (see page 264), or large-curd cottage cheese pureed very smooth

1½ cups (375 ml) mascarpone cheese

3 tablespoons vanilla sugar

¼ teaspoon freshly grated nutmeg, or to taste

6 small (about 1 pound 3 ounces; 540 g) ripe, very flavorful white or yellow peaches, peeled

Fresh mint leaves

1. Preheat the oven to 400°F (200°C).

2. Press the pastry evenly into a 9½-inch (24-cm) tart pan with a removable bottom. The pastry should be about ⅛ inch (0.3 cm) thick. The pastry will extend up and over the sides of the pan; remove this and reserve to make cookies. Line the pastry with aluminum foil and weight it with pastry weights or rice or beans.

3. Bake the pastry shell in the center of the oven until the edges of the pastry are golden, 10 to 12 minutes. Remove the pastry from the oven and remove the foil and weights, then return the pastry to the oven and bake until it is golden and baked through, an additional 10 to 12 minutes. Remove from the oven and cool on a wire rack.

4. If using cottage cheese, place it in a food processor and puree until it is very, very smooth. If using fromage blanc, add the mascarpone and sugar and process in a ford processor until thoroughly combined. Season to taste with nutmeg. Spread the mascarpone mixture in the cooled pastry shell and refrigerate, loosely covered, for 1 hour.

5. Slice the peaches into eighths and arrange the slices attractively atop the mascarpone filling. Garnish the tart with mint leaves, and serve immediately.

> **ASTUCES:** There will be some excess pastry after you press it into the pan. Shape it into a log, wrap, and chill it, then slice it into disks to bake for cookies. Expect enough extra pastry to make about 12 ⅛-inch (0.3 cm) cookies. ✿ When baking the pastry for a tart, bake it thoroughly, until it is crisp. Fill it with the mascarpone mixture an hour or two before you serve the tart, so the pastry softens slightly. Add the peaches at the very last minute. ✿ To peel peaches, bring a pan of water to a boil over high heat. Add the peaches and leave them in the water a scant minute, then remove them. The skins will slip right off. Don't leave them in the water too long, or else they will start to cook. If your peaches are are white and slightly blushing, blanching may darken the blush, so you may want to peel them by hand.

Lemon Meringue Tart

Tarte au Citron Meringuée

❧ The tang of lemon is a universal favorite, as I discover again and again whenever I serve this exceptional tart. I make it throughout the winter when lemons are abundant and full of juice.

8 to 10 servings

For the pastry

1½ cups (210 g) all-purpose flour

¼ teaspoon fine sea salt

7 tablespoons (105 g) chilled unsalted butter, cut into 7 pieces

⅓ to ½ cup (80 to 125 ml) ice water

For the lemon cream

7 tablespoons (105 g) unsalted butter

1 cup (200 g) sugar

4 large eggs

¾ cup (185 ml) freshly squeezed lemon juice (from about 3 large lemons)

Grated or finely minced zest of 1 lemon

For the meringue

2 large eggs, separated

Pinch fine sea salt

⅓ cup (65 g) vanilla sugar

1. To make the pastry, place the flour and salt in a food processor and process to mix. Add the butter and process until the mixture looks like coarse cornmeal. With the processor running, drizzle in ⅓ cup (80 ml) of the water and process just until the mixture comes together, but not until it forms a ball; if necessary, add some or all of the remaining water. The pastry should be quite moist. Turn it out onto a work surface, form it into a flat disk, cover and let rest for 1 hour.

2. On a floured surface, roll out the pastry to about 14 inches (35 cm) and fit it into a 10½-inch (26.5-cm) tart pan with a removable bottom. Refrigerate for 1 hour, or freeze for 20 minutes.

3. Preheat the oven to 425°F (220°C).

4. Prick the bottom of the pastry all over with the tines of a fork, then line it with aluminum foil and weight it with pastry weights, or rice or beans. Bake in the center of the oven until the pastry is golden around the edges, about 12 minutes. Remove from the oven and remove the aluminum foil and weights from the pastry, then return to the oven to bake until it is golden all over, about 10 additional minutes. Remove from the oven and let cool.

5. To make the lemon cream; place the butter and sugar in a *bain marie*, or water bath, and stir until the butter is melted. Add the eggs one at a time, whisking well after each addition so they are thoroughly blended into the

butter and sugar. Add the lemon juice, whisk, and cook, stirring gently, until the mixture is thickened, 6 to 7 minutes. Remove the bowl from the water bath and let it cool to room temperature, then stir in the lemon zest.

6. Spread the lemon cream into the cooled tart shell. Refrigerate for 2 to 3 hours.

7. Right before serving, make the meringue: In a large bowl or the bowl of an electric mixer, whisk the egg whites with the pinch of salt until they are foamy. Whisking constantly, or with the mixer running, slowly add the sugar, and continue whisking until the egg whites form smooth peaks but aren't whisked so hard that they are chunky.

8. Preheat the broiler. Spread the meringue over the top of the tart, and place under the broiler until the meringue is golden on top. Remove from the broiler, transfer to a serving platter, and serve immediately.

To Zest or to Rasp

A lemon zester is a small tool with a row of sharp holes at its metal end that removes long strips of zest—the colored part of citrus peel—from the fruit. The strips of zest have texture and flavor that explodes when bitten into.

A rasp, manufactured by Microplane, removes zest from citrus too. Rasped zest is very fine and almost fluffy, and it gives a more subtle, pervasive flavor.

When I want the texture of lemon zest as well as its sunny flavor—in a cake or a cookie, or in a savory dish—I use a zester, then I mince the strips of zest. You may use a box or other grater with tiny holes, then scrape off the zest into your preparation, but a zester or Microplane is best. When I want the essence of the zest—in a soufflé, cream, or other delicate dish—I use the rasp.

Chocolate Chocolate Cake

Gâteau au Chocolat Chocolat

❧ When a friend I'd invited over for dinner one evening asked if she could bring dessert, she arrived with this glistening cake. Since then it has become a favorite, for it is moist, deeply chocolate, and dense without being heavy, as well as easy to make and impressive to serve.

The secret to the cake is, of course, top-quality chocolate and cocoa. I recommend several excellent brands below. If you cannot find any of them, make sure that the chocolate you use is made with pure cocoa butter, as inferior chocolate contains vegetables oils.

10 to 12 servings

For the cake

3 ounces (90 g) high-quality milk chocolate, preferably Lindt, Scharffen Berger, or Valrhona, cut into small pieces

14 tablespoons (1¾ sticks; 210 g) unsalted butter, softened

1¾ cups (350 g) vanilla sugar

1 teaspoon vanilla extract

4 large eggs

¾ cup plus 3 tablespoons (125 g) cake flour

¾ cup (75 g) cocoa

1 teaspoon baking powder

¼ teaspoon fine sea salt

For the ganache

1¼ cups (310 ml) crème fraîche or heavy cream, preferably not ultra-pasteurized

1. Preheat the oven to 350°F (180°C). Butter and flour two 8-inch (20-cm) round cake pans. Line them with parchment paper, and lightly butter and flour the parchment paper.

2. Melt the milk chocolate in the top of a double boiler over medium heat, uncovered. Remove the pan of chocolate from the double boiler and cool until it is tepid.

3. Whisk together the butter and sugar in a large bowl or the bowl of an electric mixer until pale yellow and light. Whisk in the vanilla extract, then whisk in the eggs one at a time until thoroughly combined and very light.

4. Sift the flour, cocoa, baking powder, and salt onto a piece of parchment paper, then whisk the dry ingredients into the butter and sugar mixture until thoroughly combined. Fold in the milk chocolate.

5. Transfer half the batter to each prepared pan and bake in the center of the oven until the cakes are slightly puffed, 30 minutes. To test for doneness, gently touch the cake on top; if the cake feels firm but is obviously a bit moist and your finger cracks the surface easily, re-

12 ounces (360 g) semisweet
chocolate, such as Lindt,
Valrhona, or Scharffen Berger,
broken into small bits

For the optional filling

¼ cup (60 ml) red currant jelly
or orange marmalade,
homemade (page 290) or
store-bought

move it from the oven and let cool on a wire rack for
15 minutes, then turn the cakes out onto the cooling
rack and remove the parchment paper. Let cool to room
temperature.

6. While the cake is baking, make the ganache: In a
small saucepan, scald the crème fraîche over low heat.
Remove the pan from the heat, add the chocolate, and
swirl the pan from time to time as the chocolate melts
into the crème fraîche. When the chocolate is completely melted, transfer the mixture to a medium bowl
and whisk so it is smooth and homogeneous. Let it cool
to room temperature. Just before using, whisk the
ganache so it lightens in color and consistency. It should
have the consistency of a thick but spreadable frosting.

7. If using the jelly or marmalade, warm it in a small
saucepan over low heat until you can easily mix it.
Transfer to a small bowl and whisk in 2 tablespoons of
the whipped ganache. Reserve.

8. Dust any excess crumbs from the cake layers with a
pastry brush. Place one layer on a metal cooling rack set
over a serving plate. Spread a thin, even layer of
ganache over the top and sides of the cake. Spread the
filling, if using, over the top layer. Using a pastry bag
fitted with a ¼-inch (0.6-cm) plain pastry tip, pipe a
ring of ganache around the top of the layer just in from
the edge. Set the second layer atop the first layer, pressing it gently but firmly onto the tube of ganache, which
acts both as a wall to keep in the filling, and a glue to
stick the layers together. Frost the second layer with a
thin layer of ganache, then let it sit for about 30 min-

utes. Soften the remaining ganache over low heat until it will pour, then pour it in the center of the cake. Using a flexible spatula, urge the ganache evenly over the top and down the sides of the cake. Smooth it quickly over the top and sides so it covers them completely, then let the cake sit for several hours, or preferably overnight, at cool room temperature so the ganache solidifies. Carefully transfer the cake to a serving platter and serve.

ASTUCES: This cake is slightly underbaked, which gives it a texture not unlike a good brownie. ✣ When you melt chocolate in a double boiler leave it uncovered, to prevent any condensation forming on the lid and dropping into the chocolate, which will make it "seize" and ruin its texture. ✣ Ganache, the chocolate and cream icing for this cake, is very easy to work with. Pouring it over the cake and letting it run down the sides, then smoothing it lightly over the surface of the cake allows the ganache to retain a professional luster. There will be leftover ganache, which will keep for about one week, refrigerated, or two months in the freezer. You can use it to make wonderful hot chocolate. Simply whisk a nob of it into milk that has heated just to the boiling point. If you prefer a sweeter ganache, you can reduce the amount of chocolate by up to 3 ounces (90 g). ✣ To scald means to heat a liquid over medium heat just until a ring of tiny bubbles forms around the edges of the pan.

Caramelized Apple Cake

Gâteau aux Pommes Caramelisé

⚜ This recipe from Pierre-Yves Pieto, a friend who practices medicine in the small Breton town of Lamballe, reminds me of all the pound cakes I made while I was a cooking apprentice in Paris. Into the welcoming batter I would fold walnuts and dried currants, praline and anise seed, lemon zest, candied lemon, scented geranium leaves, just about anything else I thought would be tasty. This cake, however, beats them all. It is dense and buttery with a pure flavor.

Serves 6 to 8 servings

For the apples

⅓ cup (65 g) vanilla sugar

1¾ pounds (875 g) tart apples, such as Gravensteins, Cox Orange Pippins, Criterions, Melroses, or Winesaps, peeled, cored, and cut into eighths

For the batter

½ cup (70 g) plus 3 teaspoons all-purpose flour

½ teaspoon baking powder

Pinch fine sea salt

6 tablespoons (90 g) salted butter, softened

½ cup (100 g) vanilla sugar

3 large eggs

Seeds from 1 vanilla bean

Geranium blossoms, optional

1. Preheat the oven to 350°F (180°C).

2. To prepare the apples, sprinkle sugar in an 8-inch (20-cm) cake pan (you can use a nonstick pan here), and place it over medium heat. Using kitchen tongs, tilt and swirl the pan slightly as necessary to melt and caramelize the sugar evenly, being very careful not to burn yourself. When the sugar is a deep golden, add the apples, stir them around so they are covered in caramelized sugar, and transfer the pan to a heatproof surface. If the caramel hardens when you add the apples, don't be concerned. It will melt again and coat them.

3. To make the batter, sift together the dry ingredients onto a piece of parchment or waxed paper.

4. Place the butter and sugar in a large bowl or the bowl of an electric mixer and beat until the mixture is pale yellow and light. Add the eggs one at a time, beating well after each addition, then add the vanilla seeds. Fold in the dry ingredients until they are thoroughly incorporated.

5. Pour the batter over the apples and spread it evenly right to the edge of the pan, so it covers them. Bake the

cake in the center of the oven until it is golden and slightly puffed and your finger leaves a slight indentation on the top when you press on it, about 30 minutes. A knife inserted into the cake should come out clean (it may come out slightly moist if it pierces a piece of fruit, but it shouldn't have any uncooked batter on it).

6. Remove the cake from the oven. Run a knife around the edge of the cake to loosen it from the pan, then invert a large platter atop the cake pan. Working carefully so you don't burn your hands, turn the cake pan over so the platter is on the bottom and the cake falls out onto the platter. You may need to give the cake pan a sharp shake or two to release the cake from the pan; if some of the fruit sticks to the pan, just remove it and place it atop the cake. Let the cake cool to room temperature, then serve, garnished with geranium blossoms, if desired.

CUSTARDS, COMPOTES, CAKES, TARTS, AND MORE

Crème Anglaise, Compotes, Gâteaux, Tartes, et Encore

If you are not feeling well, if you have
not slept, chocolate will revive you.
But you have no chocolate! I think of
that again and again! My dear,
how will you ever manage?

Marie, Marquise de Sévigné
(1626–1696), French writer and lady of fashion,
February 11, 1677

Baked Apples from the Market

Pommes au Four du Marché

❧ This simple dessert is very common in Normandy, where dozens of varieties of flavorful apples hang heavy on the trees each year. Boscop, a large, tart, firm-fleshed apple that tastes of flowers and perfume, is a favorite for baking, and this recipe comes directly from a farmer at the Louviers market who raises some of the best.

This is a particularly nice and simple way to prepare baked apples—the almonds, which bake to a golden crisp, set them apart.

6 servings

6 large apples (about 8 ounces; 250 g each), such as Winesaps, Macouns, or Cox Orange Pippins

3 tablespoons (45 g) light brown sugar

3 tablespoons red currant, black currant, or raspberry jelly

⅓ cup (45 g) whole, unblanched almonds, coarsely chopped

1½ tablespoons (22 g) unsalted butter

About 2 cups (500 ml) hard apple cider or water

6 small (4 inches; 10 cm in diameter) ½-inch (1.3-cm)-thick slices brioche

Crème fraîche for serving, optional

1. Preheat the oven to 400°F (200°C).

2. Core the apples, leaving the base intact, and peel off a ½-inch (1.3-cm) ribbon of skin around the circumference of each one. Place the apples in a baking pan just large enough to hold them so they are touching but are not packed in, and place 1½ teaspoons of the brown sugar in the cavity of each one. Place 1½ teaspoons of the jelly in each cavity and divide the almonds evenly among the apples, pressing on them gently so they fill the cavity and mound just slightly above it. Divide the butter evenly among the apples, placing it on top of the almonds, and pour enough cider around the apples to come one-third of the way up their sides.

3. Bake the apples in the center of the oven until they are tender through, about 45 minutes.

4. While the apples are baking, lightly toast the slices of brioche on both sides. Place one slice on each of six dessert plates.

5. When the apples are baked, remove them from the oven and place one atop each piece of brioche. Serve immediately, with crème fraîche on the side, if desired, and the cooking juices drizzled on and around the apples.

THE SWEET STORY

Sugar. It tenderizes, it sweetens, it moistens, it makes most things just a little bit better. More than 120 million tons of refined sugar are produced each year. About seventy percent of it comes from sugarcane, a gracious and sturdy grass that grows in more than 120 tropical countries and four states—Texas, Louisiana, Florida, and Hawaii.

The rest comes from the sugar beet, a tuber that looks like a bloated parsnip and is grown in more temperate zones. When I drive outside of Louviers in just about any direction in the fall, I see sugar beets being dug from the ground and mounded in enormous, long piles in the fields that surround the town. Some are destined for sugar refineries in the north; others are manufactured into animal feed.

Chemically, cane and beet sugar are the same, for they are both sucrose, a carbohydrate. Cane sugar contains trace minerals lacking in beet sugar, however, and it may be these that account for its round, gentler, pure and less sweet flavor, making it taste more like a food than a simple sweetener. Cane sugar also melts more quickly than beet sugar, which makes it easier to cook with.

Crumble
Crumble

❧ *Le crumble* is quickly replacing the simple apple tart as one of the most popular desserts in the French repertoire. It consists simply of a pile of apples in a baking dish topped with a butter-sugar-flour mixture that bakes to a crisp golden brown. What makes it very French indeed, and richly flavored and delicious, is the caramelized butter and sugar on the bottom of the baking dish, and the crème fraîche that is served *d'office*, or obligatorily.

6 to 8 servings

For the topping

1¼ cups (175 g) all-purpose flour

½ teaspoon ground cinnamon

Scant ½ teaspoon fine sea salt

2 tablespoons finely ground almonds

8 tablespoons (1 stick; 120 g) unsalted butter, softened

¾ cup (150 g) vanilla sugar

3 tablespoons (45 g) unsalted butter, melted

¼ cup (50 g) vanilla sugar

3 pounds (1.5 kg) apples such as Cox Orange Pippins, Winesaps, Gravensteins, or Criterions, cored, peeled, and cut into thin slices

Crème fraîche for serving

1. Preheat the oven to 400°F (200°C).

2. To make the topping, sift together the flour, cinnamon, and salt onto a piece of parchment paper. Add the ground almonds and mix well. In a medium bowl, mix the butter with the sugar until smooth and thoroughly combined. Using your fingers or a wooden spoon, mix in the dry ingredients until thoroughly combined. The mixture will be lumpy and fairly soft, like cookie dough.

3. Pour the melted butter into a 8 × 12-inch (20 × 30-cm) baking dish and spread it evenly over the bottom. Sprinkle the vanilla sugar evenly over the bottom of the dish. Heap the apples in the baking dish. Crumble the topping evenly over the apples.

4. Bake in the lower third of the oven until the topping is deep golden and the apples are tender through, about 55 minutes. Remove the crumble from the oven and let it sit for at least 15 minutes, preferably 30, before serving, as it will be very hot. The crumble is delicious both warm and at room temperature. Whatever the temperature, be sure to serve the crème fraîche alongside.

> **ASTUCE:** For the best caramelization, use an enamelled baking dish rather than a glass baking dish.

Cherry Clafoutis
Clafoutis aux Cerises

❧ Clafoutis, a simple, homey dessert from the Limousin region in southwest France, is perhaps the easiest, most familiar and comforting dessert in the French repertoire. Traditionally made with the cherries that grow so profusely in the Limousin, it can be prepared with all kinds of fruit, from apples to raisins to flavorful grapes.

6 to 8 servings

About 1 teaspoon unsalted butter for buttering the pan

2 tablespoons (30 g) light brown sugar

¾ cup (105 g) unbleached all-purpose flour

¾ teaspoon fine sea salt

2 cups (500 ml) whole milk

3 large eggs

¼ cup (50 g) vanilla sugar

Seeds from 1 vanilla bean

1 pound (500 g) sweet, flavorful cherries, stemmed, rinsed, patted dry, and pitted

1½ tablespoons (22 g) unsalted butter, cut into 6 pieces, optional

1. Preheat the oven to 450°F (230°C). Butter and lightly flour a 9½-inch (24-cm) round nonreactive tart pan without a removable bottom or a baking dish. Sprinkle the pan with 1 tablespoon of the brown sugar.

2. Sift together the flour and salt into a large bowl. Whisk in 1 cup (250 ml) of the milk to make a smooth batter, then add the eggs one at a time, whisking briefly after each addition. Whisk in the vanilla sugar and vanilla seeds until combined, then whisk in the remaining 1 cup (250 ml) milk.

3. Place the cherries in the tart pan. Pour the batter over them, and dot the batter with the pieces of butter, if using. Bake in the center of the oven until the clafoutis is golden and puffed, about 25 minutes.

4. Remove the clafoutis from the oven and immediately sprinkle it with the remaining tablespoon of brown sugar. Let it cool to lukewarm before serving.

ASTUCE: Some cooks insist that the cherries impart more flavor when the pits are left in. I've tried it both ways, and I can honestly say that there is so little difference in flavor that I see no reason at all to leave them in.

Dried and Fresh Apricot Compote

Compôte à l'Abricots dans Tous Ses États

❧ I can always tell it's July by the scent of apricots in the air. The *épicerie*, or grocery, that is a stone's throw away has crate after crate of them in their quaint sidewalk display, piled precariously so the apricots threaten to tumble off as people walk by. There are the small, red-speckled Rouge de Roussillon, the furry, sunset-hued Rouge Gorge, and the plump, pale apricot-hued Bergerac. Each has a different aroma, texture, and taste.

I make everything with apricots, from thick golden jam, to tarts, sorbets, and custards, to this sweet and tart compote. Dreamy on its own, I also put some compote in a shallow soup dish with a scoop of homemade Vanilla Ice Cream (page 241) or Red Currant Sorbet (page 245) on it, then drape the whole affair with fresh red currants.

6 to 8 servings

6 ounces (180 g) dried apricots, cut into thin strips

2 pounds (1 kg) fresh apricots, halved and pitted

1 cup (250 ml) orange juice, preferably freshly squeezed

½ vanilla bean, split lengthwise in half

1. Place all of the ingredients in a medium heavy-bottomed nonreactive saucepan, stir, and bring to a boil, covered, over medium heat. Reduce the heat so the juice is simmering and cook, stirring occasionally, until the fresh apricots have softened to a thick puree and the dried apricots are tender, about 20 minutes.

2. Remove from the heat and let the compote sit in a cool place or in the refrigerator for at least 2 hours, and up to 12 hours, before serving so the flavors can ripen. Remove the vanilla bean before serving.

ASTUCES: Use unsulphured dried apricots, which are a rusty orange color with deep, pure flavor. Sulphured apricots are pale in color, puckery tart, and unripe tasting, a pale version of their unsulphured cousins. ❧ To pit a ripe apricot, simply pull it apart and flick out the stone. ❧ If you cannot find a juicy orange in summer, use a high-quality frozen concentrate or commercial freshly squeezed juice. ❧ There is no sugar in this recipe. When fresh apricots are sweetly ripe and dried apricots are high quality, no added sugar is needed. Sweeten this to your taste if necessary. This compote freezes perfectly.

Normandy Apricot Custard

Fondant Normand aux Abricots

❧ **This dessert is a signature dish in Normandy when made with apples. I have tried it with all sorts of fruit—plums, grapes, even raisins—but prefer it best with apricots, for their slight tartness is a perfect foil to the rich custard.**

6 to 8 servings

For the fruit

3 tablespoons (45 g) unsalted butter

2 pounds (1 kg) slightly tart apricots, pitted

¼ cup (55 g) gently packed light brown sugar

For the custard

6 tablespoons (75 g) vanilla sugar

2 tablespoons (30 g) unsalted butter, softened

2 large eggs

¾ cup (105 g) unbleached all-purpose flour

1 teaspoon baking powder

¾ cup (185 ml) whole milk

For the topping

⅓ cup (65 g) vanilla sugar

4 tablespoons (60 g) unsalted butter, softened

1 large egg

1. Preheat the oven to 400°F (205°C). Generously butter and flour a 2-quart (2-1) soufflé dish about 4 inches (10 cm) deep.

2. Melt the butter in a skillet over medium heat. Add the apricots and brown sugar, stir, and sauté until the apricots are hot and the sugar has melted and begun to caramelize, about 8 minutes. Remove from the heat and reserve.

3. To prepare the custard: in a large bowl, beat together the vanilla sugar and butter until the mixture is pale yellow and light, 3 to 5 minutes. Beat in the eggs one at a time until they are thoroughly combined. Using a whisk, whisk the mixture until light and pale yellow. Sift the flour and baking powder together over the mixture, whisking as you do so that it incorporates smoothly into the mixture, then whisk in the milk. Fold in the apricots and their cooking juices. Pour the mixture into the prepared baking dish.

4. Bake the custard in the center of the oven until it begins to puff and look golden, about 30 minutes.

5. While the custard is baking, prepare the topping: In a small bowl, whisk together the vanilla sugar and butter until light and fluffy. Whisk in the egg until combined.

ASTUCE: Sautéing the apricots before adding them to the custard caramelizes them, and they give up some of their juices, which blend with the custard for extra apricot flavor.

6. Remove the custard from the oven and spread the topping over it. Return it to the oven to bake until golden and bubbling, an additional 20 minutes. Remove from the oven and let cool to room temperature before serving.

Chocolate Mousse

Mousse au Chocolat

❖ Given the salted butter used in this chocolate mousse, it could only come from Brittany, where there is virtually no other kind of butter. The salt (sea salt, of course!) here is subtle, adding a lovely counterpoint to the deep chocolate.

Chocolate mousse is such a universal favorite, and so simple to make. I vary the flavor by adding minced orange zest, strong coffee, a bit of ground fennel seed, and a tiny dice of candied ginger. You can suit it to your whim, and to your menu.

4 to 6 servings

7 ounces (200 g) semisweet chocolate, preferably Lindt or Scharffen Berger

4 tablespoons (60 g) lightly salted butter

3 large eggs, separated

1 tablespoon very strong coffee, Grand Marnier, Cognac, or rum, or more to taste

Tiny pinch of fine sea salt

1. Melt the chocolate and butter in a double boiler over medium-high heat, uncovered. Remove from the heat, stir until blended, then whisk in the egg yolks and coffee. Let cool.

2. Place the egg whites and salt in a large bowl, or the bowl of an electric mixer fitted with a whisk, and whisk them until they form soft peaks. Fold one-quarter of the egg whites into the chocolate mixture, then fold in the remaining egg whites. Taste for flavoring—you can carefully fold in additional flavoring at this point, if you like. Transfer the mousse to a serving dish or to individual serving dishes, and refrigerate for at least 2 hours, tightly covered. (The mousse can be made up to 1 day ahead.)

ASTUCE: When melting ingredients, such as chocolate and butter, in a double boiler, don't put on the cover, as the condensation that would form on it could drip onto the ingredients and alter their taste and texture.

Easy Chocolate Sauce
Sauce au Chocolat "Hyper-Simple"

❧ If you are in need of a quick, smooth, and rich-tasting chocolate sauce, this is your recipe. I learned to make this simply by watching French home cooks whip it up at the last minute, without a care.

Try the sauce over homemade vanilla ice cream, sandwiched between two sablés once it has firmed up, or as a dip for fresh fruit. You will, no doubt, find many other uses for this as well.

1 scant cup (250 ml)

5 ounces (150 g) semisweet chocolate, preferably Lindt, Scharffen Berger, or Valrhona, coarsely chopped

3 tablespoons water

3 tablespoons heavy cream or crème fraiche, preferably not ultra-pasturized

Place the chocolate and water in a small heavy-bottomed saucepan over medium heat and melt the chocolate, stirring constantly. When the chocolate is melted and the mixture is smooth, remove it from the heat and stir in the cream. Use immediately.

ASTUCE: You can make the sauce as bitter or as sweet as you like, depending on the chocolate you use. I make it with semisweet chocolate when I'm serving it to the children. When it is destined for more adult palates, I use a more intense bittersweet chocolate.

Tips for Perfect Custard and Ice Cream

Ice cream is so, so simple to make, and nothing is better! Not only can you make any flavor you want, but even if you stick to plain old vanilla it will be fresh, creamy, and so vivid you won't believe it!

Most ice cream is made with a custard base. Here are tips for ensuring that your custard, and your ice cream, are perfect every time.

❖ If you are making a cooked custard, the basis of most luscious ice creams, the key is not to overcook the custard, which will curdle the yolks. To avoid this, make sure the heat under the custard is moderate, not too hot. As the custard cooks you must stir it in a figure-eight pattern—this keeps all of the custard moving across the bottom of the pan, which allows it to cook evenly. Don't stir too fast—the custard needs contact with the bottom and sides of the hot pan to cook, and if you whip it around in the pan too quickly, it won't cook.

❖ Rest a sieve over a bowl large enough to hold the custard, and place the bowl into a larger bowl that is filled with ice. Set the bowls next to you. As you make the custard you will take it to the exquisite point where it is thick, velvety, and perfectly cooked, yet a split second from curdling. When it reaches this stage you need to act quickly by immediately pouring the custard through the sieve into the waiting bowl. The sieve will catch any hint of a curdle and the chilled bowl will immediately begin cooling the custard, which will be perfect.

❖ If you are making a spice ice cream, infuse the milk with the spice before you make the custard, which the recipes here will instruct you to do. Make your custard with the flavored milk that has the spices still in it, then strain it into the waiting bowl. Remove the spices from the strainer, rinse and pat them dry if necessary, and return them to the custard. They will continue to add their flavor to the custard as it cools and chills.

❖ Whatever mixture is the basis of your ice cream, it needs to be thoroughly chilled before it goes into the ice cream maker. This means it must rest in the refrigerator for at least two hours, and up to eight. Stir it before putting it into the ice cream maker.

❧ Most home ice cream makers freeze ice cream to the soft stage and not much further. To firm up the ice cream and mellow its flavor, remove it from the ice cream maker and place it in the freezer for at least an hour, preferably two hours. Before you serve it, check its consistency. If it has frozen too hard just set it in the refrigerator until it softens slightly. Sorbets, on the other hand, generally freeze to the perfect texture in the ice cream maker. If you do have leftover sorbet and freeze it, it is imperative to remove it from the freezer well before you plan to serve it, for it will have frozen iceberg-hard.

❧ Finally, ice cream is the very, very best the day it is made. It will still be good on subsequent days, but that wonderful texture won't be the same! So, eat up!

Vanilla Ice Cream

Glace à la Vanille

Ice cream is exquisite. What a pity it isn't illegal.

Voltaire (1694–1778)

⚜ **I've made ice cream for so many years it is almost a reflexive action. I love the whole process, from infusing the milk with vanilla, which scents the entire house, to feeling the custard thicken under my wooden spoon.**

Vanilla is a basic recipe that can be infinitely varied. We all love it plain but it is also delicious with fresh summer fruit stirred into it, right after it has turned in the ice maker and before it goes into the freezer to ripen.

About 1 generous quart (1 l)

4 cups (1 l) half-and-half, preferably not ultra-pasteurized

1 vanilla bean, split lengthwise

10 large egg yolks

1¼ cups (250 g) vanilla sugar

Small pinch of fine salt

1. Place the half-and-half in a large heavy-bottomed saucepan. Scrape the seeds from the vanilla bean into the half-and-half, and add the bean as well. Stir, and scald over medium heat. Remove from the heat, cover, and let infuse for 20 minutes.

2. Set a sieve in a large bowl.

3. In another large bowl, whisk the egg yolks with the sugar and salt until they are pale yellow and light. Slowly whisk in the warm infused half-and-half, with the vanilla bean, then return the mixture to the pan.

4. Cook the mixture over medium heat, stirring constantly in a figure-eight pattern, until it is thickened and coats the back of the spoon (a line made by running your finger through the custard on the back of the spoon stays clear). Strain the custard into the waiting bowl. Remove the vanilla bean from the strainer, rinse it and pat it dry, and return it to the custard.

5. Let the custard cool to room temperature, then refrigerate it until it is chilled through. Remove the vanilla bean and freeze the ice cream in an ice cream maker according to the manufacturer's instructions. Transfer to an airtight container and freeze for at least 1 hour and up to 2 hours before serving.

> **ASTUCES:** Keep vanilla beans in an airtight container out of the light. Occasionally, vanilla beans develop vanillin on them, which looks like crystalline frost and is a sign that they are pure and of excellent quality. Don't wipe off the frost, for it is filled with flavor! (But if a bean develops a white mildew on it, discard it.)
> ✤ Adding a pinch of salt to the custard base livens up its flavor. ✤ Freshly made ice cream generally has the texture of soft-serve ice cream. Its texture is best if it is transferred from the ice cream maker to an airtight container and frozen for an hour or two. If you freeze it overnight, you will need to transfer the ice cream to the refrigerator about 1 hour before you plan to serve it, so it softens enough to scoop it into bowls.

Vanilla Beans

The sensuous fruit of the vanilla orchid (*Vanilla planifolia*), which we call Bourbon vanilla, blooms far away in Madagascar, Indonesia, Mexico, Comoros, Tahiti, Guadeloupe, the Antilles, and Réunion Island (Ile de la Réunion)—and the plant must be hand-pollinated on the very day the flower opens. The flower wilts and the seed pod, a fat green bean, grows to maturity, eventually to become the vanilla bean we are familiar with. In Madagascar, where the finest vanilla comes from, the green pods are so valuable they are branded to foil vanilla rustlers.

The pods mature on the vine for up to nine months before they are harvested. Then for five months they are cured in the sun by day and tucked away at night so they sweat, which helps them develop rich flavor and shrivel to their rich, deep, oily brown. If they've been left on the vine long enough, the seeds that fill them develop the characteristic flavor we are all familiar with.

Though Madagascar vanilla is the highest quality, the Mexican bean, also the Bourbon variety, is thick and rich smelling. The Tahitian bean (*Vanilla tahitiensis*) is the fattest but least flavorful. Vanilla from Guadeloupe and the Antilles (*V. pompona*) is not highly regarded.

When you buy vanilla beans, look for fleshy, oily, shiny, beans with a pure aroma. Avoid dry, thin, brittle, or smoky beans. Heavy beans are a good sign, for it means they are full of flavorful seeds. High-quality vanilla beans can develop vanilla crystals on them over time, called *givre*, or frost, in French. These fine, sparkling crystals are enormously flavorful, so should you find them on your vanilla beans, don't scrape them off. However, vanilla beans are also subject to mildew, a white substance that forms on their surface; discard them, as their flavor is compromised.

Vanilla beans will keep almost indefinitely if they are stored in an airtight container in a cool, dark place or in the freezer. I keep mine in an airtight jar in my spice drawer because I always use them in a relatively short amount of time. After I've used a vanilla bean once, I dry it, then add it to my sugar to make vanilla sugar. Or, if I've left in the seeds and used it only to flavor something mildly, I rinse it, dry it out, and if it is still moist and fragrant, use it again to flavor a custard or syrup.

Honey Ice Cream
Glace au Miel

⚜ **This elegant ice cream is delicate yet intense, purely flavored with honey and a subtle touch of vanilla. It is delicious all on its own, better yet as a foil for Dried and Fresh Apricot Compote (page 234), or sitting in a pool of Easy Chocolate Sauce (page 238).**

About 1 generous quart (1 l)

4 cups (1 l) half-and-half, preferably not ultra-pasteurized

10 large egg yolks

1¼ cups (250 g) vanilla sugar

Small pinch of fine sea salt

¼ cup (60 ml) lavender or other lovely honey

ASTUCES: Cooking with honey can be tricky, for if honey isn't made under perfectly pristine conditions, by happy bees that have harvested flavorful nectar, the result can be a muted, almost "dirty" flavor. I use a top-quality lavender honey from Provence, but good honey is available just about everywhere; look for locally produced ones. ❧ Do not cook the honey with the custard, but stir it in while the custard is still hot. The honey will melt gently into the custard and impart its flavor. ❧ To scald milk means to heat it over low to medium heat just until a ring of tiny bubbles forms around the edges of the pan.

1. In a large heavy-bottomed saucepan, scald the half-and-half over medium heat. Remove from the heat.

2. Set a sieve in a large bowl.

3. In another large bowl, whisk together the egg yolks with the sugar and salt until they are pale yellow and light. Slowly whisk in the warm half-and-half, then return the mixture to the pan.

4. Cook the mixture over medium heat, stirring constantly in a figure-eight pattern, until it is thickened and coats the back of the spoon (a line made by running your finger through the custard on the back of the spoon stays clear). Strain the custard into the waiting bowl. Whisk in the honey.

5. Cool the custard to room temperature, then refrigerate it until it is chilled through. Freeze the ice cream in an ice cream maker according to the manufacturer's instructions. Transfer the ice cream to an airtight container and freeze for at least 1 hour and up to 2 hours before serving.

Red Currant Sorbet

Sorbet aux Groseilles

⚜ **From late June to late July, round red currants tumble like translucent jewels into market stalls, saucepans, and mouths all over France. I use currant juice to make a flavorful sorbet, which I serve by itself or with a halo of fresh currants, both red and white.**

About 1¼ quarts (1.25 l)

4 pounds (2 kg) red currants, stemmed

1 cup (200 g) sugar

¾ cup (200 ml) water

ASTUCE: You can substitute any berry for the red currants here, adjusting the amount of sugar you use to the sweetness of the berries.

---

1. Rinse the currants and place them, with the water still clinging to them, in a large saucepan and cook over medium heat, stirring and pressing on them, until they have burst and released their juice. Remove from the heat and strain the berries into a large bowl. You should have 4 cups (1 l) of juice.

2. Place the sugar and water in a small saucepan over medium heat and cook, stirring frequently, just until the sugar dissolves. Remove the sugar syrup from the heat and let it cool to room temperature.

3. Add the sugar syrup to the currant juice, stir well, and refrigerate until chilled through. Freeze the sorbet in an ice cream maker according to the manufacturer's instructions.

Lychee, Lime, and Candied Ginger Salad

Salade de Litchi au Citron Vert et au Gingembre Confit

❧ High, dusty-rose piles of lychees from Madagascar and Ile de la Réunion flood France just before Christmas. Those from Madagascar are very juicy and slightly tart with a flavor somewhere between fragrant roses and Muscat grapes. Those from Ile de la Réunion, which arrive on the stem, are more subtle in flavor, less vibrant in color, but still delicious and alluring.

I buy lychees by the kilo and we eat them as fast as I bring them home. They are delicious, and they are also little vitamin balls, high in vitamin C and potassium. This salad enhances their floral, delicate flavor and acts as an antidote to winter too.

4 to 6 servings

2 pounds (1 kg) lychees (or two 20-ounce; 565-gm cans lychees, drained)

2 tablespoons (30 ml) freshly squeezed lime juice

2 tablespoons diced candied ginger (½ ounce; 15 g)

4 to 6 thin curls of lime zest

Peel the lychees, if using fresh ones. Place the lychees in a medium bowl, drizzle the lime juice over them, add the diced ginger, and toss until all the ingredients are combined. Serve immediately, garnished with the curls of lime zest.

> **ASTUCES:** Pitting a lychee is nearly impossible, as the pearly flesh clings mightily to the dark, shiny, elongated pit. I leave the pits in, which does nothing to detract from the quality of this salad! ❧ You can also use canned lychees, which are, surprisingly, luscious.

Peaches in Orange Flower Water
Pêches de Vigne à l'Eau de Fleur d'Oranger

❧ *Pêches de vigne* (peaches of the vine) are a late-summer delicacy. Their flesh is deep red, their skin fragile and lightly furred, their flavor intensely perfumed and deep, with a pleasant tannic bitterness. They are a connoisseur's peach, an older variety so named because the trees were once planted among the grapevines in the vineyards of the Rhône Valley. They are still cultivated there, harvested at near-total ripeness, packed carefully in wooden crates, and shipped in small quantities to distant destinations like Normandy.

Whenever *pêches de vigne* make their appearance at the market or the local *épicerie,* I buy them. One year, as one of the young apprentices who works at the *épicerie* was carefully choosing my peaches for me, a woman standing nearby suggested I prepare them this way. It has become a favorite, and it illustrates the most important tenet of all French cooking—when you have fabulous ingredients, get out of their way and let them speak for themselves!

Try this recipe with your local tree-ripened peaches or the best, most juicy and floral peaches you can find. I like it served by itself, but it is also good with a small dollop of homemade Vanilla Ice Cream (page 241).

4 servings

1½ pounds (750 g) peaches, chilled for 30 to 45 minutes, peeled, and pitted

2 to 3 teaspoons orange flower water

Fresh mint sprigs, preferably peppermint

Slice the peaches into ¼-inch (0.6-cm)-thick slices and arrange them in a shallow serving dish. Drizzle them with the orange flower water, and garnish with mint sprigs. Serve immediately, so they are still lightly chilled.

> ASTUCE: Lightly chilling the peaches makes them easier to slice nicely and gives a refreshing edge to their flavor.

Caramelized Oranges

Oranges Caramelisées

❧ **Picture sunshine on a plate and you've got this simple, bright dessert. It is the brainchild of Eloise Peret, a young schoolteacher who often invites us for supper so she can exercise her passion for cooking. She served this to us one night along with chocolate mousse, and I liked it so much I've made it regularly since, the ideal dessert to cheer up a winter evening. You can omit the candied zest if you are making this for a casual meal, though its bright sparkle is gorgeous.**

6 to 8 servings

4 pounds (2 kg) oranges

For the orange zest

¾ cup (180 ml) mineral or filtered water

¾ cup (150 g) vanilla sugar

3 tablespoons (45 g) light brown sugar

For the caramel

½ cup (100 g) vanilla sugar

2 tablespoons hot water

1. Using a vegetable peeler, remove the zest from 1 orange. Cut the strips into julienne (very fine strips).

2. Bring 2 cups (500 ml) water to a boil in a medium saucepan over medium-high heat. Add the zest and return to the boil, then drain. Repeat. Spread the zest out on a tea towel to drain.

3. Bring the mineral water and sugar to a boil in a medium saucepan over medium heat, stirring occasionally until the sugar dissolves. Add the orange zest, bring the syrup to a boil, and cook until the zest is translucent through, about 8 minutes. Using tongs or a slotted spoon, transfer the zest to a plate and let cool.

4. Remove the pith from the zested orange and the pith and skin from the remaining oranges. Slice the oranges into ¼-inch (0.6-cm)-thick slices, scraping the juices from the cutting board from time to time into a bowl to use later.

5. Cover the bottom of a 1½-quart (1.5-l) heatproof serving dish or attractive soufflé dish with a layer of oranges, and sprinkle them lightly with brown sugar. Repeat, sprinkling each layer except for the last one with sugar. Sprinkle with ¼ cup (60 ml) of the orange juice, and set aside.

6. Make the caramel: In a small heavy saucepan, mix the sugar with the water and heat over medium heat, swirling the pan, until the sugar dissolves and the mixture caramelizes evenly. Don't be tempted to stir the caramel once it is bubbling; it will gradually turn golden, and you are looking for a deep golden color. The minute it is deep golden, remove it from the heat and pour it evenly over the oranges. Let the oranges sit until the caramel has cooled and hardened, then cover and refrigerate for at least 2 hours.

7. Remove from the refrigerator and serve chilled. Garnish with the zest.

MINERAL WATER VERSUS TAP WATER

I often specify using mineral water in a recipe, because tap water, depending where you live, can taste of too much chlorine, which can adversely affect the flavor of many dishes. If your water system is filtered to remove chlorine and other minerals, you needn't worry about using mineral water. If not, heed my advice. Using pure water will make a huge difference in the flavor of the dish, particularly when the other flavors are subtle.

BASICS AND PRESERVES
Bases et Réserves

In truth, cooking is an art. Isn't it a work
of art that approaches the dignity of nature?
Culinary successes—a soup, a sauce, a
cream—come close to the essence of an egg
yolk or a fruit juice. Therefore, the closer
cooking comes to the freshness of nature,
the more it will be an art.

Henri Pourrat,
French writer (1887–1959)

Chicken Stock

Fond de Volaille

❧ **This recipe gives a light, sweet stock that can be used in any recipe calling for chicken stock. It can also be turned into a marvelous soup. I like to add a couple of coins of ginger, some star anise, a bird's-eye pepper, and simmer these in the stock, then right before serving add a tablespoon or two of freshly squeezed lime juice, some lime zest, and angel hair pasta.**

About 6 cups (1.5 l)

1 medium onion

2 whole cloves

1 medium carrot, peeled, trimmed, and diced

2 leeks, trimmed and diced

1 tablespoon extra virgin olive oil

1 bouquet garni

2 cloves garlic, peeled

10 black peppercorns, preferably Tellicherry or Vietnamese

One 3½- to 4-pound (1.75- to 2-kg) chicken, cut into serving pieces

10 cups (2.5 l) mineral or filtered water

1. Pierce the onion with the cloves, then cut the onion into 8 wedges. Place it, with the carrot, the leeks, and the oil, in a heavy stockpot over medium heat, and cook until the onion is translucent and beginning to brown, about 15 minutes.

2. Add the remaining ingredients, cover with the water and bring to a boil over medium-high heat. Reduce the heat so the liquid is simmering merrily and cook, with the lid of the stockpot slightly ajar, for about 2½ hours.

> **ASTUCE:** If you would like a more intensely flavored stock, you can cook it for an additional hour or, once strained, you can reduce the stock to the intensity you like. Stock freezes very well, and will keep for several months. It keeps just 2 or 3 days in the refrigerator.

A Well-Stocked Pantry

I used to ask myself how my French friends put such marvelous meals on the table seemingly with so little effort. Along with top-notch organizational skills, one of the most important keys to successful entertaining is a well-stocked pantry. This list below guarantees that whether guests are expected or simply drop by, a meal can always be put together.

In the freezer: fish fillets; meat such as steak, lamb chops, or a pork roast; chicken; bread; puff pastry, pâte brisée, and pâte sucrée; herbs; meat, poultry; fish stock; bread crumbs; nuts; specialty flours such as chickpea and corn

In the refrigerator: crème fraîche, milk, and yogurt; butter; eggs; mustard, Gruyère, and Parmigiano-Reggiano; lemons; yeast; slab bacon; nut oils

In the cupboard: pastas; lentils and dried beans; dried wild mushrooms; white and brown rice; olives; cornichons; extra-virgin olive oil; vinegars, including sherry, balsamic, and cider; soy sauce; capers; anchovies; rice flour (for thickening sauces); canned tuna, tomatoes, artichoke hearts, rillettes, and pâte

In the spice cupboard: powdered and candied ginger; ground and stick cinnamon; whole cloves; coriander; white, black, and green peppercorns; saffron; dried oregano; piment d'Espelette; sweet and hot paprika; cumin seeds; Madras curry powder; turmeric; coarse and fine sea salt; vanilla beans

In the baking cupboard: organic flours: all-purpose, whole wheat, whole wheat pastry, and spelt; organic sugars: white, white vanilla, brown, brown vanilla, muscovado (a barely refined deep brown sugar with the taste of molasses); molasses; baking powder; baking soda; chocolate: bittersweet, semisweet, and milk; cocoa powder

In the garden: Herbs: thyme, sage, tarragon, bay leaf (*Laurus nobilis*), sweet cicely, borage, chives, garlic chives, sorrel, basil, lovage, parsley, and chervil; lettuces, including arugula; shallots; garlic

In the root cellar: onions, shallots, garlic, potatoes, squash (in winter)

INDISPENSABLE KITCHEN TOOLS

The typical French home kitchen is surprisingly ill-equipped when it comes to kitchen tools and gadgets. In my friend Edith's kitchen, for instance, which has been the scene of many large family meals, fêtes, mayoral dinners, and other culinary performances, there are, I believe, two sharp knives, one four-burner stove with oven, a large refrigerator (which is usually empty), and a long maple counter no one is allowed to cut on, in favor of the tiny, elephant-shaped cutting board her son Elie made in woodworking class. It is amazing what comes from this kitchen despite the lack of tools.

I admire the economy of the French home chef, but when one is a professional as well as a home chef, tools are essential for efficiency. Here is my personal list of tools I would have a hard time cooking without.

American vegetable peeler (removes thin layer of peel)

Baking sheets with an air-cushion so the cookies don't burn

Boning knife, one 10-inch (25-cm) chef's knife, and one 8-inch (20-cm) chef's knife

Cast-iron skillets

Cheese grater

Culinary torch for caramelizing

Electric ice cream maker

European vegetable peeler (removes thick layer of peel)

Fish scale remover

Food processor with multiple blades

Heavy steel for keeping an edge on my knives

Immersion blender

Kitchen shears

Kitchen twine

Large, medium, and small mixing bowls

Large nonstick baking sheet

Large stockpot

Lemon zester

Melon ball maker

Metal skewers of all sizes

Mixer

Mortar and pestle

Multiple baking dishes

Multiple cake pans

Multiple cotton towels

Multiple measuring cups

Multiple measuring spoons

Multiple plastic scrapers called *cornes*

Multiple rectangular baking pans

Multiple rubber spatulas

Multiple saucepans

Multiple wooden spoons and spatulas

Nonstick skillet

Oyster knife

Oyster mitt, for protecting hand

Pepper grinder

Pliers or strawberry huller for pulling out bones from fish fillets

Poultry shears

Removable-bottom tart tins

Rubber gloves

Scale

Several different heavy-bottomed skillets

Small dishes for holding prepared ingredients (minced garlic or shallots, capers, spices, etc.)

Souffle mold

Springform cake pan

Stainless steel knives, including a fish fillet knife and a tiny-bladed paring knife

Pâte Brisée

❧ *Pâte brisée* is the classic French pastry, used for both sweet and savory dishes such as tarts and quiches. The classic recipe calls for half the weight of butter to flour. When I ran a small *salon de thé* in Paris, savory tarts were my specialty and I dutifully used the classic recipe for my pastry. But it was so unpredictable, turning out short and luscious one day, dry as cardboard the next. Needing a reliable and flexible pastry, I played around with the formula and this is the result. Now the pastry is perfect every time. It is best if made in a food processor.

Pastry for one 10½-inch (26.5-cm) tart

1½ cups (210 g) unbleached all-purpose flour

¼ teaspoon fine sea salt

12 tablespoons (1½ sticks; 180 g) chilled unsalted butter, cut into 12 pieces

⅓ to ½ cup (80 to 125 ml) ice water

1. Place the flour and salt in a food processor and pulse once to mix. Add the butter and pulse 10 to 15 times, until the mixture resembles coarse meal. Add ⅓ cup (80 ml) ice water and pulse just until the pastry begins to hold together, no more than 9 or 10 times. Add some or all of the remaining water if the pastry seems dry.

2. Transfer the pastry to your work surface and form it into a flat disk. Let it rest on the work surface in cool room temperature, covered with an upside-down bowl, for at least 1 hour, and up to 3 hours, so the gluten in the flour relaxes.

3. Roll out the pastry on a lightly floured surface until it is about ⅛ inch (0.3 cm) thick. Line a tart pan. Refrigerate the pastry for at least 1 hour or freeze it for at least 20 minutes.

4. Preheat the oven to 425°F (220°C).

5. Prick the pastry several times with the tines of a fork or a sharp knife. (This isn't possible to do if the pastry is frozen—do not be concerned.) Line the pastry with aluminum foil and fill the foil with an even layer of pastry weights. Place the baking pan on a baking sheet, and bake in the center of the oven until the edges of the pastry are golden, about 15 minutes. Remove the pastry

from the oven, remove the foil and weights from the pastry, and return to the oven to continue baking until the bottom is pale golden, about 8 minutes. (Check the pastry once while it is baking for the second time. Should it puff up in the center, simply pierce the bubble with a sharp knife in one or two places.)

ASTUCES: Chill the butter and water, or use ice water. Cold ingredients make for much more tender pastry. Making it in a food processor helps the ingredients stay cool. ❖ It is impossible to give an exact amount of how much water to add to pastry dough. If it is a dry day, you will probably add the maximum; on a humid day, much less will be necessary. Add just enough water so the pastry is pliable and soft. ❖ Another secret to tender pastry is to let it rest at room temperature for at least 1 and up to 3 hours before you roll it out, to allow the gluten to relax. Gluten is like microscopic elastic bands, which develop in flour as it is worked. Right after you've made pastry, the gluten is excited and ready to snap back if you roll it out. An hour later, it has calmed down. Three hours later, it has gone to sleep. If instead you chill the pastry and then try to roll it out, it will crumble and break apart. This is why most people are convinced that they can't make pastry. ❖ Once the baking pan is lined with pastry, then it can be chilled, and it will bake up flakier. ❖ Before rolling out the pastry, lightly but thoroughly flour your work surface and the top of the dough. As you roll, don't press down but "urge" the pastry outward. Avoid rolling over the edges, or you'll flatten them out, but move the rolling pin just up to them.

Pâte Sablée

❧ This pastry is the basis for many of the gorgeous, sparkling fruit tarts that sit so proudly in French pâtisserie windows, or emerge from a home kitchen at the end of a delicious meal. Simple, tender, and sweet, it is easy to work with, requires no rolling, and highlights the flavor of any fruit that goes into it. This pastry is the basis of tarts made with uncooked fruit.

Pastry for one 10½- to 11-inch (26.5- to 27.5-cm) tart

1¾ cups (245 g) all-purpose flour

½ heaping teaspoon fine sea salt

½ cup (100 g) vanilla sugar

8 tablespoons (1 stick; 120 g) unsalted butter, cut into small pieces, at cool room temperature

4 large egg yolks

> **ASTUCE:** If you have excess pastry, roll it into a 1½-inch (3.75-cm)-diameter log, wrap it in aluminum foil, and refrigerate until firm, then cut it into rounds to bake as cookies at 350°F (180°C) until the cookies are firm and golden, 10 to 12 minutes.

1. Place the flour, salt, and sugar in a food processor and pulse just to mix. Add the butter and process until the mixture resembles coarse meal. Add the egg yolks and pulse just until the pastry holds together in clumps.

2. Turn the pastry out onto a work surface. To fully blend the ingredients, using the heel of your hand, press the pastry away from you, applying pressure against the work surface as you do so, then scrape it back together, and continue to work it this way until you can gather the pastry into a ball. If the dough is very sticky, refrigerate it for about 30 minutes to allow it firm up. If it is not too sticky, press it evenly into a 10½-inch (26.5-cm) tart pan with a removable bottom and trim off any excess. (Do not be concerned if the pastry looks lumpy—imperfections will disappear during baking.)

3. To prebake the pastry, preheat the oven to 400°F (200°C).

4. Line the pastry with aluminum foil and fill with pastry weights or beans. Bake in the center of the oven until the edges of the pastry are golden, about 12 minutes. Remove the aluminum foil and weights, and using the tip of a knife pierce the bottom of the pastry several times to allow the steam to escape so that it doesn't bubble. Continue baking until the pastry is golden and baked through, about 8 minutes. Remove and let cool.

To Prick or Not to Prick

Pricking the pastry once it has been rolled out and fitted into the pan prevents air pockets from forming between it and the pan, making it bubble up. If it were left to bake with a big bubble in it, it would be impossible to fill.

When I prebake pastry, I prick it before I lay the aluminum foil in it and fill it with pastry weights. I often prick it again after I've removed the foil and weights, before returning it to the oven. Then I check it once more and if I see it has puffed up, I simply jab it with a sharp knife blade two or three times where it is puffing up. It will heave a sigh and fall right back down where it should be.

Making Pastry by Hand

If you want to make pastry by hand, simply place the flour in a mound on a work surface and mix in the salt with your fingers. Place the pieces of butter atop the flour and quickly work it into the flour with your fingertips until the mixture resembles coarse meal. Drizzle ⅓ cup (80 ml) of the water over the flour and butter mixture, then mix it in by pulling up and through it with your fingers, until it is blended. Remember to handle the ingredients very gently as you work the water into the flour and butter. Try to form the pastry into a ball—if it doesn't hold together, work in enough remaining water until it does hold together. Transfer the pastry to a work surface, form it into a flat disk, cover, and let stand for at least 1 hour.

Pâte Sucrée

❧ This easy pastry is technically a sweet pâte brisée, since it is a pâte brisée but with less butter and a bit of sugar (*sucre*) added. I call it pâte sucrée (sweet pastry) to make things simple. Use it for tarts that call for a slightly sweet pastry that is a bit more sturdy and less "short" than pâte brisée.

Pastry for one 10½-inch (26.5-cm) tart

1½ cups (210 g) all-purpose flour

1 tablespoon sugar

Pinch fine sea salt

8 tablespoons (1 stick; 120 g) chilled unsalted butter, cut in tablespoon-sized pieces

⅓ to ½ cup (80 to 125 ml) ice water

1. Place the flour, sugar, and salt in a food processor and pulse once or twice to mix. Add the butter and process until the mixture resembles coarse sand.

2. With the food processor running, add ⅓ cup (80 ml) of the water, then pulse until the pastry begins to clump together. Pinch the pastry to see if it holds together—if it is still a bit crumbly, add some or all of the remaining water.

3. Transfer the pastry to a work surface, form it into a flat disk, cover, and let stand for at least 1 hour, and up to 3 hours.

ASTUCES: It is next to impossible to determine exactly how much cold water to use in pastry. I always have ½ cup (125 ml) available, but I more often than not use closer to ⅓ cup (80 ml); it all depends on the weather. ❧ Let the pastry rest for at least 1 hour or up to 3 hours at room temperature. Make it the day before you plan to use it, if you like. Wrap it well and refrigerate it, then remove it from the refrigerator about 2 hours before you plan to use it so it is easy to work.

Herb Broth
Bouillon d'Aromates

❧ **I use this herb broth (in favor of any other sort of broth), for it is light and aromatic, and it lends these same characteristics to soups and sauces.**

About 6 cups (1.5 l)

20 sprigs fresh thyme or lemon thyme

One 2-inch (5-cm) sprig fresh rosemary

1 sprig fresh sage (or about 10 leaves)

4 fresh bay leaves from the *Laurus nobilis*, or dried imported bay leaves

4 fresh lovage leaves or leaves from 2 celery stalks

4 garlic cloves, green germ removed if necessary

½ teaspoon fine sea salt

2 quarts (2 l) water

1. Place the herbs, garlic, salt, and water in a large heavy saucepan over medium-high heat, cover, and bring to a boil. Reduce the heat and simmer merrily for 15 minutes.

2. Strain the broth and use immediately.

> **ASTUCE:** I do not advise making the broth ahead of time, for its flavor is best when freshly made.

Court Bouillon

✦ Court bouillon is the perfect poaching liquid for any kind of fish, for its lightly acidic nature balances the delicacy of most fish. You can vary the herbs and spices depending on the flavor you are trying to achieve, but do keep the balance of acid in the liquid.

This amount of court bouillon is enough for poaching approximately 2 pounds (1 kg) of fish.

About 7 cups (1.75 l)

1 bottle (750 ml) dry white wine, such as Sancerre or Vouvray

¼ cup (60 ml) white wine vinegar

4 cups (1 l) water

1 small onion, cut into thin rings

10 black peppercorns, preferably Tellicherry or Vietnamese

2 whole cloves

3 bay leaves

Pinch fine sea salt

Three 3 × ¼-inch (7.5 × 0.6-cm) strips lemon zest

10 sprigs flat-leaf parsley

Place all the ingredients in a large saucepan or skillet with sides at least 3 inches (7.5 cm) high. Bring to a boil over medium-high heat, then cover, reduce the heat so the liquid is simmering, and simmer for 20 minutes. The court bouillon is ready to use.

Crème Fraîche

⚜ Ethereal crème fraîche is one of the cornerstones of French cooking. It is used as a seasoning, as a basis for sauces, as a condiment, or as a cloud atop fresh berries. Nothing more than top cream, when first brought to market crème fraîche pours like thick milk. As one or two days pass, it thickens and its flavor becomes even more voluptuous.

Crème fraîche is now easy to find in North America, as is double cream, which is a fine substitute. If you cannot find it, though, you can make a reasonable facsimile with the following recipe.

2 cups (500 ml)

2 cups (500 ml) heavy cream, preferably not ultra-pasteurized

3 tablespoons cultured buttermilk

1. Whisk the cream and buttermilk together in a medium bowl. Cover with a cotton tea towel and let stand in a warm spot (on top of the refrigerator or furnace) until the cream thickens, 8 to 12 hours, depending on the temperature.

2. Cover the crème fraîche and refrigerate it for several hours to further thicken it. It will keep in the refrigerator, tightly covered, for up to 1 week.

ASTUCE: Ultra-pasteurized dairy products have had the living daylights heated out of them to extend their shelf life. Such high heat destroys their gustatory quality. If you can avoid these products, your dishes will taste better.

Fromage Blanc

❧ Fromage blanc is similar to cottage cheese, although it isn't curdled until firm. It is fresh cow's milk cheese with some of the whey still in it, so it is loose. It is widely used in French cooking in everything from tarts to savory preparations, but I like it best as a dessert, doused with heavy cream and sugar or honey.

About 1½ cups (750 ml)

1 quart (1 l) fresh whole milk, unpasteurized if possible

4 drops rennet, available at a pharmacy, or on the Internet

1. In a medium saucepan, heat the milk to about 95°F (35°C). Whisk in the rennet, remove from the heat, and let stand at cool room temperature (68°F; 20°C) until the milk has curdled, about 12 hours.

2. Line a sieve with cheesecloth. Pour the curdled milk into the sieve and let it drain for about 2 hours, until the cheese has a texture similar to large-curd cottage cheese. There will still be quite a bit of liquid left with the cheese. The fromage blanc is fragile; it will keep 24 to 48 hours, refrigerated.

ASTUCES: The whey, or liquid that remains after draining the fromage blanc, can be used in place of water in a bread recipe. ❧ Use pureed large-curd cottage cheese as a substitute for fromage blanc.

Basic Vinaigrette
Vinaigrette de Base

❧ **What is it that makes French green salads, those simple mounds of green lettuce leaves served after a meal, so unique? Great lettuce and a simple vinaigrette. Toss your greens slowly and thoroughly, so they are evenly coated with a sheen of vinaigrette. By doing this you will *fatiguée,* or "tire" the salad so it is ready to be eaten!**

About ⅓ cup (80 ml); enough for about 14 cups (350 g) greens

2 teaspoons sherry vinegar

1 teaspoon Dijon mustard

Fine sea salt and freshly ground black pepper

1 shallot, minced

¼ cup (60 ml) extra virgin olive oil

1. Whisk together the vinegar, mustard, salt and pepper to taste, and the shallot in a large salad bowl. Slowly whisk in the oil until the mixture is emulsified. Use the dressing immediately, or refrigerate.

2. To make a salad, place the vinaigrette in a large bowl. Add the salad ingredients and toss well, until all the salad ingredients are throughly coated with vinaigrette. Serve immediately.

ASTUCES: This basic vinaigrette can be infinitely modified by adding herbs, varying the amount of mustard, and/or using flavored vinegars and oils. This one is light on the vinegar. If you prefer more, increase the amount by 1 teaspoon, but no more. Also, use just enough vinaigrette to coat the leaves and not leave them dripping—about 5 tablespoons (40 ml) vinaigrette per 8 cups salad. ✤ Double the ingredients so you have some extra vinaigrette on hand. To do this, omit the shallots and add them to the salad just before tossing. Refrigerate the vinaigrette, but remove it at least 15 minutes before using it, then shake the jar before tossing it with the salad. Vinaigrette also goes well on steamed vegetables, grilled fish, meat, or bread.

Balsamic Vinaigrette
Vinaigrette Balsamique

❧ **A classic vinaigrette with a twist—sweet balsamic vinegar.**

About ⅓ cup (80 ml); enough for about 14 cups (350 g) greens

1 tablespoon balsamic vinegar

Fine sea salt

1 shallot, sliced paper-thin

¼ cup (60 ml) extra virgin olive oil

Freshly ground black pepper

Whisk the vinegar, a large pinch of salt, and shallot together in a small bowl. Slowly whisk in the oil until the mixture is emulsified. Taste for seasoning. Add freshly ground black pepper to taste.

ASTUCES: I prefer gutsy lettuces that can stand up to this vinaigrette. I go out to my garden and pick a handful of arugula, another of curly endive, two or three sorrel leaves, some new, shiny Swiss chard leaves, fennel fronds, two or three sage leaves, and some sweet cicely, but any combination will do. I wash, dry, and tear them into tiny, bite-sized pieces. To serve this as a first course, I top the dressed salad with shavings of Parmigiano-Reggiano. As a palate cleanser after the meal, serve as is. ❧ Refrigerate any leftover vinaigrette and use it within a day or two, while the shallot is still fresh. ❧ For a special occasion, I part with some of my cache of five-year-old balsamic vinegar, called *condimento,* from the Leonardi Acetaia (vinegar factory) outside of Modena in Emilia-Romagna, which is available from www.chefshop.com. In any case, use the best-quality balsamic vinegar you can afford.

SALAD SEASONING

An axiom that is as French as the *Marseillaise:*

It takes four men to season a salad: a generous man for the oil, a miser for the vinegar, a wise man for the salt, and a crazy man for the pepper.

Vanilla Sugar
Sucre Vanillé

❧ Vanilla sugar is essential to French home-baked goods. Although I can buy it in pretty little packets at the supermarket, the flavor isn't as fresh as when it is home-made.

When I have a vanilla bean left over from making custard sauce or vanilla sugar syrup, I rinse it, let it dry thoroughly, and then pop it in my sugar jar. I often have as many as a dozen vanilla beans in the jar. I check through the beans, and when they have turned pale brown and brittle after several months, discard them.

8 cups (1 kg 600 g)

8 cups (3½ pounds; 1 kg 600 g) sugar

2 fresh vanilla beans or 4 used vanilla beans (see Astuces)

1. Pour the sugar into an airtight container, and push the vanilla beans down into it. Cover and let ripen for at least 1 week.

2. Replenish the sugar as you use it—pour out the sugar that is already flavored, add new sugar to the container, and top it with the flavored sugar. Replace the vanilla beans every 2 months or so.

ASTUCES: Add vanilla beans to your brown sugar too. ❖ Keep some plain sugar on hand for making jellies and jams and savory dishes.

Four Spices
Quatre-Épices

❧ *Quatre-épices* — four spices — is a foundation of the French spice repertoire, used most frequently to flavor terrines, pâtés, and other pork dishes. I keep some on hand to sprinkle on roasts or grilled pork, poultry, or fish.

4 teaspoons

1 teaspoon freshly ground cinnamon

1 teaspoon freshly ground cloves

1 teaspoon freshly ground allspice

1 teaspoon freshly grated nutmeg

Throughly blend all the spices together in a small bowl, and transfer to an airtight container. Store in a cool, dark place.

ASTUCE: Ground spices rapidly lose their freshness unless they are kept in an airtight container in a cool, dark place. Then they will stay fresh for up to 3 months. If you aren't going to use up your *quatre-épices* quickly, store it in the freezer, where it will keep indefinitely. To test for freshness, open the jar and inhale — if the spices don't smell fresh, they won't taste fresh.

Herbes de Provence

❧ *Herbes de Provence* is a mixture of dried herbs that reflects the rocky, dry land-scape of the gorgeous region in southern France east of the Rhone River, extending all the way to the Mediterranean. On a hot day there you can smell the mixture in the air, for the wind often blows over the rocks and through the vineyards where these herbs grow, rattling them just slightly so they give off their perfume.

This is the only dried herb mixture I use, because I prefer fresh herbs for most of my cooking. But here, the herbs emit a sweet aroma and flavor. They are ideal for strewing over any food destined for the grill or the oven.

About ⅓ cup (80 ml)

1 tablespoon dried thyme

1½ tablespoons dried marjoram or oregano

2 tablespoons dried rosemary

1 tablespoon dried savory

Blend the herbs in a small bowl, then place them in an airtight container. Store them in a cool, dark place, and the herbs will stay fresh for about 6 months. Check before using them, however, to be sure they still offer all of their flavor. To use them, measure out what you need and coarsely grind them in a spice grinder or mortar and pestle.

ASTUCES: There are as many different blends of herbes de Provence as there are Provençal cooks. Some include lavender, a contemporary affectation I think, for lavender is considered a medicinal herb noted for its calming and antiseptic properties, rather than an edible one. Lavender can overpower the other herbs as well. ❧ Use very fresh dried herbs here, and as with any herb or spice, keep the mix in an airtight jar in a dark spot. I keep most of my herbs and spices in a drawer, but freeze those I use infrequently.

Marinated Anchovies

Anchois Marinés

⚜ **If you can get fresh anchovies, marinate them to use in any recipe that calls for anchovies.**

40 anchovy fillets

20 fresh anchovies

⅓ cup (80 ml) freshly squeezed lemon juice

1. To clean the anchovies, simply cut through the backbone behind the head, and when you pull off the head, the viscera will come with it. Anchovies are very fragile and won't always withstand rinsing, so you may need to carefully wipe them clean with a damp paper towel instead. Remove the backbone by slipping a knife blade under the end nearest the head and gently pulling it from the fillets; this will leave the fillets attached at the tail end, which is what you want.

2. Lay the anchovies in a single layer in a flat nonreactive dish. Cover them with the lemon juice and refrigerate until they are opaque through, 12 to 14 hours, depending on the size of the anchovies.

3. Remove the anchovies from the lemon juice and pat them dry. They can be used immediately. Or, to keep the anchovies, place them in a wide-mouth jar or other container, cover them with olive oil, and seal tightly. They will keep well for a week or two, refrigerated.

> **ASTUCE:** When buying anchovies, make sure they are freshly caught and very firm. When prepared this way, the anchovies are cooked by the acid in the lemon juice. They are unbelievably fresh and delicate tasting, and you may end up using more than are called for in a recipe, for they aren't as intensely salty, nor is their flavor as intensely concentrated as commercially preserved anchovies.

Cumin Salt
Sel au Cumin

❖ I keep various seasoning mixtures such as this salt on hand to dress up certain dishes. I sprinkle a pinch over sliced cucumbers dressed with Lemon Oil (page 272), on avocados drizzled with pistachio oil, on fish fillets, or on a potato gratin straight from the oven.

About 3 tablespoons

2 tablespoons fragrant cumin seeds

4 teaspoons fleur de sel

1. Place the cumin seeds in a small heavy skillet over low heat and toast them, stirring, until they turn golden and are fragrant, 3 to 4 minutes. Transfer them to a mortar or a spice or coffee grinder, add the salt, and grind together until uniformly but coarsely ground. The salt should be very "sprinkable."

2. Place the mixture in an airtight jar, and keep in a cool, dark place.

> **ASTUCES:** I keep small quantities of this mixture in an airtight jar in my spice drawer because it doesn't last forever. ❖ I prefer to grind the cumin and salt in a mortar and pestle, resulting in a coarse blend that retains its delicate crunch. If you don't have a mortar and pestle, do this in a spice grinder.

Lemon Oil

L'Huile Citronée

⚜ On a visit to the Abruzzo region in southern Italy while researching a book, I heard the story of how the olive presses were cleaned at the end of the pressing season by squeezing kilos of lemons in them. As the lemon juice flowed through, it blended with the remaining olive oil in the press, emerging as an elixir that found its way to the table.

I pursued this story, which ultimately was not true, but the idea of lemon-flavored olive oil stayed with me, and I decided to make my own, using lemon zest, the bright yellow part of the peel that is full of flavorful oil.

This scented oil is as good on a salad as it is on toasted bread rubbed with garlic, or on seafood, meat, or vegetables that have been steamed, roasted, or grilled. I often blend some into fresh goat or feta cheese.

1 quart (1 l)

Minced zest of 4 lemons

4 cups (1 l) extra virgin olive oil

1. Place the zest and oil in a medium heavy-bottomed saucepan and heat very slowly over low heat until the oil is hot to the touch but nowhere near smoking point. Remove from the heat and let steep for 48 hours.

2. Strain the oil and transfer it to an airtight container. The oil will keep for 1 month at room temperature, and for several months in the refrigerator. Remove the oil from the refrigerator at least 1 hour before you plan to use it.

ASTUCE: Use organic lemons or those that have not been treated with a fungicide wax after harvest. Wash them in hot water and rub them dry.

Cilantro Oil
L'Huile de Coriandre

✤ Cilantro, *coriandre*, has become a common herb in France. I have learned to use it the way the French do—in an oil like this, on fish fillets cooked in parchment, tucked under the skin of a chicken for roasting—rather than in its raw state.

The intense color and soft flavor of this oil make it versatile, ideal for adding to everything from crème fraîche to a salad.

About 1 cup (250 ml)

4 cups (about 40 g) gently packed cilantro leaves

1 cup (250 ml) extra virgin olive oil

1. Prepare a bowl of ice water. Bring a large pot of lightly salted water to a boil. Add the cilantro to the boiling water and stir gently, then, the minute the water returns to the boil, transfer the cilantro to the ice water to cool; the cilantro should remain in the boiling water for approximately 30 seconds. As soon as the cilantro leaves are chilled, drain and transfer them to a wire cooling rack covered with a cotton towel. Let them drain and dry slightly, then pat them dry.

2. Place the leaves in a food processor, add ¼ cup (60 ml) of the olive oil, and process to make a thick paste. With the processor running, add the remaining ¾ cup (190 ml) oil. Transfer the oil to a container and refrigerate, tightly covered, if not using immediately. The oil can be refrigerated for a day or two.

ASTUCES: Blanching herbs softens them and allows their flavor and color to blend more easily with oil. ✤ This oil maintains its flavor for about 48 hours in the refrigerator, so waste no time using it. It will thicken on chilling, so remove it about 30 minutes before you plan to use it.

Onion Marmalade

Marmelade aux Oignons

⚜ Onion marmalade is a classic French condiment, used with everything from the Breton pork stew *kig ha farz* to pâtés and roasted pork. Here, I've added my own touch in the form of grenadine, which adds soft sweetness and color. For a simple lunch, spread some on a piece of fresh bread to accompany a green salad.

Any good-quality yellow onion makes a fine marmalade. It keeps for several weeks in the refrigerator. Heat it slightly before you use it, to melt the butter.

About 1 cup (250 g)

2 tablespoons (30 g) unsalted butter

2 pounds (1 kg) onions, very thinly sliced

Generous pinch of fine sea salt

1 tablespoon grenadine

2 tablespoons sherry wine vinegar

1. Melt the butter in a large heavy-bottomed saucepan over medium heat. Add the onions and stir until they are coated with butter. Season with the salt and stir, cover, and cook until the onions begin to sizzle and slightly stick to the pan. Add 3 tablespoons (45 ml) water, stir, cover and continue cooking until the onions are almost thoroughly tender and "melted," about 1 hour and 15 minutes.

2. Mix together the grenadine and vinegar and add to the onions. Stir so the liquid is thoroughly mixed into the onions and cook, stirring almost constantly, until the onions are completely caramelized, about an additional 10 minutes. Remove from the heat and transfer the onions to a serving bowl so they don't continue to caramelize and burn in the heat of the pan. Serve the onions warm or at room temperature. Once cooled, the onions can be refrigerated, tightly covered. They will keep well for 1 month.

ASTUCES: Three things affect the pungency of onions: high growing temperatures, dry soil, and length of storage. Onions are best when used within 3 months after being harvested, though they keep well for about 6 months in a cool spot. ⚜ Onions are high in sugar and can easily burn, so do watch them carefully as they cook.

Eggplant Caviar
Caviar d'Aubergines

A staple in the French culinary repertoire, eggplant caviar was one of the first things I made as a cooking apprentice in Paris at La Varenne Ecole de Cuisine. It remains one of my favorite ways to prepare eggplant, although my recipe is more rustic and flavorful than the typical French version. The extra flavor comes from grilling eggplant right over a flame, or roasting it in the oven or under the broiler, rather than steaming it, as many French cooks do. And I blend the eggplant with the other ingredients in a mortar and pestle rather than in a food processor, because I prefer the resulting texture.

Eggplant caviar can be used in dozens of ways. Spread it on toast, use it as a dip with breadsticks, layer it with thinly sliced peeled, fresh tomatoes and goat cheese for an appetizer, or use it for Eggplant Caviar and Red Pepper Toasts (page 25).

Scant 1½ cups (375 ml)

2 medium eggplant (about 11 ounces; 330 g each)

2 garlic cloves, green germ removed if necessary

Cumin Salt (page 271) to taste

2 teaspoons freshly squeezed lemon juice

Generous 1 tablespoon tahini (sesame paste)

1 tablespoon extra virgin olive oil

Fresh basil or cilantro leaves

1. Prick the eggplant all over with a skewer or fork so they won't explode during cooking, and cook by whichever method suits you. To broil the eggplant, set them about 3 inches (7.5 cm) from the heat source, or roast them in the oven at about 450°F (230°C) until they are tender through (about 40 minutes). To grill the eggplant, set them over a gas flame or on a grill and turn them frequently until the skin is charred and cracked and the eggplant are cooked through, about 20 minutes. Once the eggplant are cooked, let them sit until they are cool enough to handle before removing the skin.

2. While the eggplant are cooking, place the garlic and cumin salt in a large mortar or in a bowl. Using a pestle or a wooden spoon, mash the garlic and salt together to a coarse puree.

3. When the eggplant are cool enough to handle, halve them lengthwise and scrape the flesh into the mortar or the bowl. Mash it into the garlic until it is a coarse puree. Add the lemon juice and tahini and mix until they are thoroughly combined. Stir in the oil and taste for seasoning. Let the eggplant sit for at least 30 minutes, covered, before serving so the flavors have a chance to mellow.

4. Transfer to a serving bowl and garnish with basil leaves just before serving.

Steamed Couscous

Couscous à la Vapeur

❧ Couscous came to France from North Africa, underlying the axiom that when you go out to conquer the world, the world comes back to become part of you!

My Algerian friend Dalila Boufercha is a passionate cook and has held my hand through numerous makings of couscous. "Somehow, Suzanne," she says, "when you and I make couscous together, it tastes the way my grandmother's couscous tasted. I can't make it that good myself."

Couscous isn't difficult to make but it takes time and attention. If you follow this recipe carefully, it will be your road map to success. Remember, though, that it takes a few times to get the couscous *coup de main,* or knack. When you've got it, you will know immediately, for the couscous threatens to float off the plate!

8 to 10 servings

6 cups (2 pounds; 1 kg) fine couscous

1 tablespoon extra virgin olive oil

2 teaspoons fine sea salt

9 tablespoons (135 g) unsalted butter

1. Pour the couscous into a large shallow bowl or onto a work surface. Drizzle the olive oil over the couscous, and thoroughly blend the oil into the grain with your fingers and between your palms, gently rubbing and working until the oil is completely blended into the couscous.

2. Place 1¼ cups (310 ml) warm water in a small bowl, add the salt, and stir until it is dissolved. Sprinkle the salted water over the couscous 2 to 3 tablespoons at a time, then work the water into the couscous with your fingers and palms as you did with the oil, but even more gently, until the water disappears into and slightly softens the grain. Let the couscous sit for 10 minutes.

3. Prepare a couscous or other two-part steamer by wrapping a wet cotton tea towel around the seam where the top and the bottom come together, to prevent the steam from escaping. Bring the water in the bottom to a rolling boil, and place the couscous in the top of the steamer. Steam, uncovered, for 30 minutes.

4. Turn the couscous out into a large shallow bowl or onto a work surface and, using a wooden spoon, a plastic dough scraper, or your fingers (the couscous is very hot, so be careful), gently break up any clumps in the couscous, without mashing it. If you do not plan to serve the couscous soon, you may let it sit at this point for several hours before proceeding. Otherwise, spread out the couscous slightly, and sprinkle over it an additional 1½ cups (375 ml) hot water, 2 to 3 tablespoons at a time. Work it in using a wooden spoon and your fingers by lifting up the couscous and letting it fall through your fingers or from the bowl of the spoon. As soon as the couscous is cool enough for you to handle, work with only your fingers, handling the couscous very gently, until all the water is absorbed. The couscous should have expanded and feel slightly tender, though it will still be quite firm. Let it rest for 10 minutes.

5. Check the cloth tied around the steamer—if it needs moistening, do so. Return the couscous to the top of the steamer, bring the water in the steamer to a boil over medium-high heat, and steam the couscous, uncovered, for 30 minutes.

6. Turn out the couscous into a shallow bowl or onto a work surface and add 1 cup (250 ml) hot water, 2 to 3 tablespoons at a time, working it as before. Let the couscous sit for 10 minutes.

7. Return the couscous to the steamer to steam until it is fluffy and tender, about 15 minutes. Turn out the couscous into a large shallow bowl or onto a work surface. Cut the butter into tablespoon-sized pieces atop the couscous. Gently work the butter into the couscous with your fingers and a wooden spoon, breaking up any lumps and urging the butter into the grain the same way you urged the oil and the water into it. When all the butter has been absorbed, transfer the couscous to a warmed shallow bowl and serve. If you have prepared the Soup for Couscous (page 46), transfer the meat and vegetables, with the broth, to a large warmed serving bowl. To serve, place couscous on a warmed plate or in a shallow soup bowl, and top it with meat, vegetables, and broth.

Harissa

✤ Harissa is a pepper sauce used in North African cuisine that is widely available commercially. It's good on its own, but to make it truly lively and vibrant I doctor it up, a trick I learned from Dalila, who does this for the harissa she serves with couscous (see page 278). It makes a world of difference to the flavor.

Harissa is traditionally served alongside couscous, but once you've tasted it, you'll think of dozens of other ways to use it!

1⅓ cups (330 ml)

2 teaspoons cumin seeds

10 garlic cloves, green germ removed if necessary

Pinch fine sea salt

¾ cup (185 ml) top-quality prepared harissa

½ cup (125 ml) extra virgin olive oil

1. Toast the cumin seeds in a small, heavy skillet over medium heat, shaking the pan gently until they begin to give off a toasty aroma, 2 to 3 minutes. Transfer the seeds to a mortar and pestle or spice grinder and roughly crush or grind them.

2. Add the garlic cloves and salt to the mortar and crush them to a rough paste. Add the harissa, stir, then slowly add the olive oil, stirring to make a thick sauce. Taste for seasoning, and serve.

ASTUCE: This harissa will keep, tightly covered, for several weeks in the refrigerator. It makes a wonderful accompaniment to steamed or roasted vegetables, or grilled meats or poultry.

Spicy Paste from Ile de la Réunion
Pâte Épicée de l'Ile de la Réunion

❧ Ile de la Réunion is a small island in the Indian Ocean that remains under French rule. Everything, from the language to the postal system, is the same as in France.

This recipe comes from our neighbor's daughter, Claire Mutrelle, who lives on Ile de la Réunion. Every time she comes home she brings a jar of this spicy paste, for she claims she can no longer live without it! She gave me a jar of it along with the recipe, and since then I've made it part of my repertoire too. It's fabulous on roast meats and poultry, alongside Chicken with Turmeric and Coconut Milk (page 122), or anywhere you want a bit of spice. Just opening the jar is like taking a little breather on an exotic isle.

1¾ cups (435 ml)

5 ounces (150 g) firm fresh ginger, peeled and cut into chunks

5 ounces (150 g) garlic cloves (about 64), green germ removed if necessary

5 ounces (150 g) hot peppers (about 3), trimmed, seeds and pith removed as desired, and coarsely chopped

1 lime, coarsely chopped (including the peel), seeds removed

1 teaspoon coarse sea salt

3 tablespoons mild vegetable oil, such as grapeseed or sunflower

1. Place all the ingredients except the oil in a food processor and process to a fine paste, which may take 5 minutes. The lime may tend to stay in larger pieces, which is fine.

2. With the processor running, add the oil until well blended. Use the paste immediately or store it in an airtight container in the refrigerator, where it will keep for several months. Check it from time to time, and add oil if necessary to keep it moist.

ASTUCES: Contrary to popular belief, the heat of a pepper doesn't all rest in its seeds—most of it is in what I call the pith, the pale, spongy membranes or ribs. You have to be daring to find out how hot a pepper is, for the only way to know is by tasting. Then you can make adjustments. I use long, snaky, spicy peppers that resemble paprika peppers (*Capsicum frutescens*), and I always taste them before I make this, because each pepper has a unique heat content. ❧ This paste will keep almost indefinitely in an airtight container in the refrigerator. If it gets a bit dry, simply stir in some oil to moisten it.

Bolognaise Sauce à la Francaise

Sauce Bolognaise

⚜ *Bolognaise* **is one of the basic preparations budding French home cooks learn first. With it, the possibilities are endless. Try it in Many-Layered Eggplant (page 157), or serve it over sautéed squash, pasta, or even slices of bread.**

2 quarts (2 l)

2 pounds (1 kg) tomatoes, cored and peeled (or the same weight of canned peeled tomatoes, undrained)

Generous 1 tablespoon extra virgin olive oil

1 medium onion, cut as you like

3 shallots, thinly sliced

1 medium carrot, trimmed and cut as you like

4 ounces (120 g) green beans, trimmed and cut as you like

Fine sea salt and freshly ground black pepper

1 pound (500 g) ground pork or beef

2 cups (500 ml) tomato puree

3 bay leaves

A handful of fresh thyme sprigs

3 garlic cloves, green germ removed if necessary, minced

1. Cut the tomatoes horizontally in half, and squeeze the seeds from just half of them. Coarsely chop the tomatoes.

2. Place the oil, onion, and shallots in a large heavy-bottomed saucepan over medium heat and cook, stirring occasionally, until the onion begins to turn translucent, about 5 minutes. Add the carrot and beans and cook, stirring occasionally, until they are softened, about 5 minutes. Season lightly with salt and pepper.

3. Add the ground meat, stir, and cook, stirring occasionally, just until the meat is beginning to cook through but isn't brown, 4 to 5 minutes. Add the tomato puree and tomatoes, stir, and add the bay leaves and thyme. Increase the heat and bring the sauce to a boil. Add the garlic, then reduce the heat so the sauce is simmering and cook until it is nicely thickened but still bright red, 45 to 55 minutes; the sauce shouldn't be dry. Remove from the heat and correct the seasoning.

> **ASTUCES:** Note that just half of the tomato seeds are removed; the remaining seeds carry flavor and a pleasant acidity, which are essential to the sauce. ⚜ This amount of sauce will dress about 2 pounds (1 kg) cooked pasta.

Quince Paste

Pâte de Coing

⚜ The quince is an old-fashioned fruit of my grandmother and mother's generations. Even in France, where it is popular, it is sometimes very hard to find because there is no commercial cultivation. What quinces do appear at the market are the knobby, pistachio green to bright yellow fruits of the home garden. When they are in good supply, I buy bags full and store them in baskets in the kitchen and the entry way, and their flowery perfume fills the house.

I make quince jelly; add quince to applesauce, which turns it the color of a hot sunset; and make this quince paste, which is not really a paste at all, for it isn't spreadable. Instead, it is a candy with a texture like very thick gelatin, and a flavor that is very alluring, very sweet and tart. In France, it is part of the of *les Treize Desserts*, or the Thirteen Desserts of Christmas, served after a meal along with nuts, dried fruit, fresh oranges, and special breads.

About 72 pieces

2 pounds (1 kg) quinces

4 cups plus 4 tablespoons (850 g) vanilla sugar

The zest of 1 lemon, minced

1. Scrub the quinces with a damp towel to remove all the fuzz from the skin. Cut them into quarters and remove the core and any hard pith, then cut each quarter lengthwise in half. Leave the skins on the quinces—it adds flavor and pectin.

2. Bring about 4 cups (1 l) water to a boil in the bottom half of a steamer. Place the quinces in the top half, cover, and steam the quinces until they are completely soft, about 25 minutes.

3. Transfer the quinces to a food processor and puree. Strain the puree through a fine sieve so it is completely smooth, and transfer it to a large heavy-bottomed saucepan. Add 4 cups (800 g) of the sugar and stir until thoroughly combined, then stir in the lemon zest. Bring to a boil over medium heat, reduce the heat to medium-low, and cook, stirring, until the mixture becomes very thick and gelatinous and turns the color of terra cotta, about 30 minutes.

4. Sprinkle 2 tablespoons sugar evenly over a 13 × 16-inch (32.5 × 40-cm) surface (you can also use a nonreactive baking sheet of this size or larger).

5. When the quince paste is cooked, turn it onto the prepared surface and smooth it out as rapidly as possible until it is approximately ¼ inch (0.6 cm) thick. Sprinkle it evenly with the remaining 2 tablespoons sugar, and leave to cool and solidify completely.

6. When the quince paste is cool, cut it into 2-inch diamond shapes. Store in an airtight container, layered with parchment paper, in a cool place (but not in the refrigerator).

Red and Black Currant Jelly
Gelée de Groseilles et de Cassis

✦ Black and red currants ripen simultaneously, and when they are ripe, it is as if they've exploded off the bushes for suddenly, they are everywhere. Temporary stands—often simply a folding table—appear at our local market and are laden with currants that glisten like small jewels.

The berries are all turned into homemade jelly. At the market customers talk, comparing recipes. Everything I know about making jelly has come from standing in line at the market: the quantity of sugar to fruit (I use less than most), whether to press the fruit or not (pressing gives more juice, but results in cloudy rather than clear jelly), whether to use new or used jars (most of us use commercial jam jars because their size is perfect, and the seal on their lids works for years on end).

Look for currants in farmers' markets during the summer. If you cannot find black currants, use all red currants.

5 cups (1.25 l)

2¾ pounds (1 kg 360 g) red currants, stemmed

1¼ pounds (620 g) black currants, stemmed

½ cup (125 ml) water

2½ cups (500 g) sugar

1. Place the currants and water in a medium heavy-bottomed saucepan or pot over medium-high heat and cook until they are steaming, stirring and pressing on them gently so they release their juices. When the berries are hot and have released a great deal of their juices, remove them from the heat and gradually pass them all through a food mill to further crush them so they release as much juice as possible (the pulp left from the berries should still be somewhat moist, not totally dry). Or, if you don't have a food mill, continue pressing on the berries in the pan until they've given up as much juice as they are going to. Line a strainer with damp cheesecloth, set it over a large bowl, and pour the berries and their juices into the strainer. Gather up the edges of the cheesecloth and tie them together, then hang the cheesecloth bag above the bowl and let the juices drip from it. You can press quite firmly on the bag of berries once the juice has dripped from it, as you aren't concerned here with the clarity of the juice since

black currant juice is inky blue. Strain the juice through a fine-mesh sieve.

2. Place the juice and sugar in a large heavy-bottomed saucepan and bring to a boil over medium-high heat. As the juices boil, foam will form on the top; skim off these impurities. Boil for exactly 3 minutes, then remove the pan from the heat. Fill the hot jars to within ¼ inch (0.6 cm) of the top and seal according to the jar manufacturer's instructions.

Jam and Jelly-Making Tips

When going to the effort of making jams and jellies, I want them to taste as much like fresh fruit as possible when I eat them with my morning toast. To ensure this, I follow these few simple guidelines:

Before cooking the fruit, have the sterilized jars and lids hot, a clean towel to wipe the jars before you put the jelly into them, a wide-mouth funnel for filling the jars, a paper towel to wipe off the jar rims, and a cotton kitchen towel for handling the hot jars.

Never add commercial pectin, because it acts as a flavor filter. Instead, I use pectin-rich peaches, apples, currants, quinces, and plums in combination with other fruits to help them jell.

Use less sugar than the standard French jam or jelly rule, which is equal parts sugar and fruit or fruit juice, because this quantity of sugar dulls the flavor of the fruit.

Make small batches so the fruit doesn't have to cook long, which helps preserve flavor and color.

Avoid using overripe fruit, because the height of its flavor has passed and the natural pectin will have lost its jelling power.

Use a food mill to crush the cooked fruit so it releases as much juice as possible. This is a gentle way to encourage the juice from the fruit without pressing too hard on seeds, pits, and stems that have cooked with the fruit and which can give a bitter flavor if the fruit is pressed too hard. If you do not own a food mill, crush the fruit with a wooden spoon.

To further extract juice from the fruit, I set a strainer or colander in a large bowl and line it with damp cheesecloth. I put the fruit in the cheesecloth, tie the corners of the cheesecloth together to make a bag, and hang the bag over the bowl—from a faucet, pot rack, or whatever you can rig up—so that the juice can drip into it.

Skim away the foam that rises to the surface while the fruit and sugar are cooking, so these impurities do not mask the flavor in the jam.

To test the texture of jams and jellies, put a plate in the refrigerator. When I think the jelly or jam has reached the right stage of jelling, I drizzle a bit on the plate and return it to the refrigerator. Within moments, it will tell me if the texture is right.

When the jelly or jam is ready, I turn off the heat under it, but I leave the pilot light on so the mixture will stay hot. If you don't have a pilot light, leave the pan over very low heat as you fill the jars, working as quickly as possible. Then I fill and seal the jars according to the manufacturer's instructions, working carefully. I store the fruits of my labor in a dark place so their color and flavor stays pure, and I try to make them last throughout the year.

Bitter Orange Marmalade
Marmelade d'Oranges Amères

❦ Homemade orange marmalade has rich texture, flavor, and color; it is perfect on toast with an ever-so-thin layer of lightly salted butter.

I also use this marmalade as a filling for Chocolate Chocolate Cake (page 223), or heat it slightly and pour it over vanilla ice cream with fresh orange segments.

Babette Dewaele, a friend who owns Louvier's *herboristerie*, or healing herb and organic foods store, got me started making this marmalade when she gave me a jar of hers to sample. Since then, when she places her winter order for organic bitter oranges, she automatically orders some for me too.

6 cups (1.5 l)

2 pounds (1 kg) bitter oranges, preferably organic, well washed

2 lemons, preferably organic, well washed

6 cups (1.5 l) water

3¾ cups (825 g) packed light brown sugar

ASTUCES: Soaking the cut-up oranges in water for 24 hours results in a smooth, uniformly flavored marmalade. When preparing the oranges, cut them into quarters then into paper-thin slices, to expose more of the fruit's surface allowing more of its flavor to emerge. ❦ No bitter oranges? Sweet ones can be used instead. Whichever oranges you use, make sure they are organic, or at least untreated with a fungicide wax after harvest.

1. Cut each orange and lemon into quarters, then cut the quarters into paper-thin slices; discard the seeds. Place the fruit in a large bowl or nonreactive stockpot, add the water, cover, and let sit for 24 hours.

2. Transfer the fruit and water to a large stockpot, if necessary, and bring to a boil over medium-high heat. Reduce the heat so the mixture is boiling gently and cook until the fruit is translucent and tender through, about 1 hour. Remove from the heat and let sit for 1 day, covered, which allows the fruit flavor to mellow and soften.

3. Add the sugar to the fruit, stir, and bring to a boil over medium-high heat. Reduce the heat so the mixture is boiling gently and cook, stirring from time to time and scooping off any foam that rises to the surface, until the mixture is thick and a little jells softly when drizzled on a cold plate, about 25 minutes.

4. When the marmalade is thickened to your liking, ladle it into sterilized jars and seal according to the manufacturer's instructions.

Raspberry Jelly

Gelée de Framboise

⚜ **In France, raspberries might as well be gold ingots unless you grow your own. Fortunately I know plenty of people with raspberry bushes, and if I cajole them into generosity, I can pick just enough berries to make this jelly.**

About 5 cups (580 ml)

4 pounds (2 kg) raspberries, carefully picked through

3¾ cups (1½ pounds; 750 g) sugar

ASTUCE: Use organic berries whenever possible, because their flavor will be more intense. Also, avoid overripe fruit; the flavor won't be as pure. Rinse the berries quickly and carefully so as not to bruise them.

1. Place the raspberries in a large heavy pot and cook over medium heat, shaking the pot and stirring gently, until the berries have broken down, 10 to 15 minutes. Remove them from the heat and put them through a food mill, or in a strainer, then press on them with a wooden spoon to extract the juice. Strain the juice. You should have about 5 cups (1.25 l) juice.

2. Place the juice and sugar in the pot and cook over medium heat, stirring, until the sugar has dissolved and the mixture is boiling gently. Skim off any impurities (there aren't likely to be many), and cook at a gentle, rolling boil until the mixture falls thickly from the spoon, and jells softly when drizzled on a cold plate, 20 to 30 minutes.

3. Remove from the heat. Ladle the jelly into sterilized jars and seal according to the jar manufacturer's instructions.

Tapenade

❧ Nothing says Provence more than this savory, highly flavored combination of that region's finest ingredients—olives, garlic, anchovies, capers, and olive oil. That said, tapenade is served as an appetizer all over France.

While there are many excellent commercial brands, tapenade is easy to make and so much fresher and better than anything bought in a store.

Best of all, tapenade has a multitude of uses: as a dip for fresh bread, vegetables, or hearty crackers; spread on pizza dough; or kneaded into bread dough to make an olive-rich loaf. Sometimes I smooth some under the skin of a chicken before roasting it, or add a teaspoon atop steamed fillets of turbot or flounder.

Tapenade is best when accompanied by a good, lightly chilled rosé, such as a Riversaltes Tuilé from Domain Dol-Payré.

About 1⅓ cups; 10 servings

1 tablespoon capers, preferably packed in salt

8 best-quality anchovy fillets, from Collioure or Sicily

¼ cup (60 ml) dry white wine (optional, for soaking anchovies if necessary)

2 cups (300 g) best-quality black olives, preferably Nyons, pitted

2 teaspoons Dijon mustard

2 garlic cloves, green germ removed if necessary

2 to 3 tablespoons (30 to 45 ml) extra virgin olive oil

Freshly ground black pepper

1 teaspoon fresh thyme leaves, optional

Fresh thyme sprigs, for garnish also optional

1. If using salt-packed capers, rinse them, then place them in a small bowl and cover them with warm water. Let sit for 1 hour; drain and pat dry.

2. Meanwhile, if using anchovy fillets packed in salt, place them in a shallow bowl and cover them with the wine. Let sit for 15 minutes, then drain and pat dry.

3. Place the capers, anchovies, olives, mustard, and garlic in a mortar and pestle or in a food processor and grind or process until the olives are ground to a thick puree. Slowly add the oil until the puree loosens just slightly and the oil is fully incorporated. Season to taste with black pepper and the thyme, if using.

4. Transfer the tapenade to a dish, garnish with the thyme sprigs, and serve with toasted bread or crackers.

ASTUCES: Salted capers need to be soaked for an hour, so plan accordingly. Anchovies packed in salt need to be soaked in about ¼ cup (60 ml) dry white wine for 15 minutes. ✿ Now, for pitting those olives. Don't spend money on an olive pitter—olives are too varied in size to fit just one, and none of them work very well anyway. The best way to pit olives is to lay the flat side of a chef's knife atop each olive and smack the knife with your fist. The olive will split; the pit will pop out. Once you get the hang of it, you will be able to pit enough olives for tapenade in no time. ✿ I prefer to make tapenade in a mortar with a pestle because its texture is more irregular. It can be made in a food processor, but pulse the mixture just until coarse—it shouldn't be a fine puree. ✿ To store tapenade, place it in a jar or crock and cover it with a thin layer of extra virgin olive oil, to seal in its flavor. It will keep well for a week or two in the refrigerator or in a cool place. To serve it, simply stir in the olive oil on the surface, and add a teaspoon or so of fresh minced garlic.

A NOTE ABOUT ANCHOVIES

Some of the best preserved anchovies come from the small French Mediterranean town of Collioure. Packed in oil, the fillets are firm and reddish, and they have the taste and texture of tiny fish rather than the fishy, salty substance that so often goes under the name *anchovy*. Whole Collioure anchovies are also available, packed in a salt brine—they are excellent.

If you cannot find anchovies from Collioure, look for other good-quality anchovies packed in oil, or for anchovies packed in sea salt. The best of these come from Sicily.

Anchovies packed in salt should be soaked in white wine for 15 minutes, then rinsed quickly under cool water and patted dry.

Roquefort's Last, Delicious Gasp
Le Délicieux Dernier Soufflé au Roquefort

In all my years of living in France, I have never seen an empty cheese platter at the end of a meal, which begs the question—what to do with the leftovers? There's usually a small stub or slice of each variety, not enough for another meal, but too much to throw away.

Like any good French cook, I have figured out many ways to use these morsels: goat cheese atop pizza, or Camembert, Livarot, and Neufchâtel folded into a custard and baked in a tart shell, or added to a salad right before serving.

Leftover Roquefort gets this smooth, silken treatment, which is ideal with a glass of port or Pommeau as an apéritif. You may add minced walnuts, and either port, Calvados, or marc de Bourgogne, but frankly, I prefer it just like this. It is so mellow and delicious it tastes almost illicit!

About 1 cup (250 g)

4 ounces (120 g) Roquefort, at room temperature

3 ounces (90 g) unsalted butter, softened

Flat-leaf parsley leaves

Place the Roquefort and butter in a food processor and process until the mixture is smooth. Transfer it to a serving dish, garnish with the parsley, and serve immediately. Or transfer it to a small crock, bowl, or jar, cover, and refrigerate until ready to serve.

ASTUCE: This mixture keeps, tightly covered in the refrigerator, for several weeks. Remove it from the refrigerator at least an hour before serving, so it is spreadable, and be sure to serve with warm toasts. Serve with freshly cracked walnuts.

The Brave Shepherd

Many years ago, a shepherd near the town of Roquefort, in the southern part of the Massif Central, took shelter from a storm inside a mountain cave. While there, he ate his lunch of rye bread and curdled sheep's milk. He probably took a nap, and then was awakened by the bleating of his herd letting him know that the sun was shining and they needed to get home. In a rush, he left the cave and went on his merry way.

Some time later, he was back in the same vicinity when another storm hit. He once again took shelter in the cave, but this time had nothing to assuage his hunger. Sitting there as the thunder crashed and the rain came down, he spied a small package that, when opened, revealed leftovers from his lunch of weeks before. The curdled cheese was no longer fresh and white, but firm and riddled with blue mold. The rye bread, too, was furry and blue.

Despite the way it looked, the cheese smelled creamy and delicious, and the shepherd was overcome with hunger. He took a bite and to his astonishment, the flavors that met his palate were extraordinary. In disbelief, he took another bite, then wrapped up the remaining blue-veined curds and stuck them in his pocket. This was news too good to keep to himself.

When he arrived back in his village, he told everyone about his find, which changed the world forever. What the shepherd had discovered was a cheese that would become legendary worldwide.

To this day, Roquefort cheese is still made from ewe's milk and the spores from rye bread, which are injected into the fresh curds to riddle them with blue.

The shepherd was brave to eat that first morsel of moldy cheese. If he hadn't, where would the world of French cheese be today?

Cornichons

❧ Cornichons are dainty pickles that are an obligatory—and appropriate—accompaniment to a *charcuterie,* or cold-cut, platter. Pâté is always served with cornichons, too.

In late summer, the rush to buy the minuscule cucumbers used for making cornichons might be likened to a stampede, for they are always in short supply. I order the quantity I want well before the season begins so I am sure to get an ample supply.

2 quarts (2 l)

1 pound 9 ounces (770 g) cornichons (tiny, thumb-sized cucumbers)

2 tablespoons coarse sea salt

Four 6-inch (15-cm) leafy sprigs fresh tarragon, rinsed and patted dry

2 garlic cloves, green germ removed if necessary, cut lengthwise into quarters

12 tiny pearl onions

10 peppercorns, preferably Vietnamese or Tellicherry

2 to 3 whole cloves

1 teaspoon mustard seeds

2 fresh bay leaves from the *Laurus nobilis,* or dried imported bay leaves

2¾ cups (685 ml) white vinegar

¼ cup (60 ml) filtered or bottled water

1. In a large bowl, toss the cornichons with the salt. Turn them out into a tea towel, gather the towel by the four corners, and tie it into a bag. Attach it to a faucet to drain into the sink for 2 hours, or set the cornichons in their towel in a strainer in the sink.

2. Once the cornichons have drained, vigorously rub them with the salt in the towel, to remove any spines. Rinse the cornichons, then pat them thoroughly dry.

3. Place the tarragon sprigs in a 1.5-quart (1.5-l) jar, then layer the cornichons with the garlic, onions, and other herbs and spices until they come to about 1 inch (2.5 cm) below the top of the jar.

4. In a medium saucepan, bring the vinegar and water to a boil. Pour the hot liquid over the ingredients in the jar, making sure to cover them and leaving about ½ inch (1.3 cm) headroom. Seal the jar, and let it stand in a cool, dark spot for at least 3 weeks before opening. The cornichons should be refrigerated after opening.

ASTUCES: Marcerating the cucumbers softens and seasons them. The salt rub removes their sharp little spines, cleans them up, and gets them ready for pickling. If you cannot find tiny cucumbers, use pickle-sized cucumbers. You may need to adjust the amounts, however, and the ripening time. ❧ The amount of water and vinegar called for may be slightly more than is needed, though this can vary depending on the size of the cucumber.

Orange Flower Water and Lemon Ice Cubes

Glaçons d'Eau de Fleur d'Oranger et de Citron

❧ Dropped into a glass of mineral water, these flavorful little ice cubes melt into an exotically flavored and refreshing drink. I keep these on hand in summer, so they are ready on the hottest days. Three cubes per 6 ounces (180 ml) mineral water usually does the trick, though you must use the number of ice cubes that flavors the water to your taste.

These cubes also turn sparkling water and certain fruit juices into an apéritif for those who don't drink alcohol.

36 ice cubes

1 cup (120 g) vanilla confectioners' sugar

2½ cups (625 ml) mineral water

1 cup (250 ml) freshly squeezed lemon juice (from 4 to 5 large lemons)

2 tablespoons orange flower water

Place all of the ingredients in a medium bowl and whisk together until the sugar is dissolved. Freeze the mixture in two ice cube trays. (If you are using rose petals, place a petal atop each cube and gently push it under the surface of the mixture, then freeze.)

ASTUCES: To dress these up, add a rose petal (unsprayed) to each ice cube. As the cubes melt, the petals will float fetchingly in the glass. ❧ I like to pour room-temperature liquid over the ice cubes, which will melt and both chill and flavor the liquid.

Mellow Orange Wine

Vin d'Orange Doux

❧ Like many of my French friends, I make orange wine every year, and my recipe has evolved over the years. This is my current favorite, with a deep and alluring flavor thanks to the coffee and vanilla beans.

Serve this as an apéritif along with something lovely to eat from "The Apéritif Hour" chapter. It is best just cooler than room temperature in winter, lightly chilled in summer.

About 2½ quarts (2½ l)

10 good-sized oranges, preferably organic, scrubbed

8 cups (2 l) dry white wine, such as Sancerre

2 cups (500 ml) vodka

44 coffee beans

1 vanilla bean, left unsplit

2 cups minus 2 tablespoons (375 g) sugar

1. Peel the oranges right down to the fruit, reserving the peel. Reserve the fruit for another use.

2. Place the orange peel in a large nonreactive pot or heatproof bowl. Add the wine, vodka, coffee beans, vanilla bean, and half the sugar, and stir. Set aside.

3. Caramelize the remaining sugar: Place the sugar in a small heavy saucepan and set it over medium-high heat. The sugar will melt and begin to bubble, then gradually liquefy, turning a pale golden color; this will take about 7 minutes. Continue cooking, swirling the pan occasionally so it colors evenly, until the caramel is a deep golden color, like light molasses, about 5 minutes.

4. Remove the pan from the heat and pour the caramelized sugar into the orange mixture, scraping as much of the sugar as possible from the pan with a wooden spoon. Be careful; the caramel will sizzle and send up steam as it hits the liquid so stand back, and it will instantly harden—don't be concerned, it will gradually dissolve. To remove any remaining caramel in the pan, ladle some of the wine and vodka mixture into it, swirl it around, scrape a bit, and pour it back into the orange mixture. Cover the mixture and let it sit in a

cool, dark place for at least 3 weeks, stirring from time to time.

5. Strain the wine through a fine-mesh sieve lined with several layers of cheesecloth. Discard the solids and bottle the wine, corking it so it is well sealed. Let it stand in a cool, dark place for at least 3 weeks, preferably for up to a year before serving.

GLOSSARY
Le Lexique

À blanc: The operative word in this cooking term is *blanc,* or white. It refers to a mixture of flour and water used to cook white or pale foods so they retain their color. Other ingredients, such as lemon juice and salt, may be added to season the food.

À la meunière: A classic French technique for cooking fish. The fish is seasoned, lightly dredged in flour, and fried in butter; lemon juice is squeezed over it before serving.

Apéritif: A drink served before a meal. Historically, an apéritif was a drink with bitter flavors served for the purpose of stimulating the appetite before the evening meal.

Bay leaves: I prefer using fresh bay leaves from the *Laurus nobilis* tree, because these are the leaves that grow throughout Europe and lend a sweet, floral aroma to so many dishes, from soups and stews to marinated olives and breads. If you cannot get the fresh leaves, use dried imported bay leaves (usually from Turkey), which are from the same genus and species of tree. Do not use California bay leaves (*Umbellularia californica*; also called Oregon myrtle), which have a strong, almost acrid, piney taste. Bay leaves generally are removed from a dish before serving.

Béchamel: A basic white sauce made by adding hot milk to a cooked mixture of butter and flour (called a *roux*). For a good béchamel, infuse the milk with herbs such as bay leaf, garlic, or thyme.

Blanching: In cooking, this term refers to briefly cooking in boiling salted water. Vegetables are generally blanched just until they are tender. The ideal ratio of salt to water is 1 rounded tablespoon of coarse sea salt per 2 quarts (2 l) water. Certain meats or meat products such as beef, calf's or pig's feet, sweetbreads, and bacon, may be blanched in water to clean or firm them.

Brioche: A yeast bread made with butter and eggs. Special molds are required to create the classic shape, with a fluted base and a topknot. Brioche dough is also used to wrap foods, particularly cheese or sausage, that are then baked.

Bouquet garni: A bundle of herbs, preferably fresh, typically including 2 bay leaves (from the *Laurus nobilis*) or dried imported bay leaves, 20 to 40 sprigs fresh thyme, parsley stems, and leek greens, used to flavor soups, stews, and sauces.

Caul fat: The membrane of thin, lacy fat that encases the organs in the abdominal cavity of the veal and the pig. Used to wrap stuffed cabbage (page 150) here, it is typically used to wrap fresh sausage patties and other pork mixtures, it melts away during cooking, basting the food to keep it moist. It can be ordered fresh or frozen from specialty butchers.

Charcuterie: Literally means product of the pig; it refers to cold cuts and other pork preparations such as pâtés, sausages, and terrines.

Chiffonnade: Refers to the technique of cutting any herb or green leaf into fine strips. To do this, stack several leaves, roll them up gently, and slice them crosswise into very fine slices.

Confit: Traditionally, confit refers to meat cooked in its own fat and then preserved in the cooking fat. Duck confit is the classic example. Today, the term is often used to describe a vegetable or fruit that has been very slowly cooked in a fat or liquid either to the consistency of marmalade or to transparency. Tomato and onion confit are common examples.

Cornichons: Tiny French cucumbers preserved in vinegar and spices, served most often as an accompaniment to pâté and charcuterie.

Coulis: A term that originally referred generally to all sauces and specifically to meat juices. It now usually means a puree—of fruit or vegetables—that often has been strained through a fine-mesh strainer.

Court bouillon: A seasoned liquid for poaching seafood. It almost always includes an acid such as vinegar or lemon juice; the quantity of acid is increased when it is used for poaching fatty fish such as salmon or mackerel. A fragrant court bouillon made with a combination of water and wine, perhaps vinegar, along with spices and herbs, will lend a subtle flavor.

Crème anglaise: Cooked custard sauce. I use crème anglaise primarily as a base for ice cream; and it also makes a delicious sauce over a warm fruit compote. It can be flavored with just about any herb or spice.

Crème fraîche: The top cream from fresh, rich milk that has been allowed to stand until it thickens. It is a staple throughout France and a particular specialty of Normandy.

Deglazing: The technique of releasing cooking juices from the bottom of a pan by putting it over the heat, adding a liquid to the pan, and scraping and stirring until the juices and the liquid are combined.

Dried plums: Formerly known as prunes. Since prunes have an unfortunate reputation, they are now referred to as dried plums.

Emulsify: To create a stable combination of two liquids that don't ordinarily mix well, such as oil and vinegar. As the oil is whisked into the vinegar, it breaks up into tiny particles that are then held by the vinegar in a suspended, or emulsified, state.

Farci(e): The French word for stuffed; *farce* is stuffing.

Feuilleté: Literally "foliated," but it is the French term for layers. *Pâte feuilletée* is the layered dough known as puff pastry.

Fromage blanc: A freshly curdled undrained cheese that is a staple of the French diet. It is used in many ways, from a tart filling (Alsatian cheesecake) to a dessert with cream and sugar, or jam, or fresh fruit. It is the basis of the Alsatian dish *bibelskaes*.

Goûter: Refers to a snack or a small bite of something, often a sweet, taken in the late afternoon in France.

Julienne: A term that refers to finely cut or grated strips of, usually, vegetables, that are about the thickness of a toothpick. It does not mean matchstick-sized pieces.

Macerate: To soften by soaking or steeping in liquid or oil.

Madeleine: A small, light, cake-like cookie, made in special scallop-shaped baking tins.

Marinade: To season foods by allowing them to sit in a seasoned liquid.

Mise-en-place: The practice of measuring and preparing all ingredients and tools before beginning to cook.

Mornay sauce: Béchamel sauce with cheese, most often Gruyére, stirred into it.

Pâte: Pastry or dough.

Pâté: Classically, a meat or seafood mixture enclosed in pastry that can be served hot or cold.

Pistou: A condiment or sauce made of fresh basil, garlic, and olive oil that often includes pine nuts and cheese.

Potage: A hearty soup, generally of vegetables and herbs, usually pureed and often finished with cream.

Rennet: Extracted from the stomach lining of cows, goats, or sheep, rennet is an essential ingredient in the production of cheese. An enzyme in rennet causes the coagulation process that separates the milk proteins from the liquid whey. A vegetable rennet is produced from plants.

Rillettes: Usually pork, but any meat or fish that has been slowly cooked in fat, then mashed or slightly processed into a spreadable paste. Rillettes are usually served cold or at room temperature as an appetizer with bread, crackers, or toast.

Sauté: Literally, "to jump," as a culinary term this refers to keeping ingredients in fat moving in a pan over medium to high heat so they cook evenly without sticking and burning; the best technique for keeping the ingredients moving is to shake the pan and toss the ingredients.

Scald: To heat a liquid just to the point where bubbles form around its edges and the surfaces ripples slightly.

Terrine: Classically and actually, a meat or seafood mixture cooked in an earthenware mold also called a terrine and served chilled.

SOURCES
Les Sources d'Approvisionnement

Ideally, of course, you will support your local merchants and shop near to where you live. But if you cannot find what you need, here is an Internet source list for some ingredients used in the recipes in this book. You will also find sites here that will lead you to producers of raw-milk dairy products, food cooperatives, and farmers' markets near you.

Happy shopping!

Cheese
www.fromages.com
www.formaggiokitchen.com
    (Italian cheeses)

Chocolate
www.chocosphere.com
www.scharffenberger.com

Dried Beans
www.indianharvest.com
www.beanbag.net

Unpasteurized Dairy Products
www.realmilk.com
    (has a state-by-state directory of sources for raw-milk products)

Farmers' Markets

www.ams.usda.gov/farmersmarkets/map.htm

    (nationwide map with directory of farmers' markets in each state)

www.localharvest.org

    (countrywide resource of farmers' markets, food coops, community

    supported agriculture, restaurants, and more)

Flours and Whole Grains

www.bobsredmill.com

    (more than four hundred products, including whole grains [quinoa, teff,

    amaranth, kamut, millet, spelt], cereals, mixes, and flour milled from a

    variety of grains)

www.kingarthurflour.com

http://sqlblue2.cul.columbia.edu/Jim/food.coop.html

General Ingredients

www.igourmet.com

    (wide range of gourmet food items)

www.deananddeluca.com

www.kalustyans.com

    (wide range of specialty and gourmet foods, including couscous)

www.amazon.com

www.ethnicgrocer.com

    (wide range of products from all over the globe)

www.dartagnan.com

    (foie gras and other French products)

www.formaggiokitchen.com

    (Italian products, including Parmigiano-Reggiano)

Goose Fat

www.chefsresource.com

    (also many other gourmet products)

www.chefshop.com

    (also many other gourmet products)

Heirloom Seeds

www.rareseeds.com

www.victoryseeds.com

www.seedstrust.com

www.treesofantiquity.com
    (heirloom fruit trees)

Nut Oils

www.zingermans.com

Organic Produce

www.diamondorganics.com
    (organic fruits and vegetables, including heirloom varieties; other
    products, including organic meat)

Pistachios (Turkish)

www.zenobianut.com

Rennet

www.cheesemaking.com

www.cheesesupply.com

Smoked Ham, Sausages, and Meat

www.nolechekmeats.com

www.usingers.com

www.smokedmeats.com

Spices

www.penzeys.com

www.thespicehouse.com

www.saffron.com
    (saffron and vanilla)

INDEX

bay leaves:
    in award-winning country pâté, 70–71
    in aromatic braised pork shoulder, 146–47
    in aromatic quinoa, 189
    in beef braised with onions, carrots, and
        dried plums, 162–164
    in Belgian endive and leek gratin, 178–79
    in bolognaise sauce à la francaise, 283
    in braised guinea hen with Savoy cabbage,
        133–34
    in brined roasted chicken, 124–25
    in Champagne chicken, 126–27
    in chicken with artichokes, 116–17
    in cornichons, 296
    in court bouillon, 262
    in goat cheeses in olive oil, 27
    in herb broth, 261
    in a homemaker's chicken liver terrine,
        16–17
    in leek potage, 54–55
    in mackrel rillettes, 30–31
    in mussels in cider vinegar, 78
    in roast duck with stuffed apricots,
        137–38
    in roasted leg of lamb with herbs and
        mustard, 170–71
    in turkey roast with shallots, 141
    in savory beef stew, 160–61
beans:
    dried, buying of, 155
    red and white shell, in provençal vegetable
        soup, 50–51
    see also specific beans
bean threads, in Franco-American spring rolls,
    76–77
beef:
    braised, with carrots, onions, and dried
        plums, 162–64
    cuts for braising, U.S., 159
    ground, in bolognaise sauce à la francaise,
        283
    shoulder and neck in soup for couscous,
        46–47
    stew, savory, 163–64
    see also steak
beer, in crêpes for "La Chandeleur" and Fat
    Tuesday, 198–99
beet mix-up (khlat), 79

bell peppers, red:
    bread, 23
    and eggplant caviar toasts, 25
    in gazpacho with mustard ice cream,
        40–41
    roasting of, 24
    tomatoes, and garlic in pastry, 182–83
bibeleskaes, 69
bifteck poêlé au coulis de poireaux, 165–66
black radish salad, 93
blanching, 83, 134
boeuf mode aux pruneaux, 162–64
bol de soupe, un, 37–55
bolognaise sauce à la francaise, 283
    in many-layered eggplant, 157
bordelaise sauce, rib-eye steak with, 158
bouillon d'aromates, 261
bouquet garni:
    in chicken stock, 252
    in frosty lentils, 184–85
    in rooster in red wine, 129–31
    in savory beef stew, 163–64
braised(ing):
    aromatic pork shoulder, 146–47
    beef with carrots, onions, and dried plums,
        162–64
    fennel, 188
    guinea hen with Savoy cabbage, 133–34
    U.S. beef cuts for, 159
bread(s), 191–227
    baking techniques for, 193
    dried fig and hazelnut, 22
    flat semolina for couscous, 196–97
    light whole wheat and flaxseed, 192–93
    red pepper, 23
    savory lemon and rosemary, 194–95
    walnut, 214–15
Brillat-Savarin, Jean-Anthelme, 95
brined roasted chicken, 124–25
broth, *see* herb broth; soups; stock
browning, 134
bulgur wheat, in chorba, 44–45
butter:
    clarified, 199
    salmon à l'unilatérale with capers and,
        111
butterbrendel, 201–2
butter cookies, Alsatian, 201–2

cabbage, Savoy, *see* Savoy cabbage
cake:
    caramelized apple, 226–27
    chocolate chocolate, 223–25
cake aux figues et aux noisettes, 22
cake aux poivrons rouges, 23
Calvados:
    in homemaker's chicken liver terrine,
        16–17
    in mussels in saffron cream, 80–81
    in rooster in red wine, 129–31
    in stuffed cabbage for after the hunt,
        150–53
canard rôti aux abricots farcis, 137–38
cannellini beans, in provençal vegetable soup,
    50–51
cantaloupe:
    in melon and lime parfait, 15
    in Michel's melon salad, 65
capers:
    salmon à l'unilatérale with butter and, 111
    in skate with potato puree, 108–10
    in tapenade, 292–93
caramel(ized):
    apple cake, 226–27
    making of, 249
    oranges, 248–49
carrés au fromage de chèvre, 67
carrots:
    beef braised with onions, and dried plums,
        162–64
    in savory beef stew, 163–64
    in soup for couscous, 46–47
    in stuffed cabbage for after the hunt, 150–53
cauliflower, potato gratin with, 176
Cavaillon melon:
    in melon and lime parfait, 15
    in Michel's melon salad, 65
caviar d'aubergines, 276–77
Cecile (Anouilh), 57
celery root:
    in Champagne chicken, 126–27
    in savory beef stew, 163–64
cervelas sausage:
    in green bean, smoked sausage, and hard-
        cooked egg salad, 86–87
    in Gruyère and smoked sausage salad,
        88–89

Champagne chicken, 126–28
chanterelle mushrooms, in wild mushrooms on
    toast, 34–35
Charentais melon:
    in melon and lime parfait, 15
    in Michel's melon salad, 65
cheese:
    course, 210
    in an Alsatian country smorgasbord, 69
    rinds of, 212
    selecting and serving of, 211–12
    see also specific cheeses
cherry clafoutis, 233
chicken:
    with artichokes, 116–17
    brined, roasted, 124–25
    Champagne, 126–28
    soup with tamarind, 52–53
    steamed, with cilantro oil, 118–19
    stock, 252
    Syrian, with Tahini, lemon, and yogurt sauce,
        120–21
    with turmeric and coconut milk, 122–23
    wings, curried, 115
chicken liver:
    pâté, not just any, 18
    terrine, a homemaker's, 16–17
chickpeas:
    in hummus, 19
    in soup for couscous, 46–47
chives:
    in Alsatian country smorgasbord, 69
    in an artichoke, a poached egg, and a dash of
        cream, 62–63
    in leek salad, 64
    in salmon rillettes, 28–29
    in simple family omelet, 60–61
chocolate:
    chocolate cake, 223–25
    melting of, 225
    mousse, 237
    sauce, easy, 238
chocolate, semisweet:
    in chocolate chocolate cake, 223–25
    in chocolate mousse, 237
    in easy chocolate sauce, 238
chocolate milk, in chocolate chocolate cake,
    223–25

homemaker's chicken liver terrine, 16–17
homous, 19
honey:
    cooking with, 244
    ice cream, 244
    and lemon thyme almonds, 10
hot and cold first courses, 57–93
huile citronée, l', 272
huile de coriandre, l', 273
hummus, 19

ice cream:
    honey, 244
    mustard, gazpacho with, 40–41
    tips for making perfect, 239–40
    vanilla, 241–42
ice cubes, orange flower water and lemon, 297

jams, tips for making of, 288–89
jellies, tips for making of, 288–89
jelly, raspberry, 291
    in baked apples from the market, 230–31
jelly, red and black currant, 286–87
    in baked apples from the market, 230–31
    in chocolate chocolate cake, 223–25

khlat (beet mix-up), 79
kidney beans, in provençal vegetable soup,
    50–51
kielbasa:
    in green bean, smoked sausage, and hard-
        cooked egg salad, 86–87
    in Gruyère and smoked sausage salad, 88–89
kitchen tools, indispensable, 254–55
"knife point" measurement, 203

lamb:
    and dried plum tagine with toasted almonds,
        167–69
    roasted leg of, with herbs and mustard,
        170–71
lamb neck:
    in chorba, 44–45
    in soup for couscous, 46–47

lamb shoulder:
    in chorba, 44–45
    in lamb and dried plum tagine with toasted
        almonds, 167–69
    marinated, grilled over the coals, 172–73
leek(s):
    and bacon quiche, 72–73
    and Belgian endive gratin, 178–79
    cleaning of, 97
    coulis, pan fried steak with, 165–66
    and monkfish for all occasions, 96–97
    potage, 54–55
    salad, 64
    in savory beef stew, 160–61
lemon(s):
    meringue tart, 220–21
    oil, 272
    and orange flower water ice cubes, 297
    and orange guinea hen, roasted, 135–36
    and rosemary bread, savory, 194–95
    Syrian chicken with tahini, and yogurt sauce,
        120–21
    zesting vs. rasping of, 222
lemon thyme:
    in goat cheeses in olive oil, 27
    in herb broth, 261
    and honey almonds, 10
    in leek salad, 64
    in mackerel rillettes, 30–31
lemon verbena madeleines, 207–8
lentilles au givre, 184–85
lentils, frosty, 184–85
lettuce:
    for balsamic vinaigrette, 266
    in Gruyère and smoked sausage salad,
        88–89
light whole wheat and flaxseed bread,
    192–93
lime(s):
    lychee, and candied ginger salad, 246
    and melon parfait, 15
    in punch from Martinique, 14
lingcod:
    in curried fish à la meunière, 98–99
    in spiced fish fillet in parchment paper,
        104–5
lotte aux poireaux pour toute occasion, 96–97
lychee, lime and candied ginger salad, 246

pistachios:
    toasting of, 13
    tomato salad with mozzarella and, 68
plum(s), dried:
    beef braised with carrots, and onions,
        162–64
    and lamb tagine with toasted almonds,
        167–69
Point, Fernand, 9
poireaux en salade, 64
Poire Williams liqueur, in rooster in red wine,
    129–30
poisson à la meunière au curry, 98–99
pommes au four du marché, 230–31
pommes de terre dans les cendres, au foie gras, 32
pork:
    chops, the vintner's wife's, 144–45
    liver, in award-winning country pâté, 70–71
pork, ground:
    in award-winning country pâté, 70–71
    in bolognaise sauce à la francaise, 283
    in a homemaker's chicken liver terrine, 16–17
    in savory stuffed tomatoes, 148–49
    in stuffed cabbage for after the hunt, 150–53
pork shoulder:
    aromatic braised, 146–47
    in a homemaker's chicken liver terrine, 16–17
port, tawny:
    in duck breast with apple sherry, 139–40
    in a homemaker's chicken liver terrine, 16–17
    in not just any chicken liver pâté, 18
potage, leek, 54–55
potage aux poireaux, 54–55
potato(es):
    gratin with cauliflower, 176
    in an Alsatian country smorgasbord, 69
    puree, skate with, 108–10
    roasted in ashes, with foie gras, 32
    slices, oven-roasted, with herbes de Provence,
        66
    in soup for couscous, 46–47
pot-au-feu, 160–61
    popularity of, 159
pot roast, chuck, in beef braised with carrots,
    onions, and dried plums, 162–64
poularde au Champagne, 126–28
poulet a la vapeur, l'huile de coriandre, 118–19

poulet au curcuma et noix de coco, 122–23
poulet aux poivrades, 116–17
poulet saumure roti, 124–25
poultry, 113–41
    free-range, 114
    perfect roast, 123
    see also specific poultry
Pourrat, Henri, 251
preserves and basics, 251–99
prosciutto, in savory feta rolls, 26
provençal tomatoes, 186–87
provençal vegetable gratin, 180–81
provençal vegetable soup, 50–51
punch de la Martinique, 14
punch from Martinique, 14

quatre-épices, 268
quiche:
    leek and bacon, 72–73
    Lorraine, 74–75
quiche aux poireaux et au lard fumé, 72–73
quince paste, 284–85
    serving of, 285
quinoa aromatique, 189

raspberry jelly, *see* jelly, raspberry
rib-eye steak with bordelaise sauce, 158
rillettes:
    mackerel, 30–31
    salmon, 28–29
rillettes de maquereaux, 30–31
rillettes de saumon, 28–29
roast(ed):
    brined chicken, 124–25
    duck with stuffed apricots, 137–38
    leg of lamb with herbs and mustard,
        170–71
    lemon and orange guinea hen, 135–36
    potatoes in ashes, with foie gras, 32
    poultry, perfect, 123
rolls, savory feta, 26
rooster in red wine, 129–31
Roquefort cheese:
    history of, 295
    last delicious gasp of, 294

rosemary:
    in goat cheese in olive oil, 27
    in herb broth, 261
    in herbes de Provence, 269
    and lemon bread, savory, 194–95
    in mackerel with dandelion greens, 106
    in marinated lamb shoulder grilled over the
        coals, 172–73
    in roasted leg of lamb with herbs and
        mustard, 170–71
rôti de dende à l'echalote, 141
rouleaux de jambon sec a la féta, 26
rum, in punch from Martinique, 14
rutabagas, in savory beef stew, 163–64

sablés de Normandie, 204–6
saffron:
    cream, mussels in, 80–81
    in lamb and dried plum tagine with toasted
        almonds, 167–69
    in soup for couscous, 46–47
sage:
    in goat cheeses in olive oil, 27
    in herb broth, 261
    in savory feta rolls, 26
salade de Gruyère au cervelas, 88–89
salade de haricots verts, saucisses fumées, et oeufs dûrs,
    86
salade de litchi au citron vert et au gingembre confit,
    246
salade de Michel au melon, 65
salade de pissenlit, 84–85
salade de radis noir, 93
salade tiède aux saucisses et aux oeufs pochés,
    90–91
salads:
    black radish, 93
    dandelion, 84–85
    green bean, smoked sausage, and hard-
        cooked egg, 86–87
    Gruyère and smoked sausage, 88–89
    khlat (beet mix-up), 79
    leek, 64
    lychee, lime, and candied ginger, 246
    Michel's melon, 65
    tomato, with mozzarella and pistachios, 68

warm green, with sausages and poached eggs,
    90–91
salmon:
    in curried fish à la meunière, 98–99
    rillettes, 28–29
    à l'unilatérale with capers and butter, 111
salt:
    cumin, 271
    fleur de sel, 49
    folkloric significance of, 125
    sea, 48–49
sand cookies, Normandy, 204–6
sauce:
    bolognaise, à la francaise, *see* bolognaise sauce
        à la francaise
    bordelaise, rib-eye steak with, 158
    easy chocolate, 238
    yogurt, *see* yogurt sauce
sauce au chocolate "hyper-simple," 238
sauce bolognaise, 283
saumon à l'unilatérale aux câpres et au beurre,
    111
sausage, smoked:
    green bean, and hard-cooked egg salad,
        86–87
    and Gruyère salad, 88–89
sausages, warm green salad with poached eggs
    and, 90–91
savory, in herbes de Provence, 269
savory beef stew, 160–61
savory feta rolls, 26
savory lemon and rosemary bread, 194–95
savory stuffed tomatoes, 148–49
Savoy cabbage:
    braised guinea hen with, 133–34
    stuffed, for after the hunt, 150–53
seafood:
    selection and care of, 102–3
    see also fish; *specific fish*
sea salt, 48–49
sel au cumin, 271
semolina bread, flat, for couscous, 196–97
shallots, turkey roast with, 141
shellfish, selection and care of, 102–3
sherry:
    apple, duck breast with, 139–40
    in a homemaker's chicken liver terrine, 16–17

simple family omelet, 60–61
skate with potato puree, 108–10
smoked salmon, in salmon rillettes, 28–29
smorgasbord, an Alsatian country, 69
snapper, in spiced fish fillet in parchment paper, 104–5
sorbet, red currant, 245
sorbet aux groseilles, 245
soupe au concombre d'été, la, 43
soupe au pistou, 50–51
soupe aux petits pois de printemps, 42
soupe de couscous, 46–47
soupe de fèves à la crème, 38–39
soupe de poulet au tamarin, 52–53
soups, 37–55
    chicken, with tamarind, 52–53
    chorba, 44–45
    for couscous, 46–47
    creamy fava bean, 38–39
    the cucumber, of summer, 43
    fresh spring pea, 42
    gazpacho with mustard ice cream, 40–41
    leek potage, 54–55
    provençal vegetable, 50–51
spelt flour, 213
spice cookies, 203
spiced fish fillet in parchment paper, 104–5
spices, four, 268
spicy paste from Ile de la Réunion, 282
spinach, in provençal vegetable gratin, 180–81
spring fava beans and turnips, 82–83
spring rolls, Franco-Vietnamese, 76–77
squares, goat cheese, 67
steak:
    pan fried, with leek coulis, 165–66
    rib-eye, with bordelaise sauce, 158
steamed:
    chicken with cilantro oil, 118–19
    couscous, 278–80
stew, savory beef, 163–64
stock:
    chicken, 252
    see also soups
stuffed:
    cabbage for after the hunt, 150–53
    savory tomatoes, 148–49
sucre vanillé, 267

sugar:
    beet and cane, 231
    vanilla, *see* vanilla sugar
sweet cicely:
    in aromatic quinoa, 189
    in leek salad, 64
swordfish with ginger yogurt sauce and cilantro coulis, 101
Syrian chicken with tahini, lemon, and yogurt sauce, 120–21

Table au Pays de Brillat-Savarin, La (Tendret), 37
tagine:
    about, 169
    lamb and dried plum, with toasted almonds, 167–69
tagine d'agneau aux pruneaux et aux armandes grillées, 167–69
tahini:
    in eggplant caviar, 276–77
    in hummus, 19
    in khlat, 79
    Syrian chicken with lemon, and yogurt sauce, 120–21
tamarind, chicken soup with, 52–53
tapenade, 292–93
    dressed fit to kill, 33
tapenade sur sa trente-et-un, 33
tarragon:
    in aromatic quinoa, 189
    in cornichons, 296
    in leek salad, 64
tart:
    apple streusel, 216–17
    lemon meringue, 220–21
    mascarpone and peach, 218–19
tarte au citron meringuée, 220–21
tarte à la pêche et au mascarpone, 218–19
tarte streusel, 216–17
tassquia, 120–21
Temps, Le (France), 191
tender white beans and air-cured ham, 154–55
terrine, a homemaker's chicken liver, 16–17
terrine de foie de volaille menagère, 16–17

watermelon, in Michel's melon salad, 65
white beans, dried:
  in provençal vegetable soup, 50–51
  tender, air-cured ham and, 154–55
whole wheat and flaxseed bread, light, 192–93
wine, mellow orange, 298–99
wine, red, rooster in, 129–31
wine, white:
  in braised guinea hen with Savoy cabbage, 133
  in court bouillon, 262
  in mackerel rillettes, 30–31
  in mellow orange wine, 298–99
  in mussels in saffron cream, 80–81
  in tapenade, 292–93
  in wild mushrooms on toast, 34–35

yogurt:
  in curried chicken wings, 115
  in khlat, 79
  in melon and lime parfait, 15
yogurt cheese:
  in tapenade dressed to kill, 33
  uses for, 33
yogurt sauce:
  ginger, tuna with cilantro coulis and, 100–101
  Syrian chicken with tahini, lemon and, 120–21

zucchini, in soup for couscous, 46–47